Out of the Blue!

A Memoir

Remembrances from a fighter pilot, before and after enduring 7 ½ years as a POW in the infamous Hanoi Hilton in Vietnam

by
COL. J. QUINCY COLLINS, JR., USAF RET.

Contents

Foreward

We are about to spend some interesting and exciting times together! The challenge of writing a Memoir is not to just list a plethora of dry facts, but to make readers aware of what is unique about this author's life that might prompt another person to want to read my story and compare it to their own life's experiences.

I have written about my life from being born on the Fourth of July to all the acts of mischief and pranks we pulled in our growing-up years in Concord, North Carolina. After high school it was on to The Citadel in Charleston, South Carolina, then into the U.S. Air Force.

I have laid out the good times, and a few of the not so good, but this is in keeping with most of us during our early years when we are trying to "grow up"! All in all, during this time, life was good to me. That is, until I volunteered to serve in Vietnam and faced the ultimate crisis of my life—I was shot down and captured by the North Vietnamese Communists. Without even trying, I became one of the longest-held POWs in American military history!

Following is an abbreviated excerpt from Chapter 32 that gives you some idea of the particular traumatic turn in my life that resulted in my being a POW in prisons in and around Hanoi for the next seven and one-half years!

On September the 2nd, 1965, I trotted out to my F-105 at Tahkli, Thailand, for my 3rd mission of the day, totally unaware of how that day would end. So, as the Air Force song says, "Off we go into the wild blue yonder," heading to a remote spot between Laos and North Vietnam. It was a beautiful day with no cloud formations so visibility was great. Even better was the report that there was "No reported flak!" Man, that was the best news my ears could have heard!

But about fifty miles out from the target I saw something that tied my stomach in a knot and caused my heart to begin pounding. It was as if a bulldozer had been clearing an area close to the target. Why was this grading necessary? My first thought was that the enemy was preparing to defend this site —and I was their target!

Well, I didn't have time to contemplate this further because I was now right over the target and it was time for me to make my bombing run. I clicked my mic to indicate I was rolling in. We would not use voice on the mic because using that electronic device would give away our exact position in the airspace over the target. So I lowered the nose of my aircraft to accelerate and rolled into a dive to begin my run.

WHAM-BANG! I was hit by antiaircraft guns on the ground. Fire and smoke filled the cockpit. I was in trouble. DEEP TROUBLE! I felt another explosion. I wasn't sure if I had been hit again or if my own bombs were going off. I couldn't see outside my aircraft or even see my cockpit instruments. I had no idea if I was inverted, going straight down or climbing toward the sun, so I commanded myself to "Get the hell out of here!"

I was sitting in an ejection seat so I reached for the handles that were on either armrest. Pulling these handles would blow the canopy off and expose triggers on each armrest that, when fired, would launch me in my rocket seat to safety in the airspace above the aircraft. I recall that all of these actions seemed to be reduced to s..l..o..w....m..o..t..i..o..n! I never remembered leaving the aircraft by ejecting or the plane exploding. I had to have been doing over

700 knots when I hit the air stream because my body later looked like I had been dumped into a cement mixer and dropped from Mt. Everest.

When I finally opened my eyes after regaining consciousness, I was sitting, leaning against a tree with nothing on but my shorts. Across from me were 4 ancient militiamen protecting their part of Vietnam. I was, for all practical purposes, naked in the jungles of Laos or North Vietnam—and I was alone. No rescue aircraft were circling to pick me up.

After checking my body I could see that I had two arms, but could only see one leg. Damn! My left leg was bent grotesquely out to the left. It was broken in several places above the knee and it made me sick to see that I did not have the means to escape—I wasn't going anywhere!

My captors wrapped vine around my entire left leg, put me in a net with poles on their shoulders, and carried me to a Russian jeep-type vehicle and literally threw me into the rear compartment. I was holding onto my left leg because I thought it might tear off. Where were we going? What would they do to me? I was in a world of hurt and these guys were in control.

God help me!

I HAVE TOLD MY story like it is with the hope that you, my readers, will juxtapose your own personal experiences with mine to evaluate how we both have performed. It was fun recalling old memories and recreating situations that not only molded my character and gave me direction, but also allowed me to laugh at myself even when I physically hurt, and at times may have wanted to quit or give up.

In the course of a lifetime, everyone becomes a prisoner of something, experiences some type of torture or other self-imposed trauma, and faces life or death type circumstances.

I hope that your personal evaluation comes out as well as mine has. God has indeed challenged me above and beyond what I expected or even thought possible. It was as if my life just fell *"Out Of The Blue!"* How about yours?

Col. James Quincy Collins, Jr., USAF (Ret.)

1
The Beginning—July 4, 1931

As I pondered about how to start my memoir, I came to a wonderful conclusion—why not start where life began for me, at the beginning, my birthday on July 4, 1931.

But first, let me go back a little: My father, James Quincy Collins, Sr., was born on April 22, 1901, on a farm near Elko, South Carolina, in Barnwell County. His father, James Augustus Collins, raised cotton, asparagus, pecans and various other crops. Grandpa had two mules to plow with, and an old Model T Ford to drive to the store and to church. Of course, the old outhouse was a prominent feature at the farm along with cows, chickens and a couple of old dogs.

Dad walked to school on the old sand-bed roads except when he cut across big fields to save time. A good-looking boy with an outgoing personality, he was smart enough to do well in school. World War I came along at about the time he turned seventeen, and somehow he matriculated to Carlisle Military Institute near Bamberg, South Carolina. It evidently was a prep school for military colleges like The Citadel, as the cadets wore West Point type uniforms. I recall Dad telling me about the day WWI ended. All the cadets mustered on their parade ground—and went AWOL for the balance of the day.

Dad began looking for a job in Augusta, Georgia. He landed one on his very first interview with Mr. Grover Maxwell, owner of the Maxwell Brothers Furniture Stores. Dad did all the right things and soon progressed from stock and delivery boy to a route salesman, then to the coveted inside salesman. Within about seven years, Dad was sent to Maxwell Brothers and Morris in Charlotte, North Carolina, the largest and most profitable store in the chain.

One day, while gazing out the big showroom window in the entrance to the store, Dad spotted a beautiful young woman with gleaming dark hair and a movie actress stride in her step as she walked by on the way to King's Business College. Yep, that beauty, Willie Marie Doggett, caught the eye of the man who was to be my father. Dad decided that the best way to meet this damsel was to play it cool and take it easy. So each morning he would stand on the sidewalk by the entrance to the store and say hello as she passed by. It didn't take him long to become bolder and let the salesman scenario take over.

Finally, she came into the store to look at a porch swing she wanted to buy for her sister who lived on Thomas Avenue just off the Plaza in Charlotte. She bought it and he delivered it—just like you thought it would happen.

They married, and their first child was stillborn at birth. This was around 1927. The American economy was really down, so my parents were having a rough road all around. Mr. Grover Maxwell saw a lot of potential in my Dad, and that is how my parents ended up in Winnsboro, SC, with him running the Maxwell Brothers store there.

By this time Mom is pregnant again with yours truly, and Dad is knocking the cover off the furniture ball in the Winnsboro area. They had a small home in town and prepared for my birth there.

Winnsboro, South Carolina, was a sleepy little place about twenty-five miles north of Columbia (the capitol of SC)—not the place where I was to grow up, but merely a starting line for my race in life. When I was born the population of Fairfield County was probably stuck at 10,000 to 15,000 people, and was a rural community plain and simple. I lived there for all of a year before moving to Concord, North Carolina. This became my training ground and what could be called *The Quincy Collins Development Center.*

I was an infant when Dad suddenly came down with diphtheria, an acutely contagious disease caused by infection of the throat and other air passages. He had to be isolated and quarantined from me in our own home. His solution for this problem was to go outside, raise a ladder up to the window in my room, climb up, and then look in at his son lying in his crib. Mom used to laugh when she would tell this story, so I suspect that several funny things happened to Dad while he was doing all this and he didn't want Mom to add it to the story.

I am happy to report that my father got well and everything returned to normal again—at least that's what I was told. As you might imagine, I remember nothing and no one from the year I spent in Winnsboro.

Within a year our little family was on the way to Concord, North Carolina, where Dad had been assigned a bigger market area and a new Maxwell Brothers and Collins Furniture Store. Dad certainly had the Midas touch, as his business operation flourished. Later, I did meet Jack and Lene Bolen, who were friends of my parents. Jack took over the Winnsboro store when Dad was promoted to Concord in 1932.

The building that Dad leased to operate the new Maxwell Brothers and Collins store in Concord was huge in comparison to the Winnsboro store. It was three stories high with a big elevator, and on a huge lot,

My parents purchased a nice brick home on Hillcrest Drive, which turned out to be a perfect place for a young stallion like me to grow up. I could walk or ride my bike to Clara Harris Grammar School, and I had the Red Hills right behind my house to get as dirty as I dared. New friends came out of the woodwork and all sorts of mischief began to happen. I was in the right place to begin the growing up process and I was raring to go!

Then I had a little sister, Carolyn. Four years younger than I, she became my wrestling partner, the bad guy when we played cowboys and Indians, and the cause of all the awful things that happened to me around the house. But my sister was a good sport and held up very well.

When World War II started, we began to have practice air raids, blackouts and USO entertainment for the soldiers stationed nearby. Every weekend, we would have several soldiers stay in our home, and many of them became good close friends.

My father's sales and management prowess led us to own a farm with a beautiful lake house, an airplane for Dad, and a wonderful home with tall white columns in the historic district of Concord. I had a pony and then a horse, and little Carolyn got a horse and stable in our backyard. The Collins family was on the move!

Dad required me to work—either around the house, out at the farm, or at the furniture store. He encouraged me to round up five or six of my buddies to work in the Concord store. Dad put us on routes knocking on doors and passing out potholders while asking what furniture or appliance needs they had. As I recall, we were paid a quarter for every prospect we landed.

My father was a member of the Rationing Board for Cabarrus County and needed four tires, but was turned down. However, he was presented an application for a new car. Finding one was not an easy task, but he found one in Columbia, SC. This purchase became our family car—a 1942 Buick Limited with a sliding glass between the front and back seats. What a fun vehicle for a high school teenager—and I took full advantage of it. I could get twelve-plus buddies in that car, so we had a traveling party ready to go to any location. The worst habit any of my friends had was smoking—no one used drugs or had alcohol problems.

Dad went out of his way to include me in as many social functions as he could: a trip on a chartered train to watch UNC-Chapel Hill play, starring Charlie Justice, in New Orleans in a College Bowl Game; many lunches at his Rotary Club at the Hotel Concord; flying with him on Civil Air Patrol missions during WWII; driving an ambulance to Columbia, S. C., when I was fifteen to pick up Grandma Collins and bring her to a nursing home in Concord. What other kid had the opportunity to do these type grown-up things?

(1.1) James Q. Collins, Sr. (Dad)

(1.2) Willie Marie Doggett Collins (Mom)

(1.3) J. Quincy Collins, Jr.

(1.4) Carolyn Doggett Collins (Sister)

2
My Mother, Willie Marie Doggett

I am embarrassed about what few facts I remember about my mother and her life. Perhaps she didn't tell me much about that, but I should have been more inquisitive. I know that she was raised in Cowpens, SC, which should put the brakes on expectations from those wanting to trace the beginnings of such a lovely lady. Lovely she was. The early photos I have found of Willie Marie Doggett reflect a Show Girl type beauty that she carried with her even into her latter years. She had other names too—like Will and Bill (used mostly by her seven siblings—four girls and three boys). But my Mom had a way about her that caused a spotlight to separate her from others.

She exuded culture and knowledge of design and decorating, plus she had a wonderful soprano voice and played the piano quite well. She loved to read and was a terrific cook. She also loved to go to church and sing the old-time hymns and catch up on all the gossip in her ladies group. She selected clothes that highlighted her girlish figure, and was a bright shining star in any social circle. She was flat good-looking and I was always proud of her in any setting.

I do remember that Mom made reference to attending Mars Hill, the name associated with the oldest college in western North Carolina, founded in 1856. About the time Will attended around 1921, it became an accredited junior college and is now a fully accredited University.

Mom loved planting things—especially vegetables—so Dad and I became her hired hands in season. Dad's success in business brought us a farm with all kinds of livestock, a well-stocked lake with a wonderful summer home, an airplane and more business expansion. Life was unbelievably good.

IF MY SISTER, CAROLYN, had been born a little later in my life instead of May 19, 1935, she could have easily been a fighter pilot. To start with, she was Daddy's girl from the very beginning. They both loved animals and being outside and growing things like vegetables, cantaloupe and watermelon. She just had to have a horse—and of course a stable and fence and all that goes with it. But most importantly, it had to be in our backyard in Concord.

Dad and Sis both loved the idea, and plotted and planned this project so that Mom and I were in the dark as to the scope of the new addition. Then came saddles and buggies and all the accessories known to man and horses—including horse blankets and riding clothes for the Princess. Finally, Sis had to have a boarding device in order to mount her charge so the carpenter customized that too. That was OK with me. I quickly grew tired of having to lift her into the saddle. The four years separation in our ages never compensated for her gain in weight from year to year. It became increasingly difficult to hoist this honey into the saddle. Now came the most important part of all this—the horse!

Dad and Carolyn combed the woods, so to speak, for weeks just trying to hand pick Carolyn's new playmate. It finally happened. The entire family journeyed out into the country to see their choice and cast our vote of approval. Lady was, indeed, a beautiful animal and seemed to fit the bill for Sis. She was a 5-gaited Pinto with patches of white and sorrel. She was a beauty and moved into her new home within a week.

As I mentioned earlier, my sister is four years behind me. As time went on, she matured into a very pretty woman, just like our mother. But she didn't possess the elegance and mannerly charm of Mom. She preferred being the tomboy type, riding Lady and taking care of all the chores around the stable. She was always motivated to ride Lady uptown to one of the theaters that might happen to be featuring a Saturday live visit by a movie cowboy—like Johnny Mack Brown or Bob Steele. She would lure the six-shooter cowboy star to climb aboard and ride over to Dad's store to show off her celebrity catch. We all enjoyed her success with this and we never knew who would ride up with Sis.

As the years passed in high school I had attained a high level of competency in playing the saxophone. Mother played the piano and Dad self-taught himself to play the accordion, the mandolin and the violin. Although Sis was taking piano lessons, she had not yet reached the level of proficiency so that she could join in the family jam sessions. I eventually taught her to play the saxophone.

At about the same time she became a good pianist. She then joined the Concord High School Band. I had been the Drum Major and encouraged her to do this. She also became active in a lot of extra curricular activities like the Dramatics Club and the Women's Chorus. She was blossoming forth as a dance teacher's assistant and loved to shag, just like her brother! Eventually it came time to select a college.

By this time, I was well established at The Citadel in Charleston, South Carolina, and had become aware that my father was an alcoholic and was losing control over a sizable retail furniture operation in Concord, Kannapolis and Albemarle. His financial resources were fading quite rapidly, thus limiting college options available to Carolyn. Fortunately, she decided early on to go to Queens College in Charlotte and enrolled there.

She entered Queens just as I graduated from The Citadel. I was commissioned a 2nd Lieutenant in the USAF, and headed off to learn the fighter pilot business.

In addition to Sis's college transition, she became heir to the greatest burden a young woman could have—being the caretaker of an alcoholic father and an aging and sickly mother. This was 1953.

The next two years were a combination of ups and downs for Carolyn as college life suited her fine—but handling our parents was depressing and disappointing. The term Bankruptcy entered their lives and selling became the operative word. Refinancing was not an option.

By this time Lady had produced a foal. Sis named her Lady's Princess. This beautiful mother-daughter team had to be sold to pay Dad's debts. Sis was devastated. She must have cried for a week.

Next, the farm just outside Concord had to go, along with our summer home on the lake there. The barn with all the animals and equipment went too. The worst part of this was that the wonderful memories of all the good times we had shared there with all our family and friends would fade into the atmosphere of life, never again to return.

Dad's businesses were being taken over to satisfy loans he had initiated—loans that probably paid for a lot of our education and most of the lifestyle we lived. It's true that nothing in life is free. Someone is always in line to pay for it. Our nation could learn a great lesson from all this, but I doubt that we will because our government can just print more money, and we will slip into the quicksand of insolvency until there is no airstream to keep us alive. Economic suffocation is a painful way to die!

Once, while Dad was in a recovery facility, mother had to sell some of her wonderful furniture in order to keep Sis in college. Finally, our beautiful home had to go. The outstanding loans could not be satisfied so the bank had no other alternative. All the people involved in my family's successes were now involved in terminating and dismantling our present existence. Lady and Lady's Princess had led the way several years earlier, and now our dream home was on the block. It was time to leave.

But having *things* doesn't make life meaningful, especially when alcohol becomes a love of one of the main participants—Dad.

God works in mysterious ways. We are rarely aware that something is behind every action and reaction. He is more dependable than a law of science. You just have to have faith and believe!

(2.1) Mom with hat and pearls

(2.2) Mom leaning against tree

(2.3) Mom as Miss St. Petersburg

(2.4) Mom and Quincy

3
The Downhill Drag

Life started a downhill drag about the time I was a high school Senior and started looking for a college to attend. I had already decided that I couldn't go in business with my father. It appeared he wouldn't have a business very long at the rate he was going. So I thought I would go into the USAF as an officer from a place like The Citadel in Charleston, SC. Dad had taught me a lot about flying so that plan looked like a natural to me. Meanwhile, mother was struggling to keep our family together.

The more Dad drank, the worse his conduct became. I was never aware of his becoming violent or physical with Mom, but he certainly cursed and shouted at her constantly. Her health and well-being were obviously affected. She would slip into periods of bad health—such as a nervous breakdown. I concluded that nothing was going to change until and unless Dad was faced with a crisis—like divorce or losing his family or something he loved.

On the other hand, he sent me to Transylvania music camp outside Brevard, North Carolina, and also to the Midwestern Music School at the University of Kansas. And every Saturday there was a country jam session at the store in Concord. Dad played the mandolin, violin, and accordion.

I had my saxophone and others joined in with guitars and every country-western instrument known to man.

He also bought me my first car, a 1931 Ford Victoria. Man, I was in high cotton, having one hell of a good time!

This wealth that Dad was producing was great for Carolyn and me, but not so good for our parents. The vows for Mom that Dad once held high seemed to fall like the leaves of autumn as he began to wander from the straight and narrow. I first noticed it when I was working at the main store in Concord. He had acquired two additional stores in Kannapolis and Albemarle, and both of them were doing well.

One day while working, I saw an attractive lady enter the store and go toward the stairway leading to the upper two floors. Dad walked over as if waiting on her, and then they disappeared up the stairs. I sensed that the other employees knew what was happening and just ignored it. This same process happened several other times, and I confronted Dad with my observation. He denied any wrongdoing and told me not to worry.

Another time, we were riding from the store heading to the farm. He stopped and asked a lady he knew if she would care to ride with us. I couldn't believe that he could do such a brazen act right in front of me. He took her into our lake house while I rode my horse. I confronted him again and he denied that anything was wrong.

There were many more incidences involving other women, and each time I confronted him there was no admission of guilt. All the while, my father was doing wonderful things for others—like passing out turkeys and other food items to poor people whom his route salesmen knew. We were both crying as we witnessed President Franklin Roosevelt's casket passing through Concord on the way to Washington toward the end of World War II. Yes, we had a really close bond, but I could not seem to save my Dad from himself.

While I was a sophomore at The Citadel, Dad was arrested for drunk driving in Albemarle, NC, and put into jail. Mother called me and I was able to come home for a few days to try to find a solution to the problem. I pleaded with Mom to threaten to divorce him. She simply would not do it.

After I bailed him out of jail, Carolyn, my younger sister, and I tried to reason with him to quit drinking, but to no avail. We were all worried that he was going to kill or injure someone or himself in a car accident since his driving was so erratic and crazy. This went on for year after year, and rehabilitation after rehabilitation.

Dad couldn't attend my graduation from The Citadel in May of 1953 because he was in yet another rehab unit trying to sober up. I might also add that many times Dad would show up at The Citadel, go to the front office, and bring a great deal of embarrassment to Mom and me by telling the authorities that he wanted them to hide certain objects because they wouldn't be safe at our home.

Finally, Mr. Grover Maxwell, Dad's boss, decided he had had enough of trying to manage a drunk so he fired him. I'm sure Dad was paid a lot of money for his part in the businesses, but all of that disappeared in the fumes of Jack Daniels and other well-known alcoholic sources.

Grover told me that I would not have to worry about my college bill, but to this day I don't know how Dad managed to pay my tuition at The Citadel. But here I was—a Citadel graduate with no outstanding college bills to pay. I think Grover took care of it and never mentioned it to me again. It certainly helps to have friends who care about you. Grover died in 1973 shortly after I was released from prison in Vietnam.

ABOUT THE TIME ALL this was happening in Concord, I had received a really plum of an assignment to open the new USAF Academy in Denver at Lowry Air Force Base, Colorado. The Air Force did not want to bring in cadets from West Point or Annapolis to run the cadet program the first three years of its existence. Instead, they decided to recruit seventy USAF officers who had just received their ratings (pilot, navigator, electronics operator, etc.) to handle the Wing of cadets and act as upperclassmen. They called us ATOs (Air Training Officers). We arrived in January of 1955 to train and get ready for the first class of 300 men in June.

By this time I was well aware of all the goings-on back home and wanted to assist Carolyn so she could have a good start in life. I had excellent connections with the airlines in Denver, and arranged for Sis to be interviewed for a Flight Attendant's job with Continental Airlines. She was accepted, came out to Denver and roomed with the fiancée of an ATO buddy of mine. Things were looking up!

Now came our parents. What to do? Where? Somehow the idea came up for them to move to Denver and rent a house. I could help with the payments and we might be able to live as a family again. They arrived. We found a suitable house, and Dad quickly found a job in the retail furniture business. Our family settled down to something resembling normal.

Being in Denver together was a direct result of my being assigned to the new USAF Academy and my bringing us all together. Again, love was in the air and we were together as a family. Dad had stopped drinking—at least for the time being—and we had all started anew. Mother was her old self again and God seemed to be smiling on our relationships.

After the 3rd class had entered the Academy and gone through the training program we ATOs administered to them, it was time for me to get another assignment and press on with my career in the USAF.

By this time Carolyn was doing well and began helping with our parent's house payments. Things appeared to be working out. Man, how long could this last? The answer came quickly.

Dad fell off the wagon again.

Meanwhile, my assignment at the USAF Academy was drawing to a close. My personal goal was to be assigned to Fighters in Europe, but we weren't certain what Carolyn would do when I left Colorado for Europe. I finally received my orders to report to Toul Rosiere Air Base in France flying F-100s. My dream was coming true!

Dad soon sobered up enough to look into the future. Through contacts he had made earlier, he found a furniture job in Cedartown, Georgia. Mother was pleased as Carolyn also used some of her past contacts in Georgia, and migrated to the Atlanta area.

Meanwhile, I had arrived in France to fly F-100s. The only constant in our family's lives was Dad's drinking. You could bet your life on that. In fact, Dad's drinking controlled Carolyn's life.

By the time in 1965 when I was shot down and captured, my sister had faced many crises, and solved them all without any help from me. It was as if I didn't exist. I was officially Missing in Action (MIA) for about 3 years. The question before my family every day of their lives was: *Is Quincy dead or alive?* I knew nothing of their current existence because I wasn't allowed to receive mail. How frustrating for all involved!

Eventually Dad died of lung cancer because he was a heavy smoker. Mom too died because of old age and the heavy burden of living with the man she loved dearly. Both were with Sis in Atlanta when they gave up the ghost and were no more—Dad in an ambulance on the way to a hospital, and Mom in Carolyn's car after a dental appointment.

I cannot praise Carolyn enough for what she has meant to our family. She has, indeed, done more than her share. Love is still the most powerful word and action in the English language.

I love you, Sis! Thank you for all you have done.

My father had been my hero and the type of man I hoped that I could become. A compassionate soul, he loved to help people who were down on their luck. Dad had done so much for me personally, and had given me every opportunity to prepare for success. He loved me and I loved him—until the Devil filled him with the liquid of death. At that point he became unlovable and seemed to stagger headlong into an abyss from which he could not recover. He was a fine man with a horrible addiction and I, to this very day, remember him for the good that he did and the joy that he spread.

James Quincy Collins, Sr., my father, was one hell of a man! May God accept him into his Kingdom, forgive him for the hurt that he rendered those who loved him, and make him worthy of the love that has come his way! Dad was buried between his mother and father in the Calvary Baptist Church cemetery outside Elko, South Carolina.

I was in the Air Force and my sister was carrying all the weight with no help from anyone. I think she still feels this burden to this very day, and still holds somewhat of a grudge against me for not being available to help them more.

⌒

IT WAS 1968 AND I was in prison in Vietnam. I knew nothing of events back home. Even if I *had* known, I could have done little to nothing to influence them. The very first letter I was given in prison, some five years from the time I was shot down, told me of Dad's death. The letter was two years old. I was floored and so disappointed, because the one thing I wanted to do was return home and tell my father how much I loved him and give him my personal thanks for all the wonderful things he had done for me. Now I would never have that opportunity. My father was dead!

Over the following weeks in prison, while lamenting my loss, I composed a poem that expressed my feelings. It came from my heart and soul. Here it is:

> *My Wonderful Friend, Dad*
> *No one will ever know the pain of sorrow and despair,*
> *That ripped my heart, tore my soul, and left me standing bare.*
> *So unprepared was I to read the startling news, so sad*
> *How death had claimed a part of me, my wonderful friend, Dad.*
>
> *Now that the darkened veil has covered one so dear to me,*
> *So many of my hopes and dreams I'll never, ever see.*
> *For all the words and deeds omitted when the chance I had,*
> *Have e'er been lost for me to do, my wonderful friend, Dad.*
>
> *So hear my word memorial, wherever you may be,*
> *I'm proud to be your son, and wear the name you gave to me.*
> *I'll ne'er forget the lessons that you taught—both good and bad.*
> *And may we meet again some day, my wonderful friend, Dad.*

My two ladies adjusted to being without Dad although his personal impact on both of them was felt for a long time. They both became involved in the POW/MIA movement to keep our status fresh in the eyes of the American public. They sold POW bracelets with my name, rank, and shoot-down date on them. When I finally returned to freedom, hundreds and hundreds of people who wore my bracelet wrote to me and sent me their bracelets. What a "Welcome Home" we all received from people who cared about us even though we were strangers. This is what America needs today.

Mom hated that my wife had already indicated to her that when— and if—I did return from Vietnam, she was going on without me—our marriage was over. This really concerned Mom.

My wife had prepared our three sons to expect me not to return alive, so my actual return was a surprise—especially to my wife.

I *did* return, and I really enjoyed having a mother and sister again, and also my three sons.

As time went on, I retired from the USAF, ran for Congress and even married again. When I told my mother about my plan to run for the U.S. House of Representatives, she hugged me and said, "Just remember that it will not be unanimous."

She also made a wise judgment on the woman I married during my second campaign for Congress. "This won't last long."

But when she met my present wife-to-be, Catherine, she said, "This is the real thing." And it has been just that for the past forty years. How do mothers know so much?

ON JANUARY 20, 1987, Carolyn had made an appointment for Mom to have her dentures checked. By this time Mom was in a nursing home near Alpharetta, Georgia. Sis took Mom to the dental facility, helped her to get situated, and waited for the work to be completed. When Mom was finished, someone assisted her to get back in the car and fastened her seat belt. As Sis drove along, Mom seemed to be perspiring profusely. Her head dropped and Carolyn put her hand on Mom's forehead. She was icy cold! Without a word or a sound, our mother was dead.

After all the tough times Mom had experienced, all the rough times she had spent with the man she adored, her life had ended quietly and with no pain. How appropriate!

Carolyn and Mom had discussed death arrangements so everything was already set when I arrived in Atlanta from Charlotte. Mom was cremated, and although it had snowed for several days, we spread her ashes over an area owned by one of Carolyn's friend who also loved our mother. To the very end my Sis was there. She had carried the burden of our parents for years.

I miss Mom. I think I was always her "little man" even when I grew to be 6'1" tall, but that didn't keep her from giving me instructions on how to behave. I never will forget one Friday evening when I was preparing to go out on a date in high school. The car was clean as could be and sparkled in the sunlight as I put on my jacket to head out.

Mom called and came toward me with that angelic countenance she sometimes had and said, "Son, remember that God is always watching, so please behave yourself!"

Of course she had referenced my date and that I should be a nice boy. I gave her a big hug and a kiss and replied, "So far I've had no complaints!"

The next morning at breakfast she asked how the evening went. I immediately replied, "It was great, Mom. My gosh—I hope *He* wasn't looking all night!" Then I hugged her and patted her on the backside as I exited the kitchen to go outside. What a gal!

I miss Dad, too, but most of all I am so very appreciative of my sister, Carolyn, and all that she has done to care for our parents. It has been a tough job all the way, and I thank her from the bottom of my heart for her devotion and love. She is an Angel!

———

My Sis, Carolyn, died unexpectedly in Marietta, GA, on Saturday, August 25, 2018. Now she is truly one of God's "Special Angels!"

(3.1) James Quincy Collins, Sr. at Carlisle Military
Institute-1917

(3.2) Mom and Dad at Myrtle Beach, SC

(3.3) Mom and Dad
sitting on bench

(3.4) Mom and
Dad at dinner

*(3.5) Parents' 25th Wedding Anniversary
at home with family and friends*

*(3.6) Carolyn, Mom, Dad and High Point,
NC Furniture Market*

*(3.7) Dad at his business desk,
Maxwell Bros. & Collins Furniture,
Concord, NC*

4

My Grandparents

The Collins: Every family has some very special people we know as grandparents. They are the mothers and fathers of our own mothers and fathers and, indeed, they are special people. They are our personal connection with the past and also our common thread with the future. In a way, they are who we have been and also who we might become. I have been told by many of Dad's relatives that I am a dead ringer for his father, my Grandpa Collins.

I really like that comparison because my Grandpa Collins was one terrific man. He didn't drink, he didn't curse, he was a big bundle of love and caring, and he was a man of God. You can't get any better than that. His favorite words to me were always, "I, I, I love you anyhow!" What an endearing phrase to tell your grandson. I loved it and I loved him.

To his many friends he was Uncle Jim. His most favorite personal trademark was the thumb on his left hand. While building his own home he smacked it with a hammer, splitting the thumbnail. It grew back as if he had two nails instead of one.

I would always say, " Grandpa, that must have hurt a lot!"

He would always reply, "Son, it shore did!"

He was such a great guy. On every visit we would make to their farm outside of Elko, SC, Grandpa would try to teach me the ways of farming and taking care of all the animals and chickens and collecting eggs, etc. I learned how to milk cows and feed the mules. I dearly loved to see him hook up a mule to the apparatus he used to squeeze the juice out of sugar cane, bring it to a boil, and bottle it to use as molasses. Now here is the best tasting deal on any farm. Allow fresh milk to cool in an icebox while the cream rises to the top. Scrape off the thick cream, pour it over a hot sugar biscuit, and then put hot molasses on top of that. Wow! That's the best!

Grandpa's house is still standing along with the barn and stables. Of course the outhouse is still standing. The old well with the chain and bucket I used to draw water is still there too. Grandpa built them right because they are a little over a hundred years old by now. Trees and vines have consumed their presence, but I would still like to go back and see the old place because I have so many fond memories there. Grandpa had an old Ford, either an "A" or a "T" model. He loved to crank it up on a Sunday and drive us all to their church, Calvary Baptist Church, up the old dirt road a mile or two.

My Dad used to drive down from Concord, our home in North Carolina, to Grandpa's and bring his parents back with him. I think that Dad might have been showing off a bit, but it was worth it to witness the pride they had in their son. Well deserved, Dad!

Grandma Collins was called Mattie by everyone. She was a character. She had a vertebrae dislocated in her back which caused a hump to develop between her shoulders. She always had a pipe in her mouth and might switch to a cigarette if her pipe wasn't convenient.

Dad had tried to provide his parents with all the modern conveniences, but that wasn't always successful. They preferred an old Ashley wood heater to electricity, and it took a while before they would use a regular refrigerator. Dad gave them a new modern bathroom for one of their anniversaries, but they still preferred the outhouse with a Sears and Roebuck catalogue hanging on a nail. Some things never change.

Grandpa had a deadly heart attack when I was a young man. I'll never forget the effect that viewing him lying in his casket had on me. An important part of my life would be no more. This was the first really important death to deal with for this little guy and the image of him in a casket will be with me forever.

After Grandpa's death, Grandma Collins had to live with her daughter, Cora Lee, in Aiken, SC. Living alone was no longer possible for her. Unfortunately, she later rolled off her bed and broke her hip. This required Dad to make arrangements for her at a hospital in Columbia, SC.

Dad was part owner of Ladies Funeral Home in Kannapolis so an ambulance was available to transport her to Columbia. Guess who her ambulance driver was destined to be? Yep, yours truly—and did I think I was something special, especially when I was allowed to turn on the siren to get around in traffic!

Eventually Dad had to bring Grandma Collins to a nursing home in Concord. Again, I got to be the driver. Two times in a row. Wow! This was something to crow about. Man, did I! Grandma would just smile at me because she knew how much it meant to me to be the one driving her to a better life. How great it was to see the sparkle in her eyes whenever she would ask me to help her light her pipe. All too soon she died. I no longer had my connection with the past. She is buried at the Calvary Baptist Church cemetery alongside my Dad and Grandpa Collins. These three souls have had a tremendous impact on my sister, Carolyn, and me. And when we walk that field in Alpharetta, Georgia, where we spread our mother's ashes, our memories are complete.

As you may conclude, the Collins clan probably had the most impact on our family. However, I will tell the story of the Doggetts and let you make your own conclusions.

The Doggetts: Mother's father and mother were the Doggetts. Their background appeared to lead back to Germany. The first recollection I have of Mom's family was when I, as a small lad, attended Grandpa Doggett's funeral at their home in Cowpens, SC. He seemed to be the patriarch of his family and lineage. I remember nothing personal about him. Photos depicted him as being rather stiff and always old. Mom never described him as being loving and caring and interested in any of his eight children (Charles, Willie Marie, Jim, Ollie, Janette, Oscar, Helen, and Ethel).

My father was the host, many times, of gatherings of the Doggett family at our lake home out from Concord. Dad's financial successes were not timely enough to include Grandpa Doggett before his death. I found out later that Grandpa Doggett had been in the cotton mill business with Colonel Tad Westmoreland, Gen. Westmoreland's father. Col. Westmoreland had become Chairman of the Board at The Citadel in Charleston. Little did I realize that he would present me my diploma when I graduated from The Citadel in 1953.

Mom's sisters and brothers loved to play poker for up to a quarter bet. Believe this or not—her sisters, except for Ethel and Mom, smoked cigars. A Sunday poker game was likely to occur on any given weekend. Fried chicken was always nearby, because Ollie and Janette were the best chicken cookers around and their dress sizes showed it. This was a social group. They loved to get together for any reason at all, and all the grand-kids were welcomed. It was like being in Las Vegas and having Mickey Mouse as a playmate. We kids loved it!

As I reflect on this part of my life, I am so appreciative that Dad made his resources available to Mom's family. That was my Dad!

(4.1) Top: Grandpa Collins
Middle: Grandma Collins
Bottom: Grandma Collins, Mom,
Grandpa Collins, Quincy

*(4.2) Grandma Collins (smoking pipe)
and Cora Lee Lybrand*

*(4.3) Quincy kneeling at his Grandfather's and
Father's graves, Calvary Baptist Church outside
Elko, SC*

(4.4)
Grandpa Doggett

(4.6) The Doggett Family
Back row: Ollie, Ethel, Helen,
Willie Marie (mom) and Jeanette.
Front row: Charles,
Oscar and Jim.

(4.5)
Grandma Doggett

5
When You Gotta Go, You Gotta Go!

Have you ever tried to go back in your life as far as you can remember? This is a perfect exercise to spend time on when you are in prison and are in that monotonous waiting period between interrogations and torture and the unknown.

First, it takes you away from the present and places you in a time frame years ago when things were, perhaps, a little more pleasant. At least different! Second, it causes you to dig into your brain and dredge out those memories that are hidden from normal recall. Some may be embarrassing to you now as an adult, and may unconsciously be repressed so that the world will never know what unseemly act you committed.

After all, of what importance is some past atrocious deed that is only remembered by your family, their friends, or other close neighbors? One thing is for sure—these people are old . . . really old, and cannot be relied on for the facts, unless what happened was funny, a disaster, or some completely unexpected occurrence. We all have them, and now it is my time to look back.

Episode #1

After combing my past and trying to look critically at some of the early events that shaped or warped my life, I have come to one conclusion. From birth to about three years old, everything that happened to me involved *doodoo*! My God, I hate to admit this but it's true! Potty training must have been a bear for my parents. I, apparently, manufactured a lot of this stuff and it had to go somewhere!

This brings me to my very first recollection. I must have been two or three years old. At least, upon closer examination, I believe I was still in diapers. Mom had enrolled me in some kind of school so she could get a break from my antics and normal body functions. I can see the location very clearly right now. A little driveway came off Church Street in Concord and led up to this delightful small white house that looked like a drawing from a kid's book.

Across the street from the entrance was Coltrane Grammar School. That always got my attention because I wanted to go there when I got bigger. I never did. I mean I *did* get bigger, but I never went there because Clara Harris Grammar School got this big guy instead, and I later made my mark there. But back to the quaint little white house with all the kids running around wild!

My Mother had dropped me off on this particular day because she was probably driving to Charlotte to shop—these items I do not recall, but they appear to be logical conclusions on my part. I was obviously still in diapers and had evidently dumped about five pounds of you-know-what into a diaper that only held about a pound—so I was in trouble! In fact, everyone around me was in trouble.

The lady in charge called my Dad at his furniture store to come get me because "my cup was running over," and just changing my diaper wasn't going to handle the situation.

Dad did what every successful executive would do—he told one of his trusted Lieutenants (salesmen) to go pick me up and bring me to the store. Ben Craven was this man's name, and I remember him well. I think Dad selected Ben because he always had a pipe in his mouth and smoke encircled him wherever he went. His bad habit would alleviate any odors that might otherwise be debilitating.

Ben arrived in his pickup delivery truck to transport baby-dumpling Collins back to the store. Yep—that pipe was really working overtime, especially after he saw my condition and began planning how he was going to handle this mess.

The Concord Tribune Newspaper provided the answer. I was placed between the frontpage headlines and the obituaries, rolled up like a homemade cigarette, and into his arms I went. Somehow, Ben got his package loaded into the front seat and drove back to Maxwell Brothers and Collins furniture store. All of Dad's employees—from secretaries to warehouse people—were waiting to greet me and also to pat Ben on the back for a job well done. But I don't think anyone wanted to touch Ben under the circumstances.

The rest of this story was told to me later—especially when I became a more sophisticated teenager and thought I was a real "ladies" man. These kinds of Moments can whittle away at your image and expose things that should be forgotten. It never was!

Episode #2

Let's move away from my diaper stage to a time when exploration and adventure became an integral part of my life—somewhere around four or five years old. We lived on Hillcrest Drive off South Union Street in Concord. Back then this was the outer perimeter of civilization. It was an area that had just been developed and was juxtaposed with the undeveloped land, and sort of in the wild area. There were lots of red hills and gullies and tons of trees for us kids to run around in, climb, and build forts in. We might leave our homes all clean and neatly pressed, but when we returned, that red dirt was in our hair, our ears and on every piece of clothing we had on. We truly looked like frontiersmen except that we had no arrows sticking in anything, and no one had a horse or a pony. We *did* have Red Ryder BB guns. I guess Congress would have had a piece of legislation outlawing them if we had been in more modern times.

The day had started out sunny and warm—which added to the excitement of running through the wilds of our neighborhood. Even back then, time could get away from you. Fun had no boundaries, as long as the weather was good! The lateness of the afternoon had slipped up on me. The first thing that brought me to reality was a big, growling black cloud that had moved in without my noticing it. I did notice that my tummy was also growling. I probably needed to be at home close to the bathroom. Reluctantly, I decided to head home. The closer I got to home, the quicker my steps became. I sensed an urgent condition was fast approaching.

Suddenly, the rain began to fall, the wind was howling, and the bright sunny day descended into darkness. I really picked up my pace then as I was on the paved sidewalk leading to my house. I was trying desperately not to slide down on the wet and soggy walkway. I was having a big gastro problem about now, so I prepared to make my final dash for the back door because it was closest to the bathroom. Out of nowhere came a flash of lightning that struck a telephone pole right beside me. It literally scared the stuffing out of me. Fortunately, I was wearing a little boy's version of Jockey underwear so nothing showed—yet! I headed up the driveway, but when things got worse I decided to go behind our newly constructed garage and slip out of my messy clothes before going inside the house.

The storm dissipated as quickly as it had developed, so that had a calming effect over me. That was short-lived as I inadvertently stepped on a nail that was driven through a board and it stuck through one of my toes. I let out a yell that could have broken a glass window! What else could happen to a kid who just missed being struck by lightning that literally scared the stuffing out of him while that stuffing clung to him like lava coming out of a volcano—and he has a nail sticking through one of his toes to boot?

I was one crying and scared mess of humanity. I needed my Mother! She took the little child in, cleaned him up, took him to the doctor for a Tetanus shot, and soothed the savage beast until it was time for another adventure at the end of the world. A Mother's love is the very best!

DOWNTOWN CONCORD, 1930s

<small>ZACK ROBERTS/COURTESY OF HISTORIC CABARRUS ASSOCIATION</small>

There were no parking places to be found on this 1930s morning in downtown Concord on Church Street. Seen at right is the rear of the Maxwell Bros. & Collins Furniture store, which faced Depot Street (now Cabarrus Avenue). This business, known in its final incarnation as Heilig-Meyers Furniture, is now empty and is the cornerstone of a proposed redevelopment of this entire city block.

(5.1) Downtown Concord 1930s - Maxwell Bros. & Collins Furniture

(5.2) Quincy at 3 months old with nurse

(5.3) Quincy with Mom

(5.4) Quincy on sliding board in backyard in Concord, NC

(5.5) Quincy, 4 ½ yrs. old, with sister Carolyn, 6 mos., on Hillcrest Dr., Concord, NC

(5.6) Grandma Doggett, Mom and Dad and Quincy, Myrtle Beach, SC

(5.7) Quincy with Mom and Dad at Grandpa Collins' home in Elko, SC

6
My First Safari

Hitler began World War II on his 50th birthday in April 1939. Over 60,000 German troops paraded in his honor and the parade lasted over 5 hours. Meanwhile, in a sleepy little city named Concord, NC, two grammar school playmates left their homes on Hillcrest Drive and headed for their favorite place—the Three-Mile Branch. It was just a small creek with sand and weeds, and it wound around an area that flooded when a lot of rain fell, but today it was calm and peaceful. Best of all, it was warm.

My best friend was Lee Kinard, and he and his family lived in a duplex apartment next door to me. Years later, Lee made a name for himself in the Greensboro area as a TV anchorman, and his name became synonymous with broadcast excellence, compassion, and good old southern charm. Yes, Lee was my buddy and we were up to no good on this beautiful April day.

Lee's mother had warned us many times about taking off our clothes down by the creek and romping up and down "au natural"—but it was exhilarating fun, and we knew we weren't supposed to do it. That was the real challenge. At any rate, off they came! We threw the clothes up on the bank of the creek. Up and down, across and jump, and two young gazelles leaped with joy and freedom as if we had just been released from our cage. We chased each other, played follow the leader, and went way beyond our normal play space just so we could say we had explored. I didn't know then what a motivational concept that would become in both of our lives—but right then we were just having a lot of fun!

We must have played for several hours without the slightest feeling of fatigue, but a quick look at the position of the sun told us that it was late, and we had better get our fannies home.

It was always a task to try to determine where we were after running blindly up and down that long stretch of creek, and then realizing that we were naked as Jaybirds with no place to hide. We searched frantically until we finally recognized the small hill where we had thrown our clothes. Yep, this was it—but our clothes weren't there! Someone had taken them. We started to panic.

Way up on the hill where the access road ended, we heard a car horn beep. There stood Lee's mother with our clothes in her hand. She yelled for us to make it home on our own. Her instructions ended with, "And be careful!"

Be careful? How in God's name were we going to walk through woods and neighborhoods and be careful? We looked at each other. Now we really were naked! Embarrassed, angry, frustrated and naked. It doesn't get much worse than that for two little boys out in the wilderness of life alone. So what were we to do?

We looked for cover—leaves, branches—anything that would hide us. We also checked the woods and the road and the paths so we could plot a course that would be hard for us to be seen. Off we went, each step like walking on eggshells. Our heads were on swivels checking for people who might see us. We were like deer running in the night—*except it was broad daylight!* A quick move here, a stop, then full speed ahead until we heard a noise or thought we saw something. This was a frightening experience—one I would never forget. But we weren't home yet.

Each of us thought about the last dash we would have to take to put us inside our homes. We each had different environments to conquer as we split up in the red hills behind our homes. We didn't even say goodbye.

We just ran as fast as our legs would carry us, and we did it without the police discovering us, or our neighbors screaming. Thank God our doors were always unlocked. We entered like Roman soldiers returning from a conquest.

Did we learn a lesson from this? Most certainly. Never head to the Three-Mile Branch when Lee's mother was home!

(6.1) Old friends meet again! Quincy with Lee Kinard

TV—4—Daily News, Sunday, December 9, 1973

BEGINNING MONDAY on the 7:30 a.m. segment of Ch. 2's "Good Morning Show," Lee Kinard (right) will present a series of interviews with Col. Quincy Collins, formerly of Concord and now of Atlanta. Collins will discuss his experiences as a POW after his fighter bomber was shot down over North Korea in 1965.

(6.2) Newspaper photo of Lee and Quincy

Obituary for Lee William Kinard Jr., *Nov. 5, 1931 - Oct. 20, 2018*

GREENSBORO - Loved by so many, Lee William Kinard, Jr. age 86 died peacefully on Saturday, October 20, 2018, surrounded by family. The family would like to thank the wonderful nurses at Cone Hospital for their compassionate care and attention.

(6.3) Lee's Obituary

Lee was the oldest of four children born to Henrietta Grace Winecoff Kinard and Lee William Kinard, Sr. on November 5, 1931.

He married the love of his life, Anne Courtney Milton on October 11, 1952. They just celebrated their 66th wedding anniversary.

Lee is survived by his wife Anne, their children Beverly Ann Kinard Marsh (Robert) of Tucson, Arizona, Valerie Grace Kinard Surasky (Charles) of Atlanta, and Lee William Kinard III (Normandee) of Canton, Georgia.

Grandchildren, Jessica Lynn Kinard Easley (John) of Charlotte and Austin M. Kinard of Greensboro. Honorary grandchildren Anna Gentry and Luke Gentry (children of Kim and Todd Gentry).

Beloved sisters and brother, Jane Coulter of Venice, Florida, Judy Thomas (Jack) of Jamestown and Glenn Kinard (Dianne) of Fairfax Station, Virginia. Sister-in-law Emily Milton Sells of San Antonio, Texas.

Nieces and nephews, Ashley Sells, Jack Thomas (Rachel), Karen Thomas, Jonathan Kinard (Lauren), Christopher Kinard (Meryl) and Mathew Kinard (Nicole).

Lee served in the Army (as Chief of the Radio and TV Section) during the Korean War at Fort Bragg and in Puerto Rico. He was particularly proud of having participated in the Army's first atomic weapons maneuver. He was awarded the Certificate of Merit and promoted to Staff Sergeant for his filmmaking efforts.

Lee got all three of his degrees at UNC-G along with his girls. He received undergraduate and graduate degrees in English and a doctorate in Education. He received six School Bell awards during his life and was committed to education in all forms.

He worked in radio in Albemarle until starting at WFMY-TV on April 16, 1956. He created the Good Morning Show in December 1957 and continued the development of that show until 1999. He produced award winning documentaries on a variety of local, national and international topics. In 2000 he became the Executive Assistant to the President of GTCC and helped to create the Larry Gatlin School of Entertainment Technology and as the Institutional Historian he oversaw the Office of Marketing and Public Information. He worked in that position until he retired finally in 2014.

He was a member of the North Carolina Association of Broadcasters Hall of Fame and a recipient of the Silver Service Award presented by the National Television Academy of Arts and Sciences. He thought his most significant award, however, was the one he most recently received, the Unsung Hero Award from the International Civil Rights Center and Museum.

He was the author of three books and traveled the world.

He loved most in life his wife Anne, their children, his fur babies Buffy and Molly, in addition, his garden, his books, his travels, his writing and his memories.

Always a wonderful teller of stories, he reveled in weaving a magical tale to whomever would listen. He interviewed everyone he ever met and was genuinely interested in their life and experiences. He loved cooking big breakfasts, going to garden stores, shopping with Anne and going to the beach. Things are much quieter without him. He will be missed.

From www.forbisanddick.com/obituaries/Lee-Kinard/

7

Tripping The Light Fantastic

Even for a five-year-old youngster named Quincy Collins, Concord, NC, afforded its citizens a wide variety of community involvement. My Dad leased a big building in Concord to house his Maxwell Brothers & Collins Furniture Company. The lady who owned the property also had a daughter in her twenties who operated a dancing school out of her mother's home. This caught my Mom's eye, and little Quince was suddenly going to dance lessons with a bunch of little girls and a boy or two.

We were taught a bit of ballet, a lot of tap dance, and a smattering of ballroom dancing. Oh, how mothers loved seeing their precious little children doing grown-up things while still having to run to the bathroom at the most inopportune times. Coming to class really was fun! I will have to admit that I looked forward to it, although I never said a word to my guy friends about my feelings. To them, this was a torture session laid on me by a repressive and dictatorial mother. But look at Fred Astaire!

The end of the season recital was the apex of all the practicing we had been doing for months. Now we had to be measured for costumes, learn routines and timing, and know what to do with ourselves while on the stage. Man! This was big time! Just like we were going to perform on Broadway.

I didn't want any of my buddies to know about this, and certainly did *not* want them to attend the event. Secrecy became very important to me, but not to Mom, who wanted everyone to know that her little angel was going to perform! I wanted to hide under the bed and not see any of her friends, but that was not going to happen.

In the meantime our dancing teacher had made contact with the folks at WBT in Charlotte and arranged to bring a group of us over to perform on some young peoples' program. The next thing I knew, I was tap dancing on a Coca-Cola carton turned upside down and singing some stupid song I just had to learn. The emcee was a gruff guy named Grady Cole. If this was what it was going to take to have fame and fortune in this business, I wanted no part of it! It was now time to put away my tap shoes and costumes and move on in life.

When I left grammar school and entered the 7th grade in 1943, World War II was coming to an end. But another important thing happened in my life—I discovered girls! This seemed like it happened overnight and I liked it! I noticed that some of my buddies had the same transformation, and suddenly afternoon movie dates and soda shop visits became fashionable. We little guys were becoming big guys, and life was getting a lot more interesting.

It is worth noting that my taste in girls was not centered on glamour or their being beautiful. I was more interested in a girl who liked the same things I did—having pets or riding ponies and horses and camping out kinds of things. Of course, going to Summer Camp became an annual event and my friendships grew tremendously.

My personal involvement with music really got me going socially. I became an accomplished saxophone player and learned to play the piano by ear. By the time I was a junior in high school, I was dating a young lady who was an accomplished dancer and ballerina. She conned me into pulling out my dancing shoes, and we became a dance team that performed at various functions in the community of Concord. The call of Fred Astaire was getting louder!

Dance band music in college really turned me on. I became the dance bandleader at the Citadel in Charleston, SC, during my final two years there. When I graduated in 1953 I carried my horn in the trunk of my car and was primed to play whenever the occasion arose. I also was aware that I was a smooth dancer and was easy to follow. So dancing was and is an activity I thoroughly enjoy.

(7.1) First grade photo (Quincy far right on next to last row)

(7.3) Quincy as Drum Major of High School Band

(7.2) Concord High School Band on front steps of school

(7.4) High school dance orchestra, The Southerners, first live TV broadcast from WBTV in Charlotte, NC

(7.6) Quincy relaxing at the piano "somewhere"

(7.5) Quincy leading the Citadel's Bulldog Orchestra in 1953

8
Boys Will Be Boys

In high school in the late 40's, a lot of clubs flourished and provided opportunities to us kids to learn various skills and gain experience in the game of Life! One of the best clubs at Concord High School was the Key Club, an offshoot of the men's Kiwanis Club. Our elders came to our campus and solicited assistance from the Principal and teachers to develop a list of students to interview for this prestigious club. Approximately fifteen guys were selected to be the Charter Members. I was one of them—along with several of my best friends.

This association was to become one of our primary social outlets, plus we were able to begin projects to help our fellow students and also to assist needy families in our community. All in all, we had a feel good group that could accomplish many worthwhile projects when we got serious about it.

Unfortunately, we weren't serious about everything! We liked to kid each other, harass other of our friends from time to time, and, in general, create havoc amongst people we liked. We liked to laugh at what we were doing—not to do anything illegal or immoral—and to push that envelope as far as we dared. One Sunday in about 1948 we hit our apex in our endeavors to be wild—maybe even weird! Here is what happened.

One of our Key Club members was quite bright and headed the Honor Society in our school. Rodney was not a good buddy type person because he was a bit arrogant about his academic status. He had become a brown-noser kind of guy to further his own personal agenda, and this was a slight irritant to many of us who knew him.

As an example: Rodney kept bragging about being selected to go to a big National Honor Society conference out of state. An idea popped into the brains of several of us that we wanted everyone to understand that our friend Rodney was, indeed, a "brown-noser"—and would lick the boots of anyone who might be able to further his causes.

One of our motley crew was a good chemistry student and told us about the effect of putting a certain chemical on human skin to turn it brown. This was *it*! He smuggled a tube of the stuff out of the Chemistry Lab, and during lunchtime we gathered around Rodney and applied the stuff all over his nose. Needless to say, he resisted, and called us every name in the book, but it worked! Rodney went to the conference with the biggest, brownest nose known to man—and no amount of scrubbing would take it off. Now, back to that fateful Sunday in 1948.

Our group would often get together on Sunday afternoon and drive around or visit someone unexpectedly. On this particular Sunday we were in my buddy Jess' Daddy's car. It was ancient, big, and looked important—and that was fine with us. We headed out towards the Concord airport until we spotted a construction site that had a mud hole in the middle of what looked like a small lake. A raft was floating around in the center, so we pulled over to survey the situation.

Our buddy Rodney was with us. He had announced at the very first that he couldn't swim. I could see the dark thoughts swirling around in a few heads as we slipped into our swimming trunks and climbed aboard a small boat that was pulled up on shore, and headed for the raft. We dove in, pushed each other into the lake and had a really great time, except we left Rodney alone because he didn't swim. But the mysterious idea was about to be exposed. And so it was.

We took Rodney's bathing trunks, climbed into the boat and left him on the raft, naked as the day he was born! And what was to be our next community project?

We climbed into the big car and headed to uptown Concord. On Sunday, everyone who had a car had cleaned it until it sparkled, then drove through and around town for hours. We were to become a part of that slow-moving line of traffic.

Jones Yorke yelled out, "Let's take off our clothes and drive through the Square!" That was all we needed, so off they came. We all tried to sit as low in the seats as possible. Jess got in the line of cars as we waved at everyone and laughed at how brave and daring we were—that is, until we saw the policeman standing at the Square.

The policeman was eyeing every car as if this was a blockade to uncover illegal drugs, guns and liquor. There wasn't enough time to put our clothes back on so we grinned, breathed heavily, and approached the stoplight at the Square. Could we make it through while it was green? The answer was *NO!* It turned red just as we were opposite the policeman.

The car became deathly quiet. All heads faced the constable, but no one spoke. Would our naked torsos cause him to step over to investigate? The seconds passed like hours as we perched there waiting for the light to change.

Eventually the "big green" appeared and we drove—oh so cautiously—until Jess felt that he could gun the big engine and take us to safety. We dressed quickly, and decided leaving Rodney naked on the raft was not the brightest decision we had ever made. So we raced out to retrieve him, apologized to him, and pledged to try to be better friends in the future. I think we have been.

(8.1) Concord, NC High School main entrance

(8.2) Concord Key Club at International Convention, Hotel Peabody 1948. Concord's members are on third row from bottom—left to right

(8.3) Concord High School Class of 1949 Reunion—(No one remembers the date of the reunion)

9

The Man with the Horn

I have a theory that most instrumental musicians begin their careers by playing the piano. Some mother, aunt, or next-door friend was teaching piano, or at least played the piano. That is how we little guys and gals came to know this instrument. My Mom played and also sang with a pretty good soprano voice. I didn't like her high notes, but all in all she was a good starter for me.

Along came Dad with his mandolin, accordion and country fiddle and I was hooked—especially when those two sat down together to knock out some country western song Dad knew. Or sweet Mom would pull an old love song out of her extensive repertoire and loving father would try to follow. So it was an established fact that I was destined to take piano and so I did!

While at Clara Harris Grammar School around the second grade our teacher, Mrs. Fundeburke, a good-looking brunette who sang in our Church Choir, introduced our class to the flute. It was a very basic instrument with, I think, six holes and a small mouthpiece to blow through. Every student got one and we dedicated about an hour a week to making noise through this metal tube.

At least I had enough of a musical ear to distinguish between a *good* and a *bad* sound coming from the flute. When all the students were blowing, it was horrible! We could have been named the *Garbage Can Symphony* and been pretty close to the sounds being produced by this untrained group of house apes, but it was a start.

As time went on, I was sent to several different teachers including my own Aunt, Janette Setzler, who lived in Concord; Mrs. Barnhardt, who lived next door to her; and several other outstanding teachers who lived close by. I lived by the tunes in the *John Thompson Book for Beginners* and such complex compositions as *Here we go, in a row, to a birthday party.* And the exotic *Darling Dear, Sandman's near, soon you will be sleeping.* These were little songs to teach me how to use my left hand and then my right and I remember the damn things to this very day! This is called Musical Impact and those reading this who have taken piano lessons know what I mean. I am a *John Thompson* product!

As I entered the 7th grade I really felt sophisticated and advanced. I was in the same building with juniors and seniors and could rub elbows with these athletic and academic giants, and see them driving cars and holding hands with pretty girls. I was in heaven—and I had all these angels close by to guide me. How could I miss?

The flute had long since vanished. Now I had the opportunity to play in a real band—the Concord High School Band! "Doc" Brausa was the director and played a heavenly trumpet. He was recruiting for the band and introduced me to a horn I would come to love and cherish—the Baritone Saxophone! It was as big as I was, and sat in a stand that I had to adjust so my mouth would be in the right place to blow into the horn. My best solution was to sit on a Coca Cola crate. That way, my mouth was in the right place to bite down on my mouthpiece and blow into my horn. I couldn't hook the horn on a strap around my neck to carry because the instrument dragged the ground if I did. I just wasn't tall enough—yet!

Although "Doc" Brausa wasn't a woodwind teacher, he obtained every *How To* book available to help me progress with my new instrument—and music in general. Later, other band directors like Mr. Warren Wilson and George Peck pushed me along and challenged me to improve.

I practiced several hours each day, driving my household wild, and ensuring approval for my attendance at summer camps to further my capabilities and progress with this horn.

I also attended many music conventions conducted by the directors of music at all the big southern colleges—plus I attended summer music camps at Brevard, conducted by James Christian Phoel of Davidson College. I also enrolled in the Midwestern Music Camp at the University of Kansas, a six-week school that also afforded me the opportunity to learn how to twirl the baton and arrange marching formations for my high school band. Wow! I was on top of the world—practicing hard to be the best Baritone Sax player in North Carolina, and also the best and highest-strutting Drum Major Concord ever had!

Our marching band received the highest ratings in every contest we entered and also in every music contest in which we competed, because we practiced so hard and had the greatest motivation to succeed.

I thought the most interesting part of these contests was the sight-reading competition. The judges passed out music that most bands had never seen or played before because their difficulty was several levels beyond our normal music library. Our Director would explain to us the most difficult parts then lead us in playing that new selection.

In addition to this, I entered every sax competition available and established a reputation for making the most difficult musical selections appear easy. I had to work my butt off to attain this status, but music gave me goals I wanted to achieve, and that carried over into all phases of my life. Lesson learned: You can achieve whatever you want if you will dedicate your time and effort to that project.

Sometimes, in life, achievement or recognition is thrust upon you without your realizing it or maybe even desiring it. The *Quincy Collins Fanny Fan Club* was one such designation! As Drum Major of my high school marching band, it was my job to strut my stuff out in front of the marching group. The Majorettes and Flag Girls marched right behind me and my rear end was always in view to them. I suppose because they had nothing better to do, they established the *Quincy Collins Fanny Fan Club!*

When I heard about this most august group, I wasn't certain how to respond, or even if I should acknowledge my esteemed status. But over time I appreciated their flattery and would give them free gum and candy when they came into the school canteen which Jackie Aerhart and I ran for the school. I finally had a *following!*

Because our band did have some outstanding musicians, I formed the first dance band at Concord High. We called ourselves *The Southerners*, and *Stars Fell on Alabama* was our theme song.

In addition to the normal dance library of love songs and jitterbug and shag songs, I decided to try my luck at writing fun presentations like Spike Jones used to do. These were more difficult than I first thought, but they were fun and required excellent timing and musical savvy to present and perform.

In my junior year I started dating Carolyn Junker, who was also in the marching band. She helped Peggy Sapp with her well-known dancing class in Concord. Carolyn was a very smart young woman and ended up being my Class Valedictorian.

She worked up several exhibition dance routines for us and we danced at several big school parties and banquets before we parted ways during our senior year.

In 1949 I graduated from Concord High and was offered several music scholarships to Davidson, Duke, UNC at Chapel Hill and several other local colleges. My thought processes led me to believe that if I followed the music route, I would starve to death—because I loved playing so much I would do it for nothing! I needed discipline and a structured life.

So, I entered The Citadel at Charleston, SC. Yes, I signed up for the Citadel marching band and also the concert band. The Bulldog Orchestra (the school's dance band) soon followed, and I really began to get with the part music was ultimately to play in my life. I sang in the Protestant choir on campus and in the choir at The Citadel Square Baptist Church in Charleston as a soloist.

One year I attended summer school at The Citadel and played with several great combos in Charleston. During other holiday breaks I played with established dance bands in Charlotte (Billy Knauff) and other small groups who might need a fill-in. I kept trying to improve my playing ability, and these opportunities gave me a lot of experience playing with different groups. My Bulldog Orchestra had as many as 17 people in it, and I played with groups as small as 3 people. This experience was invaluable to me and pushed my playing ability beyond my wildest expectation.

After graduating from The Citadel in 1953, I became a Second Lieutenant in the USAF and hit the road to becoming a Fighter Pilot. In the trunk of my car was my best friend—my Baritone Sax. It was with me every step of the way in my Air Force career. I played that horn when I was chosen to be an Air Training Officer at the new USAF Academy. Later I had opportunities to play with outstanding bands in Europe, Africa, the USA and Japan, and I loved every minute of it.

Music came with me when I was shot down in 1965 and captured by the North Vietnamese. It was a part of my life in trying to improve the status of all POWs by starting choirs while in prison. We sang Christmas songs and hymns and my own creation—the *POW Hymn!* President Nixon asked that I direct the *POW Hymn* at his White House Dinner for the returning POWs in May of 1973.

My wife had chosen not to wait for my return so I invited my loving sister, Carolyn, to be my date for that White House event. She deserved that recognition by me because she worked tirelessly to make our plight known to the American people. She also cared for our parents while I was incarcerated. This one loving and caring sister did more for my POW mates and me than my wife was ever capable of doing. God bless her and keep her in my remembrances forever!

(9.2) Photo taken in Hanoi prison by Cuban photographer. This photo identified him, changing his status from MIA to POW. Original composer would not have recognized lyrics since Quincy changed them to pass on military information.

(9.1) Fourth of July caricature after his Congressional Campaign

(9.3) Quincy at his 70th Birthday Party, playing Sax to show his grandkids what jazz is all about!

10
My Longest And Dearest Friend

Some people you seem to have known forever. Jesse Fisher was one of those. He popped up in my life during the time that we both were in grammar school. He attended Coltrane and I went to Clara Harris Grammar School in Concord, North Carolina. We both were members of our school's Safety Patrol and proudly wore the sash that indicated that we were members of that elite corps. We directed traffic, settled squabbles amongst students and anything else assigned to us by our Principal.

Jess and I met at a hearing involving two of our fellow students and a confrontation they had over some minor issue. Neither student was very bright, as I recall. I represented my student and Jess his, so we ended up becoming friends as a result of settling the issue. The next thing I recall was being invited to Jess's home on South Union Street to see his animals and have his pet billy goat pull us around the neighborhood. Now how cool is that?

It certainly made an impression on me and I returned the favor by taking Jess out to our farm several miles out of Concord. Dad had a herd of white-faced cattle, 8-10 milk cows, mules, a couple of riding horses, a pony, pigs, and a big lake to swim and boat in. Everything two little boys could have hoped for and we had a ball!

Jess and I loved to play make-believe, and our minds were fertile with ideas to try. Some worked fine, others didn't, and our parents generally guided us to some less destructive endeavor. As we grew older, bicycles became important to us as we expanded our world. It also gave our parents more concern as these two little mavericks became world travelers and would disappear for hours at a time.

Jess' parents were much older than mine, and our other friend's parents too. Being an only child, Jess caused them a lot of concern, especially when they realized that I was more of a free spirit, and Jess was the well-disciplined and "mind-your-parents" type child. That description appears to have followed us into and beyond adulthood. More and more I observed that my good friend wanted to be more like me. That was flattering, but kind of dangerous too. His folks felt, from time to time, that I was a wee bit out of control and might not be the best friend for Jess to have. Nevertheless, we pressed on fearlessly, enjoying each other and establishing a bond that would last a lifetime.

In the 7th grade we both were introduced to band music. I became interested in the baritone saxophone and Jess latched onto the trombone. Our households would never be the same again as both of us were determined to be the best that we could be. My horn was a little bigger than I was and Jess' arms could hardly accommodate the slide positions for notes at the end of the scale. A mid-teen growth spurt took care of both of these problems and we really began to excel with our instruments. Jess developed a smooth sound from his instrument that would have made Tommy Dorsey proud, and I played the big baritone sax like it was an alto with a sound like a bassoon. We won every music contest we entered each year in high school. Jess began taking voice lessons while I centered my singing with barbershop quartet type music.

In the summer of 1946, Jess and I attended Transylvania Music Camp in Brevard, North Carolina, which was run by Dr. James Christian Pfhol, Director of Music at Davidson College. During that summer, Jess met the head of vocal music at Davidson, Dr. Bird, and became his voice student. He became a very talented bass/baritone professional singer, and sang in choirs over the two Carolinas until his death in 2014.

While my good friend was making progress in his field, our Concord High School Band Director convinced me that I should go to his Alma Mater, the University of Kansas, to attend the Midwestern Music School at Lawrence, Kansas. Warren Wilson, our Band Director, was a very handsome man with a well-known Hollywood actor, Brian Donlevy, for a first cousin. (Brian was in all the World War II movies, especially those that had a lot of Marines in the plot.)

So off I went on the train by myself, to take another step in my musical ladder. Warren also wanted me to learn how to be a drum major. Not only that, he wanted me to learn how to twirl a baton. The drum major of the Kansas University Band was a national champion twirler and strutting machine—so I had my work cut out for me.

The camp was great, the music teachers were outstanding, and the drum major instructor was unbelievable. I quickly got with the program and made amazing progress in all the fields I had chosen. A new venture for me was playing in a real dance band. I could already read the musical notes, but now I was learning how to ad-lib where I put my own personal touch to the chord progressions. This was really liberating to me and caused me to develop a talent I did not previously have. The entire summer was Quincy development time, and I was anxious to show Concord what this country boy had learned.

Jess and I both continued our musical journeys, but another issue came to the forefront—acting! Mrs. Blanche Stewart was director of all Thespian activities at Concord High and she was damned good! She recruited Jess and me for every 3-act play coming down the pike, and she especially liked the chemistry we brought to the stage. What a joy this was to the both of us and we learned much that would be instrumental in bringing about other successes that would come our way.

Eventually high school graduation would separate us just when we were really rolling! Jess picked Davidson for academic reasons and I picked The Citadel because I needed a bunch of discipline. By college graduation time, Jess had picked the loveliest of the lovelies, Miss Gaye Sanders of Charlotte, to be his wife and share the future they would make together.

I was having a hell of a good time searching for Miss Perfect and turning over every stone to uncover her. Life was good and we were all meeting the challenges ahead. After all the discussions we had as kids about sex and what was involved in producing kids, Jess finally decided to put his learning to practice and suddenly two boys appeared, Powell and John. They obviously got all their good looks from Gaye.

Jess went on to get a PHD in Economics and to teach for a while at Chapel Hill and Davidson. An inheritance eventually led him to Whiteville to take over his uncle's investments and properties there. Gaye went on to become quite an acclaimed artist in watercolors with a studio on Church Street in Charleston. Catherine, my wife, and I became two of her best clients.

I suspect that as Gaye became more successful and professionally better known, Jess had a difficult time accepting this. He became more and more noticeably upset with her over the studio operation in Charleston and specific marketing expenses associated with that business. We visited with them in Charleston frequently and would go to dinner at some of the better places.

I began to notice that Jess would try to set me up for an argument just to light my fire. His position might be one that was in opposition to the current news anchors or Fox or even Department of Defense positions, since he knew that I kept abreast of developments in that area. Maybe he just liked to see me get excited and start a verbal rebuttal, but I never let an opportunity go by without voicing what I thought to be the truth.

One of his worst affronts to Gaye was at an invitation-only party to Gaye's 80th birthday and also their 60th Wedding Anniversary. Jess began by welcoming everyone, and then he started talking about me and how I was the closest thing to a brother that he had. He also reminded everyone of the sacrifice I had made for my country by being shot down, captured and remaining a POW for 7 1/2 years in Hanoi.

I was embarrassed, and getting madder and madder that he was not acknowledging Gaye's birthday or their Wedding Anniversary. Finally, I interrupted and chewed his ass somewhat gently for his oversight and rudeness. It did not faze him one bit—but the group got my point.

Now we could all see how he was changing. He would never go to a doctor for an examination, and it finally caught up with him in the form of advanced leukemia. Gaye was catching hell at every turn, but he did not ever want her to leave his sight. He knew that his days, even hours, were numbered. On Sunday, February 9, 2014, my longest and dearest friend departed this earth. Only in memories will we be able to make people laugh at our antics and insane reenactments. Perhaps, that is what we were doing in the first place. Creating memories.

Shortly before he died, Jess began to tell his two sons that their mother was stealing from the estate. Nothing could have been further from the truth. As a result of this indoctrination by Jess, the two sons have sued their mother and caused her untold misery. My love for and respect for Jess has declined appreciably, and my wife and I take every opportunity to try to lift Gaye to more positive attitudes and outlooks. I am so sorry that Jess took this path as my heart hurts for what he might be facing in his afterlife.

I think Jess may have forgotten that God is in charge and in control of what happens to us, both while we are alive and after we have departed this earth. May God Bless Us All!

Obituary for Jesse Caldwell Fisher Jr., *Jun 2, 1931 - Feb. 9, 2014*

WHITEVILLE: Dr. Jesse Caldwell Fisher, Jr., born in Concord, North Carolina, on June 2, 1931, went to his maker February 9, 2014. He was the son of the late Jesse Caldwell Fisher, Sr. and Jane Powell Fisher.

He is survived by his wife of 60 years, Gaye Sanders Fisher and two sons, Jesse Powell Fisher and his fiancé' Lori, and John Spurgeon Fisher and his wife Lisa, and three grandchildren, Jesse Powell Fisher, Jr., Cameron Bishop Fisher, and George Sanders Fisher.

(10.1) Jesse Caldwell Fisher, Jr.'s obituary

Dr. Fisher attended Davidson College as an undergraduate, and Duke University, where he received a Masters Degree in Economics. After serving two years, as an officer in the United States Army, he completed his doctoral program in Economics at the University of North Carolina at Chapel Hill.

Dr. Fisher served as Chairman of the Committee that secured Southeastern Community College for Columbus County. He was a Charter member of both the Charlotte Oratorio Society and the Southeastern Oratorio Society. He was a bass soloist in both organizations. Music has been a thread throughout his life.

Before assuming the business responsibilities and development of his Family's 138 year old company, J. L. Powell & Company, Inc., he taught economics at the University of North Carolina at Chapel Hill, and Davidson College. Dr. Fisher, was a founder of Beachwood Golf Club and served as a director. He also served as a director of Shadow Moss Golf Plantation in Charleston, as well as several miniature golf courses in Daytona Beach, Florida. Dr. Fisher also served as a director of Peoples Savings & Loan and WHQR radio station both in Wilmington, NC. He was a member of the First Presbyterian Church of Whiteville, NC, and a former member of the Cape Fear Club of Wilmington, NC.

From www.mckenziemortuary.net/notices/ DrJesse-FisherJr

(10.2) Our comic friends seem to have forgotten something—their pants!

(10.3) Guess who was the MC at the Quincy Collins Homecoming Festivities?

11

The Preacher Boy

S how me a person who acknowledges the presence of God and the mission of Jesus Christ to save the world and I will show you a human being who has considered the ministry as an occupation!

In my early years in Concord, North Carolina, my family attended the First Baptist Church. I became involved with the Baptist Training Union and attended their meetings every Sunday evening. There were some really wonderful people conducting the meetings and adding leadership to the group. Frankly, that was the reason I joined and participated on a regular basis. True, we learned about the Bible and its impressive list of characters and the many messages Jesus left to guide us in our living. But the main motivation I had was to be with the people I had come to know who were in leadership positions, who were true Christians, and followers of Christ. I wanted to be like them!

My interest in this aspect of my life diminished somewhat during my high school days, but it took a more active turn for the better when I arrived at The Citadel in the *Holy City*, Charleston, South Carolina. This name came from the fact that there were so many churches and tall, impressive church steeples looming heavenward out of the city. There was a spirit that was Godly and impressive and very noticeable exuding from one of America's most historical cities, and this young man from Concord fell under the spell.

Even though The Citadel was a military college and we wore uniforms, there were a lot of extra curricular activities available to us. One was a club named the Baptist Student Union that met every Wednesday night for one hour. Students, especially female, from other schools in Charleston were invited to our meetings so there was universal motivation to attend.

Several times each school year there would be state-wide meetings of students who were members of the BSU, thus adding to the desirability of participating. There were some outstanding people in these clubs and it provided an additional learning experience, especially in the realm of religious training.

As the first year wore on at school, I became aware of many religious activities available. I decided to volunteer to help. One was singing in the choir so I joined the Cadet Choir at school. At that time cadets did not have an option. On Sunday morning you went to Chapel. We had a great organist who also directed the choir. It really was majestically impressive to see the Corps of Cadets march en masse across the parade ground while the Citadel Band played *Onward Christian Soldiers*, then on into the Chapel, led by the Color Guard Staff with sabers drawn and flags unfurled! The acoustics were wonderful for men's voices and our anthems were outstanding.

After Chapel we all would head out to the beach, go for lunch at one of the glorious restaurants in Charleston, or sack out in the barracks. I had joined a local church so I went to sing in the Citadel Square Baptist Church choir downtown right by the Old Citadel.

This was a great church with an outstanding Pastor and Choir Director. What an enjoyable change from the military environment to a local community gathering. The choir director began to press me to sing some solos and also sing duets and in quartets. I was learning fast, enjoying the trip and looking for more challenges. I didn't have to wait long for opportunity to knock on my busy door.

It seemed there was a small gathering of mulatto citizens who were not welcome in any of the black churches or the white ones, so they decided to form their own group. My contact wanted me to sing and also deliver a message to this group. I prayed about this for about 30 seconds and gave my answer. "Yes, sir! You bet I'll do it!" In all my young years of praying and listening for God's response, He knocked me down with this one. Man, I prepared the message and asked that the good Lord allow me to know how these people felt plus help me find the right scripture to prove that God is color-blind and is only interested in our willingness to follow Him.

I selected a great song from Billy Graham's George Beverly Shea—*Yes, God Is Real!* I had no pianist so I had to sing it *a cappella*. I truly got down on my knees and prayed for God's guidance and blessing on delivering His message, not mine, to this special group of people. My singing sounded like George Beverly Shea, and the message I delivered may not have been like Billy Graham, but I could see the response in the eyes of the congregation and hear their approval from the massive chorus of *AMENS* coming from their midst.

It was I who had been moved by my own presentation. It was I who had felt the spirit of the Living God in my singing, in my message, and most of all, in my life. Every Sunday for a month, I drove to their little building to do my part in bringing them God's word. Now I had a different direction to deal with in my life and I was scared!

The dramatic moment, Col. Collins is home at First Baptist Church

Former prisoner of war for nearly eight years, Col. Quincy Collins is shown as he stepped to the pulpit at First in a quiet dramatic moment before he began to speak The Rev. Jack Hill, pastor, is seated on the rostrum

(11.1) First Baptist Church, Concord, NC

(11.2) Collins' home, 183 N. Union St., Concord, NC

12
The Date that Haunts Me

This woman was beautiful! Her spirit was enticing, her manners impeccable, and her eyes were sparkling. One gorgeous woman! I met her at a high school band clinic in Salisbury, North Carolina. She played alto saxophone. I played baritone sax, so we were in the same section and certainly had a lot of eye contact with each other, especially when actually playing. Have you ever tried to smile at someone while biting down on a mouthpiece and reading music? I learned to master this task at that band clinic in Salisbury.

Jane and I became good friends and hung out together at every break in rehearsal and at several special events scheduled during our three-day clinic. I had built up a huge desire to bring Jane into my life, even though she lived in Kannapolis and I in Concord. Even Duke and Chapel Hill couldn't compete with the rivalry between the Concord Spiders and the Little Wonders of A. L. Brown High School. But here I was trying to bridge the gap romantically.

Well, the conclusion came at the final concert of the clinic when mothers, fathers, family, friends and others drove in for the final concert—including Jane's high school boyfriend that I didn't know existed! During the concert, my eye contact with Jane kept building until the crescendo of the final theme almost made me cross-eyed. Then the volume faded as the audience rose in acclamation. But my little tune with Jane was over as we departed on our separate paths.

All of this occurred in 1948. Fast forward to Christmas leave from the rigors of military training at The Citadel, the Military College of South Carolina. Our hero, namely me, had just completed the first semester of the 4th class system—Hell Week—but after a whole semester I was ready to have something glamorous happen in my life. Jane came into my mind, even though I had not been in contact with her since the band clinic in Salisbury. But I had the hope that yesterday's boyfriend was now in the missing persons file. Perhaps now there was an opportunity for me to enter her arena with a herald of trumpets!

When I reached home, I started searching for any clue that might lead me to lady Jane. It was tough, because I could not for the life of me recall her last name. After much research, guessing and jumping to conclusions, I ended up with a telephone number in Kannapolis. That was all I needed.

Concord College students always had a Christmas Dance at the Concord Hotel, so this was to be my piece of cheese to get this darling little mouse to say *YES* and into my arms again! With my heart in my throat, I dialed the number. I had hoped for a lot of rings so I could settle down a bit, but someone picked up on the very first ring.

"Is Jane there?" I mumbled.

"Just a minute," the voice replied.

Now I'm hooked, I thought. The next voice I hear will be HERS! I became more nervous and uncertain. My confidence was fading on me.

An alluring voice said, "Hello."

Wow! It *was* her, and I was at bat. I told her who I was.

She acknowledged remembering me as Mr. Music and the strutting Drum Major at Concord High.

I had already reasoned that I didn't want to bring up the music clinic because of the boyfriend, so I got right to the point and asked her for a date to the dance.

She didn't hesitate. "Yes, of course," she said. "I'm looking forward to seeing you again."

As I hung up the phone, weak and trembling, Mom rounded the corner and asked what my problem was. I told her that I had just made a date with an angel!

The day of the dance arrived. I had worked on my car until I had rubbed the chrome off the front bumper. I had also ordered a corsage from Mrs. Mills at the floral shop and had put it in the fridge to keep it fresh. There was no MapQuest back then, so I meticulously planned the drive to her home like General Eisenhower planned the D-Day Invasion at Normandy. The time arrived for me to leave.

Mom and Dad said, "Be careful."

Off I went like a herd of turtles. I arrived right on time, rang the doorbell and stood back thinking how wise and resourceful I had been in making all these arrangements. The door opened and an attractive mother-like lady said, "You must be Quincy."

I owned up to that and gave her the corsage to pass along to Jane. After she left the room, I edged over to the beautiful piano in the living room. I play piano by ear, so I sat down and started playing one of my favorite romantic songs, "Tenderly". I mean I really got into playing this song. I could have been playing Opening Night at Carnegie Hall. I was at the high point when I heard the door open. I wheeled about like Liberace at a concert, and came to my feet as if I had been given an order to stand at attention. There in front of me was a girl I had never seen before in my life—and her name was Jane!

I must have looked like they just took my lottery winnings away from me. I was dumbfounded, but quickly decided that right then was not the time or the place for truth and honor to prevail, so I elected to play the role I had created. I got away with it until about an hour into the dance when Jane announced, "I'm not who you thought I was, correct?"

I admitted she was right, but added, "I'm having fun and hope you are too."

She asked me to take her home, and so we left the dance. The drive to her home was like a funeral procession and I was the Director. Silence prevailed. A nice lady was hurt that evening, and it has haunted me ever since. This Jane later married a friend of mine in Concord. Small world, isn't it?

(12.1) Concord High School 1999 "Spider" cover & program page

13
Jeep Ride Number One

There is not a kid alive over sixteen who doesn't dream about having his or her own personal car. By car, I mean a vehicle with four wheels and an engine, and one that is able to carry two or three other people. As a freshman at The Citadel I could not, by regulation, have an automobile on campus, but I could have one back home. So that is what I went for. I convinced Dad that the car for me should be a Jeep, one that could go through the fields, up over the ditches and high places, and take on a wilderness.

This was good thinking on my part because Dad was a farmer at heart. He was raised on a farm and owned and operated one outside Concord, NC, our hometown. The bad part was that I would have to leave it at home, and I knew full well it would get a lot of use from Quincy, Senior, out at the farm. I decided that since he was paying for it, how could I object? So a 1948 Jeep soon joined the Collins family.

I remember well the first time I came home on holiday. Dad wanted to show me how he had mastered this little machine with four-wheel drive. Out over the farm we went, and he hit every spot that could have turned us over. It reminded me of the Thanksgiving song *Over The River and Through The Woods!* Several times I really had to hold on tight or else my butt would have been on the ground outside—but dear old Dad was having fun and showing off in my presence. He finally said that he wanted to show me something.

It was a piece of land on the other side of town, off Poplar Tent Road. So off we went. At least the road was paved so he opened the machine up to check to see if it had plenty of speed available. It did, and I was happy when Dad admitted it and slowed down to the normal speed limits. I asked him where we were going. He replied that he was on the Concord Airport Authority Board, or something like that, and he had come across a tract of land that looked perfect to him for a future Concord Airport.

We pulled to the top of a hill and parked. Dad got out. I followed him and he showed me, with a swing of his arm, the land area he envisioned as the spot for the future Concord Airport. That was in about 1949-1950. Today that site is the location of the Concord Regional Airport. My Dad had identified that location as he flew over it in his own airplane—and also as he drove my jeep around that area. In 1994 I was the speaker for the dedication of the new Concord Regional Airport. I could not have been a prouder son!

Meanwhile, back at The Citadel, after time passed I was allowed to bring my Jeep to school. It provided my friends and me a lot of convenience and fun. We would drive up to Myrtle Beach and go dunes driving, chase after the local ladies, and still have time to make it back to The Citadel barracks in time for bed check.

One particular weekend comes to mind because I had volunteered to drive a couple of seniors and one of my plebe buddies up to VMI to see The Citadel play them in football. We planned to leave right after the big dance at school.

Bob Cannon, from Orangeburg, SC. was one of the seniors and also the Commander of Band Company. I had first met Bob at Transylvania Music Camp near Brevard, NC, when I was a sophomore in high school. Bob played the trumpet—and very well, I might add. He was a handsome redheaded guy who made friends easily and was a leader in whatever activity he was involved in.

When Bob graduated from The Citadel, he went right into USAF pilot training. The next thing I knew, he was in Korea flying F-86's. Within a year, Bob was killed in combat and several of us cadets who had known him were honorary Pall Bearers at his funeral. This was my first experience with death outside of my own family, and I was badly shaken over the experience. Little did I realize that many such experiences lay ahead.

There happened to be a Citadel Hop (big dance) scheduled for that Friday night, so we were not allowed to leave campus until about 11:00 PM. Plastic see-through panels that were not exactly 100% weatherproof enclosed the seating areas inside my Jeep. But that didn't deter this group from taking this midnight ride any more than it would have stopped Paul Revere.

Keep in mind that interstate highways didn't exist at that time. So we were in for a fairly long drive—something like six or seven hours—as I recall, so off we launched. Everything was going well until my navigators all went to sleep and I was drowsy as hell, even though the road noise and Jeep flaps should have been enough to keep me awake. Without *OnStar* and *Garmin* to direct me, I became disoriented and confused as to our location. To put it bluntly, I was flat-ass lost! I awakened everyone. The decision was made to keep driving until we came to something we recognized, and then get back on track. We were tired, cold and grumpy as hell, but onward we pushed. At about sunup, we identified where we were and I made the decision to drive to Concord, get my Dad's car, and then finish the trip to VMI in some semblance of comfort. All agreed. So again, off we went.

The sight of Concord's city limits could not have been a more welcomed sight. Seeing us at the front door could not have been a more *unwelcomed* sight for my Mother. But mothers will be mothers, so we had a good breakfast and off we went again, but in a different buggy this time. Packard autos drive a hell of a lot better than Jeeps and a lot smoother too, plus we had a radio and a heater. It didn't get much better than that!

We finally arrived at the VMI stadium for the last two minutes of the game. We were pissed, confused, and ignorant of the score—and I still don't recall if we won or lost! All I could think about was that we had one long drive to get back to The Citadel campus. I pulled up to a public telephone, collected all the change available amongst us, and called Dad. I pleaded for permission to drive the Packard back to school, and I would exchange it for my Jeep next weekend. He agreed, we all yelled our approval with great enthusiasm, and off we went—this time in style and comfort and with better directions to take us to our destination. I was certain that my old Jeep would get a good workout from Dad. I hoped that I would never again have to take a long trip in a Jeep.

But you never know, do you?

(13.1) 1948 Jeep

14
The Reverend Gets Closer

Before I knew it, some of my fellow cadets had come up with the scheme of running me for Vice President of The Citadel YMCA. I guess by my sophomore year word had spread about my project with the mulatto group. I was now Drum Major of The Citadel Marching Band, a leader of the school Dance Band, and was still being involved in all my Protestant Choir activities. My interest in The Baptist Student Union was still going strong and I hardly had time to go to College. At least it seemed that way!

My family back in Concord was in trouble because my Father had become a consummate alcoholic and was unable to tend to his many business interests. I had to get permission to go home one time to bail him out of jail in Albemarle, NC. I hated this … and also what it was doing to my Mom. Embarrassing, despicable behavior and an unknown financial status faced us every day. I prayed a lot and tried to have a very close relationship with God, because I didn't know what lay ahead. I had worshipped my Dad and we had a very close relationship, but he didn't act like he loved anyone any more. That really bothered me because my Dad had always been a very caring and loving person. What had happened?

I concluded that my job was to finish college and go into the USAF, since my Father's businesses would probably not exist when I was finished with school. I became closer to a couple of guys in the BSU—I think because they had become interested in my home situation and me. Joe and Doug both wanted to become ministers when they finished College, so it seemed reasonable for them to discuss forming a Youth Revival Team to tour during the next summer vacation. Both of them were dedicated Christians, good speakers and knowledgeable about the Bible. Joe's grandfather, Dr. Boone, had been head of the Southern Baptist Convention and lived in Tuscaloosa, Alabama, around the corner from Joe. Dr. Boone agreed to be our promoter and scheduler and lined us up for four engagements, beginning in Tuscaloosa.

I was to be the music leader, soloist and choir director. Now we needed a good piano man. This seemed like arranging gigs for a dance band and we had a lot of fun with it. Suddenly Leon the piano man appeared! He lived in Tuscaloosa and was very well known in those parts because of his extraordinarily long reach on the piano. He lacked one note of being able to cover an octave with one hand. This allowed him to be able to devise some beautiful and intricate chords for ordinary hymns as well as for other music pertinent to what we were doing. I loved it! His arrangements were wonderfully fascinating. Who couldn't sing with that kind of accompaniment?

With the schedule set, we gathered in Tuscaloosa when school was over and began rehearsing and working up sermons. This was in the summer of 1950. That month of working for the Lord was unbelievable, and frankly we were damned good! When we began the tour, I became aware of some of the pitfalls of doing this type work. Romance, or at least attraction, seems to develop quickly when everyone believes you are doing God's work—sin free, of course. From the local choir members to the lovely young ladies attending our services, sometimes it felt like I was a rock star in the eyes of some of our female audience who seemed to want to get close to me.

I suppose this all emanates from an atmosphere of vibrant enthusiasm coupled with a caring and loving persona. I'm not certain as to what chemical reaction results, but I knew one thing. I had to change my attitude and my technique or I was going to cause more trouble than good in my effort and goal to uplift sinners! *Wow!* The temptations were everywhere. I think the good Lord wanted me to see more clearly where I was going. That realization brought about a change in my plans and my desire to be in the ministry full time.

The next summer I went to the Baptist Summer Camp at Ridgecrest, NC, where I worked as a lifeguard with some really great people. Andy, from Baylor University, became my best friend and helped me understand what had happened the summer before. He was very much like me and was going into the ministry within a year. We became even closer one Sunday afternoon when a kid fell out of a boat in our lake and disappeared. The facility was not open, but the visitor had come in anyway. When alerted to this emergency Andy and I, and others, dove for the individual and finally found him—but it was too late to save him. To see a life slip away right in front of me was amazing and certainly influenced my future conduct around water.

Thank goodness, God knows what he's doing! Ministry was not where I should have been. However, the little experience I did have really showed me where I should be. There is a plan for us all and I think that I am right on track to do what my Lord wants me to do. My experiences as a POW in North Vietnam have provided me a platform from which to talk about God, Country and Family, and I feel more than adequately prepared to discuss these important issues. Even with this knowledge and experience and desire to help others, one pitfall rears its ugly head eventually—and that is politics!

I find it hard, if not impossible, to discuss my experiences in prison, my personal belief system, and my country and the freedom and justice it represents as separate and distinct entities. God is an integral part of everything that is life and I have come to realize this and accept it. God Bless America! God Bless Me! And lead me to what YOU want me to do and be. I'm ready to go!

(14.1) Citadel YMCA logo

15

The Confession

Ridgecrest was a lot of fun! Young people came from all parts of the U.S.—especially from the South—to spend a week or two in the beautiful mountains of North Carolina. They were great people wanting to grow in their personal relationships with Christ. They were quite easy to talk to and seemed to hang on every word that was spoken. How easy it is to converse with some one who is like a sponge, soaking up every word, every story and really wanting to get to know you in depth. The atmosphere in that camp was electric, and encased in a caring and loving bondage that was destined to produce good things. What a joy it was to witness such an amazing transformation in people.

As members of the staff, we were able to teach and learn by *doing*, and that meant being on constant alert to help others. It is really challenging to be looking for a way to help another human being or to be able to share experiences that may impact his/her life. That was our task every day and we took it seriously. Some of our senior staff members would instruct us on how best to accomplish this. We even used the techniques on each other as we practiced getting another person to open up and discuss personal things about their relationship with God and other human beings.

The very first time I had the opportunity to have an in-depth conversation that I initiated was with a female acquaintance I had met within the past several months at a gathering of BSU (Baptist Student Union) members in Columbia, SC. Both of us were about 21 years old and making plans for after graduation from college. Ashley lived in SC and seemed to be sensitive to becoming too personal in our conversations. I certainly accepted that and we talked a lot about our mutual interest in music, as she played piano and sang in a women's chorus in school. I somehow had the feeling that Ashley really wanted to tell me something—something very personal—but the right time was not now. I knew we didn't have a romantic interest in each other, but she was one fine lady. I thoroughly enjoyed our casual meetings each night after dinner in the chilly mountain air of Ridgecrest.

She seemed to struggle to laugh and show joy in her life. I wondered why? Her family appeared to be well off and she had a lot of acquaintances who would say "hello", "how are you" and other innocuous greetings, but none appeared to be real friends. Why was this?

Finally, one evening after dinner, I looked up and there she was. Ashley was smiling and had a small gleam in her eyes as she invited me for a walk. Can you imagine a young buck like me being asked by a gorgeous lady, who resembled Elizabeth Taylor, to take a walk in the evening? I was all ears as she began to ramble on about our meeting here at Ridgecrest and how much she had enjoyed our conversations. With every bounce of her coal black hair I was drawn into her web.

Then her mysterious bubble burst and she was ready to tell me the secret that was troubling her. I didn't want to appear overanxious or try to hurry up the process, so I said, "Why don't we sit down right here in these chairs where we can be comfortable?"

She agreed, and put her sweater in the rough wooden seat to make it a bit more comfortable. I did the same. We looked at each other for a moment, then with a quick twist of her head she began to tell me about an incident in her life that had received national publicity. I could hardly contain myself as she took down all the barriers to our communicating and was about to bare her soul to me. Never had I been faced with such a spiritual like confession. I decided that the only response I could give was to listen attentively and not interrupt her.

"This happened a little over a year ago," she said, "and I'm hurting a lot more now than I did then!"

Now I was on the edge of my seat ready to blurt out, "What happened?" Fortunately I hesitated long enough for her to continue. Some tears came into her eyes as she explained what happened during the late spring of the previous year. I put my hand close to hers, sensing she was going to need some moral support in order to finish her story. Sure enough, she gripped my hand as she spoke.

"My boyfriend and I were parked in his car out on a familiar Lover's Lane road just outside the city limits. Suddenly the back door opened and a black man, with a long knife, grabbed me around my neck and told us that he would kill me if we didn't do exactly as he ordered."

At this point I'm a little short of breath as I'm not certain what direction Ashley's story is about to take. So I took a deep breath and clasped her hand to let her know I was there to listen as a friend.

She continued. "This monster pulled me over the front seat into the back and told my date not to yell or talk at all or else he would slit my throat."

Damn! I couldn't help but think back at the many times I may have endangered myself and my date during my early courting years while in this very same type situation. I shuddered to listen to the rest of the story.

By this time she was crying as if it had just happened. I'm certain that in her mind she was reliving the experience. She told me of having that knife up against her throat as he ripped off her clothes. She said she wanted to really fight back, but was not sure how far the rapist would allow her to resist before cutting her throat. The young man in the front seat was terrified, but didn't want to do anything that would upset the attacker and possibly lead to her death. He became a lifeless statue observing his girlfriend's dilemma!

Finally, a sexual explosion calmed the attacker. He evidently was not planning on lingering. He gave them instructions on when to drive away and what not to do once they got back in town. With that he opened the back door and disappeared into the woods. When he opened the door, the inside car lights illuminated, thus giving the couple an opportunity to look at the attacker face to face. This would later be critical in identifying the man responsible for this horrible crime.

What the attacker didn't know was that Ashley's father was the District Attorney in their town. It took only a few days until these two young people were looking at a line-up of people who could possibly be the perpetrator. The inside car light coming on had sealed this person's fate. Every identifying mark they remembered exposed him as being the guilty one. He was identified, tried and sentenced quickly. The judge decreed death by hanging as his punishment. But that's not the end of the story. What happened next was the crux of Ashley's problem and present concern!

On the very day this man was to be executed, Ashley received a postcard from him asking for her forgiveness. He pointed out that God had forgiven him and now he wanted Ashley's pardon. What should she do? Was this a planned confrontation to put her at odds with her Christian beliefs? Why couldn't he leave her alone and take his own just medicine? Ashley pondered these things and struggled with them. She wanted advice. What would Christ do?

I, too, wondered. We prayed together. We shed tears together. We left Ridgecrest as close friends. What did she decide? The sentence was carried out, but she did not reply to his card. And yes, she forgave him. This dissolved the one obstacle standing in the way of her future happiness. Forgiveness is a sacred process and a decision that every human being needs to ponder because we will all face this same issue many times in our lives!

It is God's will that we forgive each other just like He forgives us. This is a real gift from God. One that is not easy to accept.

16
Primary Training—Bainbridge

After graduating from The Citadel in 1953, Dad and I and the finance company bought a brand new Chrysler to start me on my Air Force career. My processing center would be Sampson AFB, NY, so I had a long drive ahead of me from Concord, NC. There were at least two or three hundred of us 2nd Lieutenants reporting in and taking all kinds of tests and evaluations to determine what type flying we were best suited for. You might imagine a couple hundred studs full of p--- and vinegar descending on an Officer's Club like it belonged to them personally, and to a man all wanting the same thing—to earn the Silver Wings of a USAF pilot.

Getting together with this group was magical and quite satisfying. There was great certainty in my mind that *Fighter Pilot* was inscribed across my forehead indicating that was what I wanted to do—and *Jet Fighters* is where I wanted to go. There was no doubt in anyone's mind that this was my choice. Lots of new friends entered my life at Sampson AFB. They were guys that I would know the rest of my Air Force career. Unfortunately, many of them would go to be with their Maker along the way. Life is like that and uncertainty is around each and every corner. After several weeks of testing, counseling and psychoanalysis, we were called together to hear the results and receive assignments. It was a tense time to say the least, and all our futures were at stake.

A number of names were called to go to another room. These turned out to be the ones of us who did not pass the physical or eye exams. Some Air Force futures bit the dust that morning. It was a very emotional time for most of those guys, and there was little that they could do to rectify the situation. Meanwhile, in the other room, most of my new friends and I sat and listened to higher-ranking officers lecture us on flying, studying and dying. Can you believe that? They wanted to introduce us to the idea that a good percentage of us would not be alive in a specified future time frame if we pursued the flying game. As it turns out, they were right!

When we calmed down and discarded all this disturbing information we had just received, they started calling out names and passing out printed orders indicating where each of us was being assigned. *Bainbridge, Georgia* stuck out like a sore thumb on my set of orders. Several others had the same destination. Some went to bases in Texas and Mississippi. At least the Class of 54-N was heading toward getting the Silver Wings of a USAF Pilot. I had made it over the first hurdle. But what lay ahead for Quincy Collins?

The very first thing that lay ahead was one hell of a long drive from Sampson AFB in Geneva, NY, to Bainbridge, Georgia, where I would begin the first step in my flying training ladder. On the first leg of my trip I began a habit that has followed me to this very day—beating the steering wheel like a drum as I listened to music, particularly Jazz. My new car and steering wheel held up quite well until the wheel popped out in my lap as I turned out of the parking lot at the USAF Academy several years later.

Well, on this leg of the trip I had already decided I would stop over in Concord, my old hometown, where Jess Fisher, my best buddy from the 7th grade to the present moment, had just married Gaye Sanders. Jess, who was a very fine trombonist, graduated from Davidson and Gaye graduated from UNC at Chapel Hill. We had a great time celebrating their marriage and recalling things that we had done as kids. Jess had a goat in grammar School that pulled us all over town. We also used to race our old clunkers, he had a 1929 Ford Roadster and I had a 1931 Ford Victoria. We were Kings of the Walk!

I think I stopped drinking champagne just prior to getting back in my car to continue the trip to Bainbridge. Man, was I suffering! I kept stopping for coffee, pulling over to walk around, drinking cokes, relieving myself and repeating this schedule every couple of hours. Finally the city limits sign for Bainbridge appeared and I followed my written instructions to Bainbridge Air Base.

Whew! This was one hot southern town and I mean that literally. The temperature was in the mid-nineties and the sky was clear. There was zero traffic and I thought that maybe this was some kind of Confederate holiday. This was my introduction to the little sleepy village where I was going to learn how to fly. I was anticipating every minute and I couldn't get started quickly enough. I drove up to the Base Administration building, walked into the main office with my set of orders and signed in. The game was about to begin!

Several of my 54-N classmates had already arrived and were milling about meeting those who had arrived even earlier. I learned that in order to get the best room, bed, etc., you had to arrive early. Fortunately, the BOQ buildings (Bachelor Officers Quarters) were air-conditioned with a shared common shower and bath area. It was better than I had at The Citadel!

There was one thing that I had not planned on—foreign officers being in our class. The first guy I met in the BOQ was Yildis Ukmachley from Turkey. Yildis became one of my best friends and looked exactly like a Turk should look—big black mustache, dark skin, extremely bushy eyebrows and stained teeth. He was a peach of a guy with a loving heart and an inquiring mind. He also had a love for motorcycles that kept him broke, in the hospital, or asking me to help him get his machine to a repair shop. His broken English cracked me up, but what the hell—how much Turkish did I know? Many years later I discovered that my friend was a 4-star General in Turkey and was Commander In Chief of the Turkish Air Force. He was a joy in my life!

We had another foreign officer, let's call him Pierre. He was French, never bathed, and made little to no effort to speak English. At least once a month, the rest of us in that building would throw Pierre into the shower in order to raise our comfort level. He is probably the President of France now. I can neither acknowledge that nor deny it. Viva La France!

The class of 54-N immediately split into 2 sections. One section flew in the morning and the other section took ground school—learning about weather, aerodynamics, etc. All instructors were civilian and under contract to the USAF to take us through the primary flying and academic phases of this part of our training. All of our instructors were pilots during WWII and we held them in high esteem. Each flight instructor had 3-4 students with a mix of officers and cadets. The Piper Cub, designated the PA-18 by the USAF, was our first challenge, and my flight experience in that plane with my Dad gave me a bunch of confidence that I would solo first in my group. My very wise instructor, sensing a bit of overconfidence on my part, soloed me last while telling me why. An humbling experience to say the least! The PA-18 and our next challenge, the T-6 Texan, were both propeller driven aircraft, except the T-6 had a much bigger and powerful engine and an added pain in the rear phenomenon called *torque*. You had to stay on top of controlling this machine or it would throw you into a ground loop, but we were undaunted and pressed on fearlessly.

Several of the other members of Flying Class 54-N were from Central and South America, and one of them—let's call him Juan—had a real problem with English. Juan was a patient and understanding guy with a great sense of humor if you could follow his explanations.

One of the fun exercises in flying the T-6 after soloing was cross-country navigation. The instructors picked the route then assisted the students in drawing the route to be flown with the time and distance measurements. We were scheduled to take off at 15-minute intervals and to check in by radio at each turning point in the route. An instructor was circling each turning point to receive the student's check-in. It was so well controlled that getting lost was virtually impossible.

That is, until Juan did not check in at the very first check-in point.

Had he had engine problems and gone down? Had he had a mid-air collision with another aircraft? No one was certain, so the emergency location plan went into effect. Juan was now about 45 minutes behind schedule and the instructors were frantically calling his call sign to have him report in. Finally they started calling him by his real name. "Juan, where are you?"

Way off in the distance, barely audible, came a response.

One of the instructors said, "I can't hear you, Juan. Where are you?" Juan's response was the ultimate navigational answer. "I am over large body of water."

Indeed he was. The Atlantic Ocean is one big-ass body of water, and unless they vectored him back to shore quickly, he was going to be in it! Juan made it back and became our class hero.

Another aspect of flight training that I had not realized is that some members of our class were not yet officers. They were enlisted people from the USAF who had been through basic military training, passed all the tests and evaluations we had endured, and were trying to get to be officers and receive their pilot's wings at the same time. There were some really great human beings in this group and they added a lot of diversity and talent to our class.

As I walked out of the building after signing in, there in front of me only a hundred yards away was the flight line with all the airplanes lined up like soldiers waiting for battle. I recognized the Piper Cub because Dad had learned to fly in one just like it. He had even slipped me into the back cockpit one time and let me get my hands on the controls. Damn! I was ready to leap into one and show them that I was ready now. Well, maybe later!

As I drove over to the BOQ, found my room and unloaded my gear, it was beyond hot. I was wet as water and there was no relief in sight. I fell into the shower with the water as cold as I could get it. Relief was sweet. This was heaven!

Flying and Ground school took up a lot of our time, but there was plenty left for the reckless and daring—and I was certainly up for it. It became my habit while in the USAF of becoming involved with a local Baptist Church choir, as that was my choice of faith. Bainbridge had a large Baptist Church with a good choir and an active congregation that welcomed students from the Base.

I immediately joined the choir and became instant friends with the band director of the high school band and his wife. It turned out that Bill was a violinist, and didn't know squat about band formations, drills, etc. So I volunteered to be his assistant since the high school football season was upon us. Bill also conned me into teaching baton twirling since I had attended the University of Kansas music and twirling school to prepare me for my stint as the Drum Major for Concord High School (1947-1949). I became proficient enough to be able to keep 3 batons in the air at one time from a stationary position. Not bad for an evolving fighter pilot!

I held classes each Saturday morning for a couple of hours, and ended up with 50-60 high school girls who wanted to learn to strut and twirl. Of course I charged for this, and it certainly helped offset the cost of my social activities.

As soon as word got around town that I carried a saxophone in the trunk of my car and could play it pretty well, I received several calls from local groups who could use a sax in their combos. This became another revenue stream for my monthly car payment—a real blessing!

Then I met a fellow in church who owned the local radio station and he recognized my resonant bass voice as being well suited for broadcasting so he asked me to emcee a program of modern Jazz, and then on Sunday play and narrate a section of Sacred Music. I hardly had time for pilot training, but these activities brought such joy to my life that it was not a chore for me to be involved in them. It was a pleasure, and I thanked God that I had had the opportunity to sharpen and develop these talents in high school and college.

One other little Base function that I became involved in was handling the base Drum and Bugle Corps. There were about 16-18 people, mostly cadets, who participated. Fortunately, I could remember enough marches and bugle music from leading the marching band at The Citadel to handle the requirements for the ceremonies and parades at the base. As a matter of fact, this group was damned good and received several awards for their work.

We also had a lot of fun working together. I tried never to let serious stuff get in the way of having fun and enjoying what we were doing. These activities added immeasurably to my maturity and ability to step out front and lead. I believe it is one of my greatest talents, and it began to be a part of me in the 7th grade. Being reticent to get out front or being shy and bashful has *never* been my thing!

Bainbridge was full of lovely people who tried to make every stranger feel at home. I quickly learned that a disaster on December 7, 1946, had a lot to do with this demeanor. That was the date of the infamous Wine-coff Hotel fire in Atlanta, Georgia. Lots of cities from all over Georgia sent representatives to attend a Youth Assembly sponsored by the Georgia YMCA. Their goal was Christian Citizenship Development. Bainbridge had sent a chaperone and 7 students to this meeting. They all died along with most of the other young people staying in that hotel. Through the ensuing years, dedications, plaques, memorials and scholarships has kept the memories of those lost close to that city. I felt it and I pray that it endures to this day.

Finally I conquered the terrible Texan (T-6 Trainer), received a certificate saying as much from the USAF Commander there, and a set of orders naming Laredo AFB, Texas as my Basic Training assignment. Enough of these Kindergarten airplanes—it was time for the big boys with tricycle landing gear, a huge and even more powerful engine, and a plane built to replicate the famous WWII fighter, the P-51!

The airplane I am describing, built by North American Aviation, is the T-28. Once I master this monster, then it's on to the Lockheed T-33 Jet, a high speed, high altitude flying machine that will introduce me to speed that I can't imagine. Best of all, it has no propeller! This is a *JET* my friend, and I am about to enter a world so fast and furious that it will make my head spin.

Bring it on, baby!

(16.1) Bainbridge, Georgia Air Base

(16.2) The Piper Cub, designated the PA-18 by the USAF

(16.3) T-6 Trainer, "Terrible Texan" plane

17
Jet Fighter And Gunnery Training

The day I graduated from Bainbridge Air Base in Georgia was when I knew great experiences lay ahead—and could hardly wait for my next level of pilot training to begin. My orders read Laredo Air Force Base, Texas, where we would learn how to fly a jet. I looked at a map and saw that that place was *nowhere*. I reasoned that if the USA were to be given an enema, it would be in the Laredo area. Wow! What a desolate place.

But at least Mexico was right there beside it. I remembered the song, *In Nuevo Laredo, in old Mexico*. That meant good old beer drinking music with senoritas and caballeros would be across the Rio Grande River from where I'd be stationed. So let's unhitch my Chrysler hoss and head out west. My new coupe was gassed up and ready to go, so I signed out and hit the road.

Looking at the map, I saw that New Orleans loomed into my horizon and all kinds of fun things began to pop into my mind. The only time I had been to the Big Easy was when my Dad had taken me there on a charter train trip with a bunch of his guy friends from Concord. That was an eye-opener to say the least. But this was different because I was older and by myself and on my own. Actually, Dad paid for everything on that trip, but now I was on my own personal nickel. *There is one hell of*

*a difference in those two scenarios, but why am I sweating this? I'm not even
there yet, so relax.*

My driving procedure was to start about dawn and try to click off at
least 500 miles before shutting down for the day. My first goal: to arrive
in New Orleans in mid–afternoon, as I had no reservations at a hotel.
The closer I got to New Orleans, the more I became aware of the fact that
Mardi Gras was cranking up, and I would probably arrive right in the
middle of it. And so I did! Actually, it was the day before, and that became
my bartering chip for getting a room. I would be out of the room by 10
a.m. the next morning. It worked. So off I wandered into the streets of
the city with no plan to follow. Jazz is one of my favorite styles of music,
so that is where I lit—a New Orleans Jazz club. I remember walking into
that place, but I don't recall ever leaving. It was mystical—jazz sounds
like I never heard before, mixed drinks that I could not pronounce, and
an atmosphere that was intoxicating without booze even being a part of
it. It was as if someone had given me a mickey to remove all reality from
my being.

Somehow I made it back to my hotel room and plopped on the
bed for an hour or so before the maid came in and informed me that
I had overstayed my visit and it was time for me to vamoose for other
parts. Thank God I had a credit card, because all the money I had left
was one five-dollar bill! Damn! What had I done with all that money I
had crammed into my wallet? I quickly showered, shaved and got my car
loaded for the next and final leg of the trip.

Frankly, I was really hurting from the mysteries of the night before.
I wasn't sure I was ready to try to be the World's Greatest Fighter Pilot.
In fact, I felt like I had already been shot down, and I was having trouble
hanging on to life itself! Three hundred miles later, I felt a lot better.

There is no easy way to get to Laredo, Texas. In fact I could best describe Texas as miles and miles of miles. There isn't even a decent radio station with country music, so I tried to keep a New Orleans station tuned in
as long as I could. My steering wheel took a good beating, as I continued
to beat the drums to the music I could pick up. After one long session

with the Billy May Orchestra, I noticed that my steering wheel was just a bit loose. I decided to listen to more love songs and leave the high voltage jazz and swing songs for another time.

Driving out west does give you a wonderful panoramic view of sunsets: beautiful colors that only God can paint and hang in the sky until the light from the sun is extinguished and darkness envelops you. It seems that a car heading towards you can be seen 100 miles out, with nothing else in sight between you and those headlights. It is mesmerizing and can lull you to sleep quickly, thus making it the best time to find a motel and turn it in for the day. By the way, a good cold beer had the same effect as that mickey I got in New Orleans. Oh, so good!

Early morning driving heading west puts the sun behind you. Every piece of sand has a glistening effect that radiates the heat that will surely overtake you soon. I felt as if I was in the world's largest sandbox and there was no way out. Mexican music also added to the irritation. It seemed that every Mexican station was more powerful than any American station, so that's all my car radio could get. I had the strange feeling that my entire car must have been assembled in Mexico, and I would be stuck with this for a while.

Finally, a mileage sign appeared showing Laredo was 150 miles straight ahead. What the hell! In this part of the US, everything is straight ahead. All mileage signs read at least 100 miles to the next bit of civilization. *Are we there yet?* came into my mind. I just settled in and waited.

The Laredo city limits sign shocked me into reality, so I checked my map to try to locate the Laredo Air Force Base. Everything reminded me of scenes from a lot of TV commercials where a car out in the western plains needs gas, and there is only a solitary hut with one gas pump on it. This whole place looks like that! *Man, this is going to be a fun place to learn how to fly!* I kept telling myself, "I can hardly wait!"

I drove through the main gate, saluted the air policeman, got directions and drove over to the building to sign in. I parked and opened the car door to get out when the Texas heat hit me head-on. I staggered a moment as I tried to take a deep breath. I entered the air-conditioned building and had never been so thankful to be Air Force instead of Army and have this building and not a tent. Several other guys from Class 54-N were hanging around because, frankly, it was too damned hot to go outside. I finally got the nerve to go to my assigned room at the Bachelor Officer Quarters, then unload my car and put all my possessions away for the next six months of training. The BOQ was also air-conditioned, so things were looking up as the officers in my class began arriving.

The next day was a repeat of the day before—hot, muggy, scorching in the sun with no relief in sight. 54-N met in the administration building and introduced ourselves to those we had not previously met. This time, the cadet-enlisted types were included, so there were a lot of new faces. This part of our training was conducted by all USAF pilots and officers. Strict military bearing was compulsory. These guys meant business and had a job to do—teaching us to be jet-jocks and the enlisted types how to be officers. We weren't going to be babied or nursed through this program, as had been the case in Primary Flying School. Here, the rubber hit the runway. You were expected to cut the mustard or be eliminated.

The underlying feeling among us was that this was going to be a hard-ass group of instructors, so we had better be prepared. With the introductions over, the chain of command was explained, and our flight assignments were made. It was time to go to the flight line and meet the nasty men who were going to train this bunch of monkeys to fly jets.

As we entered the designated building, the staff NCO (non-commissioned officer) indicated which briefing table we were to be assigned to. Out of nowhere came this big booming voice, "Come to attention!" We all popped to attention with head and eyes straight ahead. Someone obviously had looked around as a Captain got in the face of one of the cadets and yelled, "Mr., do you not know what attention means?"

"Yes, Sir!" the cadet responded.

"Well, go into that corner and show the rest of your class what it means to stand at attention!"

The cadet sheepishly found his way into the corner and hit a brace a Citadel man would be proud to claim.

Other flight instructors entered the room, went to their assigned tables and took charge of their students. Five of us were looking at each other with question marks on our faces as big as our noses. Each instructor introduced himself and gave a little history of his background. Most of them were probably pilots in Korea, and this was their first station since leaving that theater of operation. The F-86 and F-84 were the primary Air Force aircraft deployed there, and some of these guys were aces, but no more than three years older than I. Impressive to say the least!

"Attention!" blared out the same voice we had heard before. All of us stiffened up and glued our eyes straight ahead. The big Kahuna, Major Robert Sowers, the commander of our section, entered and just meandered around as if looking for a lost child. Finally he commanded, "At ease."

We all sat down. This guy had a look about him that said, "Don't fool with me!" It was like a rattle on a rattlesnake. I got the message. The Major was in charge, and everyone knew it. He welcomed us (by that I mean, his rattlers stopped rattling), and he covered what our program was to be in the coming weeks.

The T-28 was our first hill to climb, but that propeller plane had been built to handle like the P-51 of WW II, and it had a tricycle landing gear, which meant it was easier to land and steer than the T-6 we had been flying in Primary Flying School. Then he asked each of us to write about ourselves. The exact subject was to be something we had done that we were very proud of having mastered.

With that, the voice called "Attention!" and Major Sowers left the room. The instructors at each table gave us a few more details for the next day's session, and then departed too. We all looked at each other and then the senior Lieutenant in our class gave us instructions on where we were to fall in for head count each day and a few other administrative reminders. That was it for the first day. We had met our masters and also heard from the head Dragon. Thank God, I had been exposed to all this at The Citadel.

Our flight was to have ground school in the mornings, then report to the flight line each afternoon. The ground school involved studying navigation subjects, weather and the basics of avionics. Of prime importance was learning to use the flight hand computer and FAA regulations. Although those courses were quite interesting and important to our flying career, we could hardly wait to get to the flight line and closer to the aircraft.

Major Sowers had given us our first written assignment. Most of us had spent that night deciding first what to write about, then secondly getting it on paper. For some reason, I chose helping the high school band director with his band's half-time formations at Bainbridge High's football games, and then teaching baton twirling to would-be majorettes. Somehow I thought this would show my versatility and unknown talents to my instructor.

The next day, we turned in the papers and spent the rest of the afternoon touring the flight line, hangers and other areas that were of interest to us. The day after that, at our afternoon flight line meeting, Major Sowers announced that he had selected two students to train himself, one officer and one cadet. The cadet he identified was a new friend of mine, Andy. I shuddered to think how he would hold up under the Dragon.

The next name he announced was enough to give me a heart attack. "Lieutenant Quincy Collins." Me! How the hell did this happen? When Sowers asked the two of us to come forward to his table, I could hardly get up to walk. My laundryman may find out why! I'm sure my classmates observed all the blood had left my face and my normal confident stride had disappeared. I did manage to give Major Sowers my best salute, as I reported in to him at the table. He actually smiled as he asked us to be seated and began telling of the program we would be following. "You will love the T-28 and how she handles," he told us. He gave us the idea that this was the fun part of the program prior to taking on our first jet, the T-33 Lockheed Trainer.

The blood was returning to my face, and I began to feel the excitement as we walked out to a T-28 and did a walk-around type pre-flight inspection. He asked Andy to climb into the seat and spend time familiarizing himself with the cockpit. Then I followed him to the tail section where we stopped and faced each other.

"So you like to lead the band and teach the little girls to twirl their batons, eh?"

I quickly decided that nothing I could say would douse the fire coming from this dragon's mouth, so I just stood at attention and waited for the next blast.

"Collins, maybe we need to trade your flight suit for a ballet outfit."

If my goal in picking the subject I wrote about was to gain some attention, I really succeeded. Now he was right in my face and he hadn't brushed his teeth that morning.

"Lieutenant Collins," he shouted. "I am going to twirl a baton right up your ass if you don't become the best pilot I ever trained. Now go get into that cockpit and know where every instrument is within the next 24 hours. Got that?"

"Yes, Sir!" I responded, and bounced up the ladder to replace Andy in the cockpit.

"What was all that yelling about?" Andy asked.

"Tell you later," I replied, and began memorizing all the instrument positions. That night, I fell asleep way after midnight with the T-28 Operator's Manual in my arms.

After such a horrendous beginning, the T-28 program went very smoothly. Andy and I felt very fortunate to have such a strict instructor teaching us. Now the big jet program faced us. The major gave each of us an orientation flight in the T-33, which amounted to doing everything that aircraft was made to do plus check our puke level. Fortunately, we both did OK, and although we felt a little wrung out afterwards, we were ready to go. The Dragon appeared to be pleased.

Flying the T-33 seemed like driving a Cadillac after learning the basics on T-model and A-model Fords. Smooth, responsive controls and plain fun best describe the feelings I had about that aircraft. I was jumping up and down to get to the point where I could solo and then get in the air by myself.

The major wouldn't give me a clue as to when he thought I would be ready, but on the day, he had put me through the paces of aerobatics he loved and then took control of the aircraft. Damn! We pulled max-G forces, then straight up into the sun. Then he stop-cocked the engine, dropped the landing gear and flaps, and yelled, "You got it!"

I got the nose down first, cleaned up the gear and flaps then air-started the engine. What a wonderful sound to hear the engine winding up and feeling the power of the engine when I advanced the throttle. "Good job," the major proclaimed. "Let's go land!"

I really greased the landing, taxied into our parking space and listened to the sweetest words I could ever hear.

"Lieutenant, you are ready. Go have fun!" He climbed out, patted me on the shoulder and saluted.

I felt like a million dollars and taxied out for my solo flight. I was on the way to getting my wings and becoming a fighter pilot. Life was good!

Andy and I and several other soloists decided to visit the world famous Cadillac Bar in Nuevo Laredo that weekend to celebrate our achievement. Their local economy got a big kick start that evening as we consumed vast quantities of tequila in every type mixed drink imaginable. A great time was had by all—until the morning after episode came upon us. Fortunately, we had Saturday and Sunday to recover and prepare to really get with the program in the weeks ahead.

Andy and I were taught to fly the tightest formation of any students in the class, and that was a great source of pride for both of us. The major put us through the toughest flying program he could devise, and we learned well.

Finally, each student had the Standardization Flight Test conducted by an inspector none of us had ever flown with before. These are the same people who flew with the students who were having problems to decide if they were good enough to keep in the program or wash them out. All of us were on edge and a bit antsy about this part of the program, but everyone in the class passed and awaited the wings ceremony and getting our orders to our next assignment.

I actually received my official orders about my next assignment prior to having my wings pinned on: F-86 Advanced Gunnery School at Nellis AFB, Nevada—exactly what I had been working toward.

Las Vegas, here I come!

(17.1) Major Sowers, Laredo, TX Air Force Base

(17.2) Aircraft: Top, the T28 and bottom, the T33.

18
Into the Clouds on My Final T-33 Flight

The Class of 54N was milling about on base at Laredo AFB while trying to pack for our next assignment. Mine was to report to Nellis AFB in Las Vegas—bright lights, great music, and the best entertainment in the world. Man, I was on cloud nine and nervous as a bride about to say, "I do!"

My section met at the flight line to hash over our accomplishments and talk about the future. Major Sowers was giving Andy and me the benefit of all the lessons he had learned from being in the USAF. We talked about our most memorable flights thus far, and mine was just hanging there ready to pick and talk about.

SHORTLY AFTER ANDY AND I soloed in the T-33, we were scheduled on a short formation flight, just the two of us. I was assigned to be the Flight lead, so I briefed us on what we were to do. The main purpose of this boondoggle was to fly close, have fun, and play around the clouds. Zooming up into a cloud was always fun, and following the cloud formations like flying into a canyon gave me a great feeling.

I put Andy in trail behind me and off we went. I pulled up into a white swirling cloud, and when I broke out on top I rolled over and put the nose of the aircraft straight down. I looked back in the rear view mirror and there was Andy flying as close as he could get to my aircraft. This guy was really good! I immediately pushed my stick to the right and pulled 4Gs to throw him off my tail, but Andy stuck in there like he was a part of my aircraft.

Now it was time to switch leads and let him challenge me. I dropped down beneath Andy and popped up directly behind him. I got on the mic and called, "Go!" He began a series of maneuvers that would have challenged Major Sowers to keep up with.

Straight up. Straight down. And everything in between. He wrung me out, but I stayed with him. Finally, I took over again and we headed back to the base. After landing and taxing in, we shut down our engines, leaped over the side of the cockpit, and met with a big embrace. We were two proud pilots and anxious for the next adventure. This was indeed a great way to end this phase of our training. I have never seen Andy again or heard of his whereabouts.

(18.2) Three Lockheed T33 trainers in formation

19
The Las Vegas Transformation

The drive from Laredo to Las Vegas was long, hot and tiresome. The music that radio stations played along the route were about as interesting as Buddha love songs—boring, boring, boring—and it was that way until a hundred or so miles out from Vegas when civilized music became available. The highlight of the trip was driving across Boulder Dam and seeing one of the true wonders of the World. The neon capital at dusk also sparked my attention as unbelievably bright marquees announced the "World's Best of Everything" and the brightest stars that the entertainment world had to offer. This was truly a play land that had to be seen to be believed.

I kept telling myself this is not what you are here for. You are here to check out in the best fighter of the day, the F-86, and learn how to deliver firepower on enemy targets and train to be the best that you can be. And then I wondered—who is starring on the strip this week? I had hoped there would be plenty of time to catch some shows after I worked on attaining my primary flying mission.

I finally located Nellis Air Force Base, signed in, and then went to the BOQ to get my room assignment. Several guys I knew from Laredo were already there, so after some small talk we all headed out to get some much-needed sleep. The real dream was about to begin!

The next morning we gathered together at the designated building. Here were all the guys of Class 54-N who had made it through the program and were selected to enter the Fighter Pilot Gunnery phase. Others in our class had gone on to multi-engines, primarily the B-25. We jokingly called them Bus Drivers, and rarely would we ever come in contact with them. No matter what section you went into or what aircraft you flew there was always paperwork involved. When we finished that, then we got down to section assignments and class schedule. My section was to report to the Flight Line every morning and have Ground School in the afternoon. All the members of our Cadet group were now officers, and most of them had bought new cars, so our parking lot had a collection of all the current cars on the market. This was more fun than any college fraternity, and besides, we were getting paid to do this!

It dawned on me that all of a sudden we were being treated as adults, not college students. We were given situations in which we had to make our own decisions. Not only that, but we were now checking out in the F-86 and it only had a single place cockpit. This meant that no longer would we be nursed along by an instructor sitting in the back seat—prepared to save our ass if we did something really stupid. There *was* no back seat. There would be *no* instructor pilot looking over my shoulder.

We were taught how to start the aircraft, taxi it, and take off strictly from the Operating Manual produced by North American Aviation, the manufacturer of the aircraft. In other words, I was to learn how to fly the fastest and most flown aircraft in the Korean War from classroom instruction. I remembered Maj. Sowers ordering me to get into the cockpit of the T-28 and T-33 to learn where all the instruments and switches were. So I decided that was what I needed to do with this bird. I spent every spare second I had in the cockpit of the F-86 because I wanted to feel comfortable there. It was going to be my second home and I needed to be certain I knew it like the back of my hand.

My assigned instructor was a Korean War veteran and a seasoned fighter pilot. He knew his business, and I was totally dependent upon him to get me checked out in this machine. I wasn't scared, but let's say I was a wee bit puckered over the issue.

The big day finally came. I was selected to be the first student to fly solo. My instructor and I, along with two of my classmates, walked out to the aircraft to complete the walk around inspection. I started a habit that I never stopped doing. I would touch every connection, hose, or any aircraft part protruding from the aircraft skin to check for tightness and cohesiveness to the airframe. That one little habit may have saved my fanny more than once. Into the cockpit I climbed and fastened my parachute.

My instructor climbed up beside me and yelled, "Crank it up!"

I started the process and when I heard the engine revving up I thought, *Damn, this machine is running and in a matter of minutes my butt is going to be powered down the runway to cast my body into the atmosphere. Wow, this is IT!* The crew chief gave me the *taxi* motion and off I went. It was pretty simple to find the end of the runway since I had already been observing all the take-offs and landings. When I was ready, I announced to the Tower over the radio, "Tiger Lead, Number 1 for take off."

When cleared, I took the runway, held my brakes, and pushed the throttle forward to check that all systems were working. Man, I really stared at the instruments to detect anything wrong. Not seeing anything, I released brakes and checked that my throttle was fully forward. I was thrust down the runway—gaining airspeed so rapidly I could hardly keep up with it. Now it was time to pull slightly back on the stick so that the nose of my aircraft would move up a bit. I was airborne before I knew it. Now it was time to raise the gear then the flaps. The instruments indicated all was well, and Lt. Quincy Collins was in charge of one hot airplane. This was heaven and this airplane was beautiful to steer.

I headed over towards Lake Meade and then to Boulder Dam. I turned 180 degrees and flew over the desert and mountains. As I recall, I climbed to 25,000 feet and went through a series of stalls so that I could get a feel for how the aircraft responded and what signals it might send under various conditions. I really developed a feel for this machine and decided it was time to return to Nellis for my first F-86 landing.

I knew the traffic pattern and the airspeed I should use. I announced, "Tiger Lead, entering the pattern!" I knew my instructor and classmates would be waiting and looking for me, so I wanted to execute a really tight Fighter Pilot pitch out and landing. "Tiger Lead in the Break," I announced, while pulling back on the stick to give me a tight turn onto downwind.

My head was on a swivel, clearing for other aircraft and getting my bird in the right position for greasing in my first landing. "Tiger Lead on final for 36," I called.

"Cleared to land, Tiger Lead," replied the Tower.

I knew where my instructor wanted me to touch down so I used all the finesse I had to hit that spot with the slickest landing I could muster. Skip-Skip went the tires touching the runway. "Whoopee!" I yelled through my oxygen mask as I slowed the aircraft and taxied off the runway to go to my slot on the flight line.

Just as I pulled into the chocks, my instructor and friends drove up in the jeep they were using. As the engine wound down, I crawled out and down the ladder to be greeted by a handshake from my instructor and a couple of hugs from my classmates.

"Great job, Quince," one of them said.

"How was it?" chimed in the other.

I noticed that my flight suit was wet as water from my sweating profusely, but I nonchalantly replied, "Piece of cake!" I could hardly wait until Happy Hour at the Officer's Club where I would expand on the heroics of the day. I was one happy guy and my career choice was getting better with each passing day

Several of my classmates panicked while trying to solo the F-86, and had to be talked down by their instructors in order to get the aircraft back on the ground. They eventually washed out. I think fear played a big part in their situation. What a shame to have come that far in the training cycle and then be forced out.

I really felt blessed to have made it this far. Frankly, I enjoyed every minute of it. I approached every phase of my training with a confident attitude, and that in itself gave me an edge over those who had some doubts. I think a good positive attitude is the key element required if one is to be successful in anything. I have tried to live by that rule for most of my life. So far, so good!

At the very end of our training period, I developed a back problem that made it difficult for me to walk, or for that matter to even sit up. I was in the base hospital for about 10 days and became concerned that the Flight Surgeon might recommend that I be evaluated for possibly being grounded (removed from flight status).

Man! Life can throw more curves than you can imagine, and I was taking this one seriously. I took all the medicine prescribed for me plus I exercised every muscle I had in my back. I also had a lot of guidance and assistance from the Flight Surgeon's Office, as they appeared quite interested in helping me overcome my present condition. This combination of medications and exercise worked like a charm and I passed the medical evaluation with flying colors.

During the time I was indisposed with my back problem, my class had graduated and received their next flying assignments. I really felt left out and pressed the Training Section to assign me to the next class so that I could be F-86 qualified and get a flying assignment. About this same time, the Base Personnel office notified me that now was the time to apply to be selected to be a regular USAF officer—in other words, a career Air Force man. I filled out all the paperwork except for the part where my Commander completes an evaluation of me as a potential career officer.

I had just been assigned to a Training Squadron to complete my required work, so I asked to meet with the Squadron Commander to get his evaluation so I could file my application to the USAF. I had never met this Major even though I was put in his Squadron to finish my training. I walked into his office, saluted and told him why I was there. I had my personnel file with me and handed it to him. I was still standing at attention as he read over my file.

He finally looked up at me, and with a slight smirk on his face blurted out, "So you went to The Citadel?"

"Yes Sir," I responded.

"Well, I have no use for anyone who attended that place!" he replied indignantly.

With that, he tossed my personnel file towards me and leaned back in his chair.

What the hell do I do now? Lick his boots or bow down? I decided not to respond to his declarations so I saluted, thanked him for his time and did an about face and walked out of his office. My application was still on his desk as I left. This is a great example of what a leader is not, I thought to myself.

Damn! I was really pissed off, bewildered and confused over what I could do. I went to the Personnel office and told a young Major there what had just happened. He was as dumbfounded as was I.

"Tell you what I would do, Lt. Collins," he said, with a slight grin on his face. "We've just received notice from a Colonel from the new USAF Academy that he will be on base here in the next 3 weeks to interview men who have just finished Gunnery School, and who might be interested in training the first 3 classes of cadets at Lowry AFB, Colorado. He is calling them ATOs (Air Training Officers). Would you be interested in meeting with him?"

My heart jumped a beat or two as I contemplated the potential for such an assignment. "Sign me up," I ordered. "This will be great!"

I finished my training requirements and got my F-86 Qualification Certificate without ever having to come face to face with Major Dumbass again, and that suited me fine. My friend in the Personnel office arranged for me to be assigned to Base Operations while awaiting the interview for the USAF Academy.

I had a great time there. My boss was a huge man who used to fly the Hump in China at the end of World War II. His name was Major Tiny Manch and his lovely red-haired wife was from North Carolina. Major Manch was killed while flying a T-33 about a year later. The aircraft developed a problem and Tiny could not get out of the cockpit cleanly because of his size. The ejection seat worked but there was too much of Tiny to launch out of the aircraft.

At any rate, I could be checked out in the H-19 helicopter, my old friend the T-6, and the C-45 transport plane. Senator Howard Cannon from Nevada was an Air Force Reserve Colonel and would come to Nellis to get his required flying time. I was always assigned to be his co-pilot and we became good friends. Once when the Senator came to fly the C-45, the Training Wing Commander, Brig. Gen. James Roberts dropped by to welcome him and bring him up to date on what was happening at the base. The Senator introduced me to Gen. Roberts. This was to be a very important contact in my career progression.

About a week later, Gen. Roberts came by Base Ops just to look around and observe the happenings of the day. I already had decided that if I ever had the opportunity, I would like to present my case. I had just received word that I was turned down on my regular Air Force appointment because Major Dumbass had written, "I do not know this man," on my application recommendation.

My opportunity stepped up in front of me and asked how I was doing. (Gen. Roberts called me by name). He wanted to know what my next assignment might be. So I thought, what the hell do I have to lose? I told him of my desire to be a regular Air Force officer and the process I went through, including the surprising meeting with Maj. Dumbass. I requested he take a look at what had transpired to see if I had received the right consideration by Dumbass. I also mentioned that I was to meet with Colonel Moose Stillman concerning being assigned to the USAF Academy.

He replied that he knew Col. Stillman very well, and that I would enjoy talking with him. I gave Gen. Roberts copies of several pertinent documents regarding my application and he thanked me, said he would look into my case, and he would be back to me soon.

This was like manna from Heaven, and I was on top of the world! At least now, I might have a chance. That's all I wanted—a fair evaluation of my potential as a regular Air Force Officer wanting to serve my country. I prayed a lot that day and evening. I might add that it was a selfish prayer request. And what about my being critical of a superior ranking officer and telling a General about it? My neck was really stretched out. I was vulnerable from a number of directions, but I felt that I had done the right thing. Calmness settled in my heart and in my mind. All I could do now was wait.

The operator at Base Ops announced, "Lt. Collins, report to Gen. Roberts' office immediately."

Everyone in the building heard it and heads started turning to see my reaction. It had only been two weeks since my impromptu meeting in Base Ops with the General, but I knew what this was about. I had serious misgivings about what the results might be. I took a deep breath and went by Tiny's office to tell him where I was going. With his good luck wish ringing in my ears I headed out the door to my car. As I drove up to the General's office my hands were shaking as I grasped the steering wheel.

When I arrived, I opened my car door, closed it tightly, stood tall, and breathed deeply to relieve the stress. I bounded into his office, and his assistant invited me to have a seat. She asked if I wanted a cool drink.

"Yes Ma'am," I quickly responded. She brought me a Coke with ice. This was like pouring water on a hot radiator. I gulped it down and tried to hide the resulting burps, but I really needed that drink.

In a moment the assistant came over and said, "The General will see you now."

His door was already open so I knocked on the side of the door as I entered and saluted. He acknowledged me and asked me to have a seat. I didn't notice anything about his face or voice that would give me a clue as to what might be coming.

Finally he asked about Major Manch and how was he doing. "You know he has had one hell of an Air Force career, and I'm pleased that he's here at Nellis running our Base Operations."

"Yes Sir," I responded. "He's a fine man and his wife is also from my home state of North Carolina."

The General said, "You're right. I had forgotten that. I think you will be pleased to see this set of orders that just arrived this morning." He pushed the paperwork in front of me.

My eyes quickly homed in on the words *We are pleased to inform you that you have been selected as a Regular Officer in the United States Air Force, effective this date.* I came up out of my chair and grasped the General's right hand, shaking it like I was pumping water in an oasis somewhere. I thanked him profusely for reviewing my case and then doing something about it. My career had begun and I had my very first mentor.

I dared not ask about Major Dumbass and his role in this play, but in the weeks ahead the Major went out of his way to be nice to me and to wish me the best in the future. What a turnaround!

As I left his office, Gen. Roberts mentioned Col. Stillman and asked me to give him his regards, as the General would not be on base during the time of his visit. That was my first clue that the interview for the Academy would be a reality soon. Prayers are answered, even selfish ones!

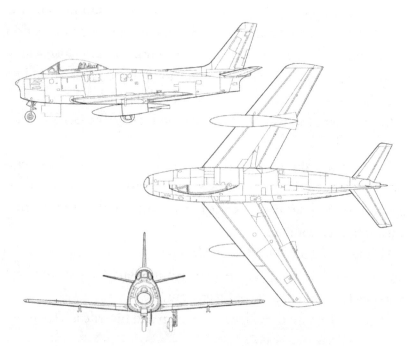

(19.1) North American Aviation F-86 Sabre (Fighter) schematic

(19.2-3) F-86 Sabre, profile and front images

20
Playing In Vegas

During the six months I was in Gunnery School flying the F-86 at Nellis AFB, hundreds—and maybe more—of major entertainers and entertainment groups played the Vegas hotel scene. In the initial phase of Gunnery School, there was no time to spend on the Strip gambling or watching and listening to the best entertainers in the world and seeing some of the most beautiful women in the world. Talk about distractions!

As the flying program continued, I think we students became accustomed to the schedule, so we made time for those special events that caught our attention. I made the personal decision to attend church in Vegas at the First Baptist Church. I had visited several times and was impressed with their music. Wednesday night choir rehearsal became another major event to add to my calendar because it was enjoyable, and I met a lot of interesting people. John and his wife, Evelyn, sang in the choir and invited me to dinner several times. He had a construction company and was kept very busy through Evelyn's connections. She was Jimmy Hoffa's Las Vegas Administrative Assistant. Since the unions were beginning to come on strong by buying a lot of hotels and other associated enterprises in that area, Evelyn was becoming a sought after person.

Choir rehearsal was a real man's outing as many of the showgirls on

The Strip attended church there and were dressed like they were to go on stage at any moment. Naturally, we had one of the largest men's singing groups in Las Vegas. The talent level in our choir was superb and because so many of the choir members could read music, we had a large repertoire of wonderful songs to present to the congregation.

One fact became obvious to me. The pit bands at the Sands Hotel, the Rancho Vegas, and the other large hotel entertainment centers had the best musicians in the world. Just to listen to them play was entertainment enough for me. In those days, you could buy one drink and nurse it through the entire evening with no harassing from the waiters. I loved to go hear Louis Prima and his wife, Keely Smith, at the Sands Hotel bar. They started around midnight and went on until about four a.m. They became an institution on the Strip and packed audiences in every night.

I also liked to hear the Big Bands like Cab Callaway. His group was loose as a goose and mingled with the crowd a lot. I got to know some of them and would accompany them to the Colored Elks Club after their normal gig on the strip. I carried my sax in the trunk of my car just so I could experience this kind of happening, and was it great! I have never had so much musical fun in my life than I had with those guys, and I learned a lot too. Meeting the flying schedule after one of these soirees was a challenge, and it took a day or two to get back to normal.

Yes, there was also a social side to this life I was leading. I met a young, beautiful schoolteacher from a very small town in South Carolina named Margaret Suber of Whitmire, SC.. Margaret was delightful and so were her circle of friends. It was 1955 when Margaret's sister, Rankin, was runner-up for Miss America. We celebrated the hell out of that, and it took several days to recover.

Margaret rented a room from an elderly lady who had lost her husband some years earlier. She was proper to a degree I felt was fake, so I had some concern about her. Eventually the curtain fell—exposing all the hidden treasure she had stashed away.

One day Margaret decided to surprise her landlady by cleaning the house while she was away for several days. Bottles of every type of booze

known to man were found in the closets, under the beds, and stored under towels, etc. in the bathroom closet. This lady was a boozer, but she really knew how to hide it. Margaret never said a word to her so the charade
continued until Margaret left Vegas.

In the meantime, several of my flying mates had met some of Margaret's schoolteacher friends, so we had a nice group of people to socialize
with. Later, when some of us went to work at the new USAF Academy
in Denver, a lot of these lovelies arranged to teach in the Denver School
System. Funny how that works. (Ain't sexual attraction fun?)

Man! I needed to get out of Vegas or my health was going to be
ruined! I hoped that the Academy assignment would materialize soon,
so I could become normal again, get some sleep at night, and regain my
health. Not only can you spend every nickel to your name—but you can
also drink yourself into oblivion. Welcome to Las Vegas!

(20.1) My favorites: Louis Prima and wife Keely Smith

(20.2) Some of the best places to visit in Las Vegas!

21
Two Surprises!

In 1955 the first class of USAF Academy cadets reported in at the temporary Academy site at Lowry AFB, Colorado. There was not an Upper Class to handle these cadets, so the first Commandant, Col. Robert M. Stillman (later Major Gen.) toured specific Air Force bases to recruit seventy Buck Lieutenants (2nd Lts.) to be the military teachers and leaders for the first three classes of cadets.

This very first class was composed of 300 males (females were not yet allowed). As you might imagine, the caliber of this class was top notch in every respect, as the best of the best wanted to be in the first class.

I was finishing up jet gunnery school in the F-86 at Nellis AFB in Las Vegas when I became aware of the recruitment opportunity. I saw this as a way to stand out and get ahead of my peers in promotions and assignments if I were to be selected for this plum of an assignment. So I volunteered to be interviewed by Col. Stillman.

I did not realize that this distinguished Airman had been captured and was a POW in World War II. Not only that, he had also been the first All American football player at West Point. When I walked into the interview room and saw this magnificent and highly decorated gentleman rise to greet me, I almost collapsed on the floor. The set of awards and medals on his chest almost blinded me as I tried to take in everything about the man. I saluted and gave him my name from a stiff position of attention. He cheerfully responded and asked me to have a seat.

My first thought upon being seated was that the Colonel could have been Santa Claus without the beard—but he made up for that by having very bushy eyebrows, chubby red cheeks and a wry little smile. This man was so pleasant and happy and interested in learning about me. Little did I realize that Santa Claus was about to change my life—forever.

His opening questions were so innocuous and easy that I found myself just bubbling away about myself, my life, and what I hoped to do during my lifetime. Then, as if by design, he switched.

"Do you like music?" he asked.

Off I went into my high school and college experiences in bands, drum majoring, playing in dance bands, and loving to sing.

"I played the tuba in high school, and for a Pep Band at West Point," he declared, a broad grin on his face. "And I sing Bass," he added.

All of a sudden we were talking and laughing and acting like two kids who had known each other in the past and were trying to catch up with each other. We were flat having fun. It was obvious we liked each other—a lot. I had learned that Col. Stillman was known to his close friends as Moose—probably because of his size when playing football at West Point.

Well, finally Moose brought us back to the task of the day. We discussed flying, leadership, military training, and other aspects of beginning the USAF's own Academy. I was blown away that he was interested in having my opinions on these issues. My energetic and forceful responses seemed to please him. I thought to myself, "You have sung the right verses to the right songs this morning!"

I think that was a correct analysis of my meeting with Moose Stillman. I received orders within a few days to report in to the new USAF Academy as an Air Training Officer. My future was beginning to unfold, and I liked what I saw.

Nearly fifty years later, the Moose was deceased and the USAF Academy was well established outside Colorado Springs, Colorado. The

Superintendent of the Academy had sent invitations to all the surviving members of that original cadre to attend the dedication of the Academy Parade Field that would honor General Stillman and bear his name.

On the specified date we all assembled on the Academy Parade Field to witness this event—the old ATOs, a few from the Commandant's Shop, some academic types who had originally taught the cadets, and some of the civilian folks who were assigned to the Academy in its infancy. We all milled around greeting one another, renewing old acquaintances, and selecting the best seats in the stands to view the parade and the flyby of jet fighters honoring our former leader, the Big Moose Stillman!

The announcer began his script telling the history that all of us had been creating. He then signaled for the band to play the USAF Academy Wing onto the field. The trumpets heralded the entrance. The drummers began, closely followed by the band playing marches most of us knew like old dance tunes. Here they came from every port at the top of the hill.

Hundreds of cadets in perfect cadence step-marched their way onto the field with their dress uniforms glistening and their feet pounding out the cadence with beautiful march music accompaniment. Wow! The sight took my breath away, and reminded me of the hours we ATOs had spent training those first three classes. Now we were witnessing the evolution of that training to present day performance. I was so proud I could hardly sit still.

The Wing was in place, the music had ceased, and commands were issued by the Cadet Wing Commanders. All movements were executed as if by "One Giant Muscle." *This*, I thought, *is how precision formation flying had its beginnings.* There were no other sounds on the plain, no noises of any kind.

Then the announcer explained the significance of Colonel Moose Stillman to the USAF Academy. How he had initiated and led the founding activities and policies that had brought this elite educational establishment from its birth to its present day status. There was a pause by the announcer and some conversations in the background.

The announcer finally came back on. "Ladies and gentlemen, at this point in the program we were to have a Jet flyby to honor General Stillman and the naming of this parade field. But due to inclement weather at the base of their origin, the flyby has been cancelled!"

The crowd gave a singular *Oh!* And a gasp. Everything became deathly quiet.

Suddenly, from the far end of the field appeared a huge V formation of geese, and their line of flight was straight down the middle of the Parade Field. The Moose had arranged his own flyby! The crowd went wild with enthusiasm, slapping each other on the back and pointing to the closest V formation any of us had ever seen. This was both fantastic and surprising. A new piece of history had just taken place that would be handed down from generation to generation. Only one word could ever describe it—UNBELIEVABLE!

The close relationship that the Moose and I had during those early years of the USAFA manifested itself in another facet of cadet life. In all the rush of planning for the first class of cadets, the Commandant's shop forgot, at least momentarily, about religious services for the Protestants. To be more specific, we had not made arrangements to have a Protestant choir to sing at the Protestant services. And, there was no music director to handle this.

The Moose called me in and announced the screw-up and asked if I could handle this chore. I agreed. We ended up with about 100 men in the first Protestant choir. Not bad as we only had 300 in the total class. My friend Blair Hennessy agreed to split this duty so that every other Sunday one of us would be off duty.

We had a great group of singers who took this commitment seriously. They performed every Sunday like they were the Mormon Tabernacle Choir. Moose loved it and attended church every Sunday. "Just to listen to the choir," he would always say to me.

This has been a fairly long dialogue to get to the surprises the chapter announces. Every military organization in the world has an Officer of the Day designated to handle anything that might come up during a time when the normal Officers In Charge are on duty or away from the base. USAFA was no different and one weekend was my time "in the barrel."

On Sunday, the Officer of the Day was assigned the job of checking each building in the complex to see if everything was in order. On this particular Sunday, I had just led the choir, heard from the Moose, and had eaten lunch in the Dining Hall.

After that, I went into all the barracks and just wandered around, observing any activities going on. Mid-afternoon I walked up to the Chapel, checked the door—it was unlocked as it was supposed to be—and walked in to look around. I heard a noise coming from a pew on the left about halfway to the front. Now the Honor System prohibited me from yelling, "Who is there?" I must actually see the unauthorized person and proceed from there.

I walked slowly toward the front, checking out both sides of the aisle as I moved along. Suddenly, down the left side, two bodies appeared that looked like they were joined in the middle. One was a beautiful blonde teenager who seemed to be embarrassed over my discovery. The other was a cadet. Not just any cadet though. He was Rex Merritt, Jr., son of the famous Rex Merritt, Sr., hero of World War II and a Congressional Medal of Honor recipient.

The names have been changed to protect whomever needs protecting, namely me! I knew Cadet Merritt quite well. He had been in the squadron I commanded earlier. I ordered him to stand at attention. I should have known that part of him was already at attention, but that didn't seem to concern him in the least.

I decided to forgo questioning him in front of his "lady" and recommended he escort her to the front gate and then come to my office for further questioning. That term means to *get your ass in gear and arrive at my office at the earliest possible moment*. The two rushed to the door of the Chapel and departed holding hands, giggling as they headed for the front gate.

Now I'm not a killjoy type person or one who tries to throw a wet blanket on those wanting to have some fun—although cooling off might have been very appropriate in this instance. I went back to my office and thought about what I might say to Cadet Rex Merritt, Jr., that might make a real positive impression on him. I liked him personally and thought his future in the USAF could be quite bright.

Knock, knock came the pounding at my door. I sat back and called out, "Come in."

Cadet Merritt entered, closed the door, popped to attention, saluted and announced, "Sir, Cadet Merritt reporting as ordered, Sir."

I returned his salute, stared at him for a moment, then rose from my chair and strolled over to look out the window that faced the drill area. After another pause, I wheeled about. Raising my voice a level or two I asked, "Mr. Merritt, what is our Chapel designed for? Why do we have a Chapel?

"Well, Sir," he started. "Chapel services are held every Sunday in the Chapel, Sir."

"Mr. Merritt," I exclaimed. "Are you trying to tell me that you and your lady friend were holding some type of religious service in the Chapel this afternoon? Is this why we have a Chapel here—so that you can use it to gratify your personal desires?"

Merritt replied, "I don't see anything wrong with that, Sir, because it's a facility for our use."

I decided that this was not the time or place for an ethics lesson. So I told him I was very disappointed in him, his answers, and his actions. I was going to report him for this infraction and complete lack of judgment. I advised him to learn from his mistakes if he expected to be successful in this world—be it in the USAF or as a civilian.

When I ordered him dismissed, his face was drenched in perspiration and his shirt was wet as water. As he wheeled about and departed, my thought was that Cadet Merritt had not heard the last of this. In fact, I was certain of it.

My assignment at the USAF Academy was to train the first 3 classes of cadets before moving on in the USAF to other flying assignments. Shortly before I departed USAF Academy for France to fly F-100s, I noted that

Cadet Merritt had just completed a long punishment of walking tours on the quadrangle. I hoped he had learned his lesson.

(21.1) Maj. Gen. Robert M. Stillman

BIO: MAJOR GENERAL ROBERT M. STILLMAN

Retired: August 01,1965   Died: May 22,1991

Robert Morris Stillman was born in Greenville, Ohio, in 1911. He graduated from high school at Pueblo, Colo., in 1929, attended Colorado College in Colorado Springs for two years, graduated from the U.S. Military Academy June 12, 1935 and was commissioned a second lieutenant of Field Artillery.

Immediately thereafter, General Stillman entered Primary Flying School at Randolph Field, Texas and graduated from Advanced Flying School at Kelly Field, Texas in October 1936. He served with the 50th Reconnaissance Squadron at Hickam Field, Hawaii from Jan. 10, 1937 to August 1940, returning to the U.S. Military Academy each fall during this period as a member of the football coaching staff.

Moving to Bolling Field, Washington, D.C., he was named officer in charge of the recruit detachment and the following Jan. 6, assumed command of the First Staff Squadron. He was appointed chief of the Overseas Section, Directorate of War Organization and Movements at Army Air Force Headquarters on May 20, 1942 and the following Jan. 20, became executive officer of the 387th Bomb Group at MacDill Field, Fla.

Going overseas that March 17, General Stillman commanded the 322nd Bomb Group of the Eighth Air Force in England until he was shot down and captured in Holland May 17, 1943, remaining a prisoner of war until April 29, 1945. He participated in two low-level B-26 bombing missions, being shot down on his second one.

Nov. 30, 1945 he was named chief of the Training Division, Headquarters, Third Air Force at Tampa, Fla., and on June 1, 1946 was appointed deputy chief of staff at Tactical Air Command Headquarters, Langley Field, Va.

General Stillman was in command of Stewart Field, N.Y., from Aug. 1, 1947 until he became deputy for operations at First Air Force Headquarters, Mitchel Air Force Base, N.Y., March 1, 1949. Entering the National War College, Washington, D.C., Aug. 28, 1950, he graduated the following June 30. Assigned to Air Force Headquarters, he then was appointed chief of the Officers' Assignment Division in the Directorate of Military Personnel.

On Sept. 1, 1954, General Stillman was designated commandant of cadets for the newly activated U.S. Air Force Academy.

(21.2) Air Force Academy sign and U.S. Flag

(21.3) Air Force Academy Chapel

(21.4) Air Force Academy Cadet Wing honoring Gen. Stillman

22
Thanks For The Memories

As a military man, I always knew my Wing Commander, Base Commander, and specific others with whom I had contact. Rarely would I even know the name of my Theater Commander if I were overseas, or my numbered Air Force Commander in the Continental USA. Those positions were just too far up the chain of command to be of any real interest to me personally. The highest-ranking military officer in the Department of Defense is the Chairman of the Joint Chiefs, and only in the past several years have I actually known who that person was.

General Hugh Shelton of Speed, North Carolina, a graduate of North Carolina State University, is a great human being. He was the 14th Chairman and was in charge when Islamic radicals destroyed the Twin Towers. Retired from the Army now, he has established a Leadership Center in Raleigh that is operated by NCSU. I serve on his Board of Trustees and know him quite well. But Hugh Shelton is not the most famous person to come into my life, although he is the person I admire most, trust the most, and believe to be the most qualified leader of men I have ever known.

The most famous person I have ever known was born in 1903 in Britain and died on July 27, 2003, at the age of 100. During his lifetime, he became recognized as the foremost comic and entertainer of his day.

Everyone the world over knew his name—Leslie Townes Hope—the renowned Bob Hope!

The question is how did a country boy from Concord, North Carolina, even come close to this entertainment media titan? Would you believe—through Cecil B. DeMille, the famous Hollywood Producer and Director at Paramount Studios? Here is how this came about ...

The first class of Air Force Academy cadets was about to report in at Lowry AFB, Colorado, in June of 1955. The Secretary of the Air Force was the Honorable Harold E. Talbott, and one of his close friends was C. B. DeMille who was completing the gigantic movie, *The Ten Commandments.* Talbott asked C.B. if he would take on the project of designing USAF Academy uniforms so that the "Top Brass" could then select the distinctive uniform for the new Academy. West Point had theirs; Annapolis had theirs; now it was time for the Air Force to have theirs. Would it look like something from Star Wars? Maybe a slight touch of the German Luftwaffe, or maybe a completely new and never-before-seen uniform? All Air Force personnel at the Academy were holding their breaths just waiting to discover what DeMille would create.

The Commandant's staff selected 6 ATOs to be models for this project and I was one of them. We would fly out to Los Angeles, go directly to Paramount Studios and meet with people from Western Costume Company, a part of Paramount. In their warehouse were costumes from every movie I had ever seen—ape suits, English noblemen outfits, cowboy pants, guns, ropes and Tarzan outfits. You name it—they had it, including Frankenstein heads! The project was classified so we always met in a special room that was not accessible to normal people traffic.

Our routine went something like this: Each of us was assigned specific pieces of clothing to model. I got good ones—the formal mess dress jacket and trousers with cummerbund, gloves and bow tie. Of course, the well-starched white formal shirt (tuxedo shirt) went with this, along with black shoes and socks.

The first fitting was to get our measurements, and I mean right down to the most personal parts. They said this was necessary if the garments were to fit correctly. In the next phase, a piece of lining was hung on us, and chalk marks showed where certain adjustments would be made. After lunch, the artisans would lay a piece of the outer garment on us, make more marks and tell us, "Nice job, see you in the morning." Now this seems like it would take only a couple of minutes, but long discussions ensued, and I concluded that these garments were the most talked about in the history of the clothing business.

Eventually we came to the final fitting. Here it was—a beautiful and distinctive Mess Dress uniform that fit me like no other piece of clothing I have ever owned. It is interesting that this Mess Dress uniform not only was selected for the academy cadets, but it was also eventually selected to be the official USAF formal dress uniform. When I was released from a Hanoi prison, I bought a current Mess Dress uniform. That was in 1973 and I am still wearing it. I know that it was made to last and I hope to be able to keep up with it. "Tight but Wearable" is my motto!

All during the time that we six spent at Paramount Studios, Mr. DeMille would take us to the various buildings (studios) to witness the current movies being filmed. One of these was *Funny Face* staring Bob Hope and Audrey Hepburn. Every time DeMille walked into a studio, all movement stopped. The Directors and staff would come directly to C.B. Most of the time we would be introduced and then everyone would go back to filming.

One time we stopped in front of an individual mobile dressing room. DeMille knocked on the door. It opened, and there stood a man I had seen hundreds of times in the movies and heard on the radio. It was Bob Hope! He was very natural and seemed quite interested in our uniform project as explained by Mr. DeMille. Lots of questions followed along with some extemporaneous humor, and then we had a photo made with these two entertainment giants. This was not the only time that Bob Hope and I crossed paths, as you will learn in other chapters. I really am thankful for all the memories this gentleman has provided me. God bless you, Bob!

(22.1) Gen. Hugh Shelton and Quincy

(22.2) Cecil B. DeMille introducing Bob Hope to Air force Academy officials. Quincy is right behind Bob Hope. Frank Drew is far left. To the left of Bob Hope is Gen. "Moose" Stillman.

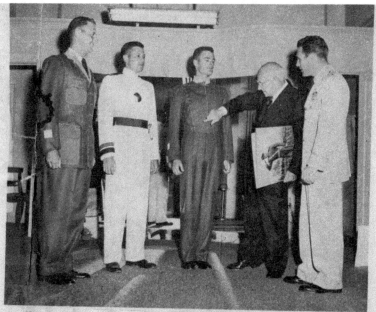

Two years in the making
Cecil deMille whips up a brilliant wardrobe for air cadets

DESIGNING and tailoring 6,400 United States Air Force Academy uniforms that will satisfy 800 cadets, the general public and senior officers and officials of the Air Force is a large order.

But Cecil B. deMille, chief designer of the 8-piece wardrobe, has succeeded admirably in pleasing everybody as head of the two-year project, now nearly completed.

He feels it's import to please the cadets. "If the man wearing the uniform is happy with it, that's the main thing," he said. "If his girl friend admires it, that's even more important."

During more than 40 years as a motion picture director and producer, deMille has acquired an unsurpassed knowledge of military wardrobes in depicting uniformed men of all branches of our armed services, from Bunker Hill to the present time.

Hours of painstaking research and infinite attention to detail have made him an outstanding authority.

Secretaries of the Air Force Donald A. Quarles and Harold E. Talbott arranged with deMille to design the cadet wardrobe in consultation with a seven-man Air Force uniform board.

The board decided that the family of uniforms and caps should not exceed $800, the price range of uniforms at Annapolis and West Point. It will include winter dress, winter dress parade, evening dress, drill, overcoat, summer parade dress, summer evening dress and a trench raincoat.

These items will be paid for by cadets from the $111.15 a month they receive while attending the academy. Khakis, fatigues, flying suits and parkas are government issue.

Materials were chosen for comfort and climatic conditions as well as for durability. Winter uniforms will be worn almost exclusively in the dry, temperate climate of the Colorado Springs area. Weight is geared to these conditions.

Six young air force lieutenant "models" were flown to California 25 times during the experimental tailoring and fitting.

The winter dress blue uniform is the work horse of the wardrobe. It will be worn to classes, meals, athletic events and during travel. To endure 12,000 hours of wear in the four-year academy program it must be made from a fabric that holds its shape.

The cap worn with most uniforms will be blue, with a darker blue braid. Its black visor has a silver-trimmed rim. White caps of similar design will be worn with summer white dress parade uniforms.

DeMille has recommended that the entire group of uniforms be analyzed from time to time. "The air force should review the cadet wardrobe at least every 20 years to eliminate outmoded items," he said.

Items in the cadet wardrobe are being shipped as soon as they are completed. All of the winter uniforms should be on hand by Christmas, with the balance of the wardrobe scheduled for completion by May, 1958.

(22.3) Air Force Academy ATOs: Quincy, Frank Drew, Andy Nial

23
GI Joe—Bill Mauldin

There is not a US Citizen who was alive during World War II who does not recognize GI Joe—the cartoon creation of Bill Mauldin. "Willie and Joe" became the heroes of WWII and the favorites of every soldier who fought for America. These two became the reflection of every GI who served in the military. The cartoon also won him a 1945 Pulitzer Prize for being the outstanding cartoonist of World War II.

I got to know Bill when he worked for Life Magazine and came to Lowry AFB to cover the new Air Force Academy that began in Denver, Colorado in the summer of 1955. I was assigned to escort him around the campus and see that everything he wanted and needed was available to him.

Bill was a civilian pilot and had just completed a coast-to-coast flight from the East to the West, and had written about his experiences for Life Magazine. He was like a sponge, soaking up every bit of knowledge about aviation and flying, and what the first class at the Academy was going to be exposed to in order to graduate.

I took him to every academic class, to drill, and to the flight line to witness the cadets getting flight time as navigators. We also spent a lot of time climbing in and out of F-86s, T-33s, B-25s and any other type aircraft that happened to be on the ramp.

Bill especially enjoyed attending meals with the cadets. I got permission for the cadets to be at ease during the meal so that Bill could carry on interviews and learn what these young fledglings really thought about making history as the first class at the USAF Academy. As I listened to them talk, I really became excited about my role as an Air Training Officer in preparing the cadets to assume important future leadership roles in the military.

I suddenly became aware of the importance we ATO's had in the overall scheme of their education. All the training and preparation we had was now in focus, and I was one proud Air Force Lieutenant!

Bill evidently felt these vibes from me and voiced his desire to meet other ATO's in a more relaxed situation, so I arranged a small party at my off-base home that I shared with 3 other guys. I invited at least 20 other ATO's and a few Flight Attendants (all women) to share time with this historic gentleman. Bill had already told me he was willing to spend some of Clare Booth Luce's money, and this was going to be a good time to do it.

Here I was—escorting a world-famous person from WWII—and we were discussing, and he was writing about, the future of the USAF. Timing is everything and man, I had the luck to be in the right place at the right time!

But now, Bill dropped a heavy mortar round on me. He wanted me to get him his first ride in a jet. This task proved to be quite easy as it was a perfect benefit for the Academy during its first year of operation. I started putting the event together. Bill was getting more and more excited. We were scheduled for a 9 AM take-off the next morning so we had a very calm evening in anticipation of the big flight.

I picked Bill up at his BOQ around 6:30 AM and we had a light breakfast before heading for the Flight Line. We did everything he had expected: checked the weather, briefed on emergency procedures, computed the take-off roll, fitted him in a parachute and covered the flight path we would be flying. He had lots of questions and was interested in all aspects of the flight—especially doing loops, rolls , wingovers and stalls.

Having spent at least an hour on all of these items, we got our helmets and chutes and walked to the T-33 Lockheed jet trainer that was to be our ride for the day. Since I had already decided we were not going to fly at a high altitude, we did not need to go through a high altitude chamber experience. I did a walk around inspection with Bill then we slid into the cockpits, Bill in the front and me in the rear. The Crew Chief explained a lot of things to Bill then gave me the signal to start the engine. Bill and I could talk to each other through the helmet microphone, but our breathing was very pronounced and sometimes interfered with our conversation. Jets are *not* as quick to start and rev-up as propeller driven planes, so Bill was concerned that we were not progressing as quickly as he thought we should.

We sort of shot the breeze as we taxied out to the end of the runway. I pulled onto the runway, locked the brakes, and pushed the throttle forward to check all of our instruments. I explained to Bill what the normal indications would be. Then, I released the brakes and went full throttle. I could hear Bill's breathing rate increase as we raced down the runway and I lifted us off and into the blue skies of Denver.

We climbed out towards Colorado Springs then turned right over Pikes Peak. I then put the nose down to build up speed and pulled back on the stick to complete a loop.

I thought it was time for my guest to take over the bird and get a feel for flying a jet so I shook the stick and told him he had it—and off we went toward Denver. It takes a few minutes for a new pilot to get into the swing of a different aircraft, but Bill did very well as we flew over the mountains west of Denver. Later, I took over the aircraft and demonstrated a fighter pilot pitch out and landing. He didn't like pulling G's that close to the ground, but I told him of the fighter pilot traditions and he settled in as we touched down, slowed and taxied in to shut down. This man really enjoyed his flight and he couldn't stop talking about it. The USAF got its money's worth for this flight. His story in Life Magazine proved it!

(23.1) Bill Mauldin

Bill Mauldin Biography

Born William Henry Mauldin, October 29, 1921, in Mountain Park, NM; died of pneumonia, January 22, 2003, in Newport Beach, CA. Cartoonist. Pulitzer Prize–winning editorial cartoonist Bill Mauldin received thousands of letters from fellow World War II veterans in the months before his 2003 death expressing enduring gratitude for his morale–boosting cartoons that ran in the Army newspaper. Mauldin's "Willie" and "Joe" were a pair of disheveled, long–suffering American soldiers with a wicked insubordinate streak, much like their creator. "Mauldin's characters offered a counterpoint to the clean–cut, gung–ho fighting man put forth by the Army publicity machine," declared Los Angeles Times writer Mike Anton.

Mauldin hailed from Mountain Park, New Mexico, where he was born in 1921. His handyman father drank, and his parents' marriage was a tempestuous one. Afflicted with rickets as a child, Mauldin was a gaunt, weak child and once overheard his father's friend say of him, "If that was my son, I would drown him," a Times of London article reported. He never forgot the sting of the remark, and later credited it with instilling in him a determination to make something of himself. By his teen years, when the family was living in Phoenix, Arizona, Mauldin was taking a correspondence course in drawing, and after being ejected from his high school for a prank involving a lit cigarette and a biology–classroom skeleton, Mauldin headed to the Chicago Academy of Fine Arts with a loan from his grandmother.

Mauldin began earning a modest income from magazine–illustration work, and considered himself ineligible for military service—because of his sickly childhood—once World War II began in 1941. He became a member of the Arizona Guard, which required no physical exam, but when it was federalized, he found himself a member of the Oklahoma–based 45th Division of the U.S. Army. Sent overseas in 1943, he participated in the invasion of Italy, was wounded at Salerno and earned a Purple Heart, and attained the rank of sergeant. He also served on the staff of Stars and Stripes, the Army newspaper, and his comical cartoons about the daily grind of Army life in Europe soon attracted a cult following. His soldiers, Willie and Joe, were ordinary infantrymen fighting the Nazi German menace, and when not dodging enemy fire were plagued by the soldiers' everyday miseries: bad food, rain, and the officious inanities of their superior officers. "During the war, he excoriated self–important generals, glamour–dripping Air Force pilots in leather jackets, and cafe owners in liberated countries who rewarded the thirsty G.I.'s who had freed them by charging them double for brandy," noted Richard Severo in the New York Times. "He was nothing short of beloved by his fellow enlisted men." Even the Allied commander in Europe, General Dwight D. Eisenhower, was a fan of the strip, and shielded Mauldin when the cartoons came under fire from General George S. Patton, who thought the duo served to depict the rank and file of the United States military in a unflattering light.

Mauldin's work also ran Stateside in several daily newspapers, and he earned his first Pulitzer Prize in 1945 for what Washington Post staff writer Claudia Levy called "a typical Mauldin effort showing dispirited infantrymen slogging through a downpour and was captioned, 'Fresh American troops, flushed with victory.'" He had actually planned to have Willie and Joe become casualties in the final days of the war, but his editors talked him out of that idea. The series made his name, but Mauldin later said he was uneasy with the fame that it brought. "I never quite could shake off the guilt feeling that I had made something good out of the war," the New York Times quoted him as saying.

After the end of the war, Mauldin found work as a syndicated newspaper cartoonist and revived Willie and Joe during the 1950–53 Korean War. He appeared in a few films, including The Red Badge of

Courage, and worked for the St. Louis Post–Dispatch as its editorial cartoonist after 1958. He won his second Pulitzer Prize the following year for a cartoon sympathetic to the plight of harassed Soviet writer Boris Pasternak, author of the Nobel prize–winning Doctor Zhivago. In 1962, Mauldin joined the Chicago Sun–Times, and his cartoons remained faithfully subversive over the next quarter–century: he poked fun at segregationists in the American South during the civil rights era, the politicians involved in the 1974 Watergate scandal, and even the staunchly conservative bent of some United States veterans' organizations. Perhaps the most famous image of Mauldin's career appeared just after the assassination of President John F. Kennedy in 1963, a captionless illustration showing the subject of Washington, D.C's stately Lincoln Memorial collapsed in grief.

Mauldin made a tour of Vietnam in 1965 when his son was serving in the military, and visited American troops stationed in Saudi Arabia during the 1991 Persian Gulf War. His pen satirized the United States' involvement in the first conflict with Iraq, and sometimes mocked the American president at the time, George H. W. Bush. Hampered by a hand injury, he retired from the Sun–Times in 1991. He was diagnosed with Alzheimer's disease and living in a nursing home in Orange County, California, in 2002 when a campaign was launched by a longtime fan of Wiille and Joe; veterans' organizations publicized his plight, and he received thousands of letters from former soldiers and fans of his World War II work.

Mauldin was married three times (and divorced twice): a brief union during World War II, a second one to Natalie Evans in 1947, who died in an automobile accident, and to Christine Lund after 1972. Mauldin died on January 22, 2003, of complications from Alzheimer's disease, pneumonia, and other ailments; he was 81. He is survived by seven sons; his daughter died in 2001. One of his sons told Anton in the Los Angeles Times, that his father's "philosophy in his work was always, 'If it's big, hit it.' He grew up a little guy. He understood the little guy." - by Carol Brennan

(23.2) A selection of several Willie & Joe cartoons, with thanks to Jerry Baker for finding them, as they were originally published by Stars and Stripes, in book form, in 1982.

24
A Foreign Affair

Would the presence of a beautiful baby blue Cadillac convertible in front of a small apartment complex in a quaint French village cause some interest for anyone passing by? I think so. But I did not give that idea a thought when I was asked to attend a wedding party in a French village outside of Toul-Rosiere Air Base, my first assignment after leaving the USAF Academy. I, like a lot of others stationed there, was a bachelor and always on the prowl for an attractive lady friend. But I am getting way ahead of myself here. Let me digress a bit.

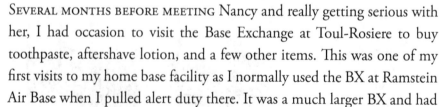

SEVERAL MONTHS BEFORE MEETING Nancy and really getting serious with her, I had occasion to visit the Base Exchange at Toul-Rosiere to buy toothpaste, aftershave lotion, and a few other items. This was one of my first visits to my home base facility as I normally used the BX at Ramstein Air Base when I pulled alert duty there. It was a much larger BX and had many more selections than our small one in France.

Late one afternoon I had occasion to visit the Base Exchange—a military facility that is somewhere between a drug store and a department store. I had a question for the clerk that she could not answer, so she went to get the Base Exchange Manager to assist me. I went about my shopping until a lovely voice said, "May I help you?"

I quickly turned around and there, standing in front of me, was a tall and very attractive Swedish blonde wanting to assist me. She was the Exchange Manager. She had a nice tan and a smile that was reflected in her sparkling blue eyes.

My first thought was: *Where the hell have you been?*

I became a little tongue-tied as I looked over this damsel who had just popped into my life. I finally settled down as she began answering my questions on whatever I was asking. This gorgeous creature had taken my breath away, and now I wanted to know more about her. I think I stayed there talking with her until the store closed.

Her name was Ingrid and she was Swedish. It was as if I had found an oasis in a blistering desert. I found a reason to visit the Base Exchange every day after that, and we became good friends. She had been told by her boss to, in general, stay away from the young officers who might find her attractive. I couldn't believe that none of my officer friends had discovered this jewel in our midst.

One day I came in late and she seemed excited to see me. She slipped me a small envelope, which turned out to be an invitation to a wedding party she and her mother were giving to honor a friend of theirs. It was to be on a late Saturday afternoon because the Base Exchange would be closed on Sunday, and that served as "Recovery Day."

I asked about her mother, as that subject had not come up before. She said they lived together because rent was high off base and they evidently got along well. *Very* well, I might say, as I discovered later.

I was really excited about this little soiree and treated my invitation as if it were top secret! I just could not believe that my horny Fighter Pilot friends had not discovered such an attractive woman.

Well, the day came. I spent a lot of time grooming both my car and myself. I really wanted to make a good impression and try to solidify my relationship with Ingrid. I studied the map she had drawn showing me how to get to her place so everything was ready for my next maneuver.

Her directions were perfect. I parked my chariot and rang the door-bell. Her Mother welcomed me with a hug and excellent English, and led me into the backyard where Ingrid was entertaining the other guests. Ingrid had mixed a hell of a drink that looked like Purple Jesus and tasted like a mix between Champagne and Wild Turkey. It was both eye opening and delicious.

I thought, "This might be a short night!"

The Bride-to-Be and her fiancé were fun people and spoke English quite well. Most of the other guests were French, and for the most part stayed to themselves. They also drank heavily. Ingrid and her Mom had prepared a virtual feast with lots of background music.

All in all, it was a great party! Everyone was enjoying it. I suddenly became aware that it was after midnight and most of the guests had left or were in the process of leaving. I already had my eye on a sofa that was long enough to accommodate yours truly, so I eased over and stretched out. Actually, passed out was more like it. I had consumed way more of Ingrid's special concoction than I could handle.

Ingrid bent down to tell me that her Mom had decided I had downed too much anti-freeze and should not drive back to the base that evening.

I agreed, and Ingrid pulled me up and led me through a door into a bedroom. She helped me out of my clothes down to my underwear, and gently helped me lie down in the middle of the bed. Yes, we did kiss before I went bye-bye.

Then it happened. Mom walked in dressed in her nightgown and crawled into bed beside me. In a second or two, in walked Ingrid in a beautiful PJ set. She lay down on the other side of me. I never sobered up as fast in my life.

This was a fighter pilot's dream!

Ingrid moved closer and whispered, "Relax and everything will be okay." Was she kidding me?

I did not know the protocol for this situation. Maybe there wasn't one. So I solved the dilemma by kissing Ingrid on the cheek and falling fast asleep. I hoped my dreams would solve the problem.

By the time I awakened the next morning and had breakfast with Ingrid and her mother, everyone stationed at Toul-Rosiere Air Base, France, knew I had spent the night with a native because my parked baby blue Cadillac convertible stood out like a billboard on the street by Ingrid's house. Most of the married officers lived off base, so I was pinpointed, recognized and convicted by noon on Sunday.

So goes the life of a Fighter Pilot … (Not bad, huh?)

(24.1) My parked, baby-blue Cadillac convertible stood out like a billboard on the street.

(24.2) Many years later, when I ran for the City Council in Charlotte, NC, I was reminded of the "billboard effect" in Toul-Rosiere, France

25
My Relationship With Nancy Begins

My relationship with Nancy began at Toul Rosier AFB in France around 1958-59. She had taken a job there as director of the Airmen's Club and was responsible for providing entertainment for the younger Air Force personnel. One night, I went to the Officer's Club to hear a band and show group that had been assigned there for the weekend. Their musicians were top notch and had a great sound. I asked the leader if I could sit in with my baritone saxophone, and he agreed. I knew a good thing when I heard it, and we really clicked. The club was packed and all seemed to be enjoying seeing one of their own playing with the group. The bandleader asked if I could join them the next afternoon at the Airmen's Club, and I agreed.

I was floored to discover the attractive woman, who was the director of the Airmen's Club, was from Charlotte, North Carolina. She was a graduate of UNC-Chapel Hill and a former cheerleader there. Being from Concord, about 18 miles from Charlotte, I found a lot to talk about and places to recall together. I knew the street she lived on, so it seemed like old home week in one way.

Between breaks in playing with the band, we would gravitate toward each other, so we planned a date in order to get better acquainted. Nancy was not a sophisticated type beauty, but more of a good-looking, whole-some, next-door-girl type demeanor. She was bright, well read and had a plan for her life. That showed in her self-confidence. I was impressed and also interested.

For a bachelor on that base, the pickin's were slim! There were a number of schoolteachers and a few female officers. Consequently, most of the pilots would go to Ramstein, Germany, or other places to do their woman chasing. There were also a few tourist spots like Malaga and Tourmalenais, Spain, that were within driving distance of our base. When a fighter pilot starts pawing the ground around the Stag bar in the Officers' Club, all of Europe opens up and the sky is the limit!

Some months earlier, General Frank Everest, Commander In Chief of the US Air Forces in Europe (USAFE), had sent out a notice that he was looking for a Junior Aide to work for him in Wiesbaden, Germany, headquarters for USAFE. While running our wing gunnery training facility at Wheelus Air Base in Tripoli, Libya, I had told my Wing Commander that I was very interested in applying for that Aide's job. Evidently, he felt that I had the talent and motivation to handle the job and sent my name in for consideration.

In the meantime, I continued flying F-100's as a flight commander, pulling nuclear alerts at Ramstein AFB Germany, and enjoying the culinary treats of restaurants in our area of France and also in Germany.

Nancy and I became a couple and we spent a lot of time together. We visited all the vineyards and resort areas within a hundred miles, and spent a lot of time investigating all the French restaurants that appeared to be worthy of our time and attention.

Eventually, I was selected to be General Everest's aide and received orders to report to Wiesbaden immediately. This was only about a three-hour drive from Toul Rosieres, so the separation would not be that bad. As the CINC's aide, I had a nice large apartment close to the headquarters' offices, and settled in while becoming accustomed to my new surroundings and different people.

Within a month, General Everest was called to return to Washington, DC and, as his aide and also pilot, I was asked to accompany him.

While in the USA, I visited Charlotte, North Carolina, to meet Nancy's mother. I spent a day with this lovely lady who eventually I came to see as my second Mom. Marjorie was a delight and very positive about life, even though she was severely crippled from polio. In the midst of the polio episode some years earlier, Nancy's father had run off with his secretary, leaving Marjorie to fend for herself. Just hearing her tell me this story pissed me off to the max, and I wondered why Nancy was still so close to him. At least that's how she sounded to me. Nancy had even said praising things about the woman who caused the break-up. This is still baffling to me to this very day.

Upon my return to Germany, I arranged for Nancy to move up to Wiesbaden, so hopefully we could determine if we had a future together. I had sent my baby blue Cadillac convertible down to France with a friend so Nancy would have a way to get her belongings up to Germany while returning my precious car. They both arrived—Nancy with a nice loving smile on her face and a warm hug—my car with one side scraped like a carrot and ready for major repairs and a new paint job.

Of course I, as Sherlock Holmes, immediately started investigating the situation. No one would claim responsibility. My friend, who delivered the car to Nancy, said it was in good shape when he turned it over to her. She had no explanation as to what had happened, and didn't remember anything being wrong with the exterior of the car. Neither did she admit to having hit or being hit by another vehicle while enroute to Wiesbaden. So I guessed a meteorite fell out of the sky right before I got the car and did all that damage. *Man, the plot was thick already and I wasn't getting any closer to the truth. Was I nuts, or what?*

I finally decided to have the car repaired and the damaged side repainted. There was no GM dealership available to do the work, so I selected a shop recommended by the local folks. My insurance company would not assist or pay, so I took the car over to the shop and left it to be put back in good shape. My precious convertible seemed to be full of bad Karma. My luck needed to change.

During the gestation period of waiting for my car to be reborn, Nancy and I continued dating, going to dinner every night. We discovered a wonderful Russian restaurant in Wiesbaden, where one waiter served the entire place and sang between servings—as we discussed the future.

From what she told me, I concluded that Nancy liked the company of older, more mature men. I somehow reasoned that this was a result of her relationship with her father—or at least what she would have liked it to be. Further, it became clear that, as a woman, she required a nurturing with some monetary requirement tied to it above the normal expected. She told me of a college friend from Dallas, Texas, who was one of her sponsors for this venture into Europe. Evidently the job as Director of the Airmen's Club at Toul was to be a temporary stop to replenish her finances and give her a jump off place to other opportunities in Europe.

These thoughts had evolved over time, but did flash by my mind from time to time while we were dating. I tried to question her further on this friend but to no avail. He became her mystery suitor as you will soon discover, and would always be in my life until Nancy and I were no more a couple.

Here is an example of what I mean. One afternoon I left the office a little early because the General was playing golf. A staff car dropped me off at my apartment, as my car was not yet ready. I hadn't been home very long when the phone rang. Upon answering it, a female started lambasting me for being associated with Nancy. "I just wanted you to know what a bitch you are dating, and I want to inform you that she is trying to steal my husband from me. Now what are you going to do about it?"

I was gasping for breath over the fervor of the person speaking to me on the other end of the line. She went on to say that this situation had been going on for some time and she wanted to bring it to a halt, right now, because it was breaking up her family!

How the hell did I get involved in this mess?

At the same time, I started defending Nancy without calling this woman a liar. I finally brought the call to a conclusion, walked over to my little bar and poured myself a scotch and soda!

What the hell do I do now?

Isn't life wonderful?

Yes, we discussed that call. Nancy informed me that this person was not dealing with all the cards in the deck, and she had made Nancy's friend quite miserable in recent years. I guess I believed her because I felt no obligation to do otherwise. But there was a question mark in my mind that would not be easy to remove! Ever!

The next significant call I would receive was from the car repair shop telling me that my wonderful baby blue convertible was ready to be picked up. A friend volunteered to drop me off at the shop after work, so we met and headed out. There she was—all gleaming and ready to go. I checked her over, saw no flaws and paid my bill. I felt on top of the world as I drove down the wide boulevards on the way to my place.

As I drove in, my normal parking area was full, so I drove around the building to a spot right below the window in my unit four stories above. I got out, stood back to admire my possession, then walked into the lobby. I gave my best regards to all the employees, called them by name and went up to my apartment. As I opened the door, the telephone was ringing. Karl, the man in charge of the apartment complex, was on the other end of the line. "Lieutenant Collins, do you drive a blue car?"

I replied, "Yes, I do. Why do you ask?"

"There has been an accident in the parking lot and your car is involved," Karl announced.

I walked over to the window overlooking that area of the parking lot. Down below were three or four people milling about my car. Then I saw it. A yellow Volkswagen was mashed into the same side of my car that had just been fixed! Evidently a car pulling out behind the Volks had touched its bumper hard enough to cause it to start a roll downhill towards my car. My lovely baby blue just repaired convertible provided the only STOP available.

I ran down to the parking lot with my heart in my throat and my hand on my wallet, again. Yes, same side, same repair and paint requirement, and I knew the way to the shop. Experience does give you some advantage, doesn't it?

The repair shop manager could not believe I was back again to have the same repair and paint job repeated. He did give me a break on the estimate for the repair and told me it would be ready in two weeks. And it was. To the day!

When I picked up my machine and headed out to my apartment, you would have thought I was part of a funeral procession—slow, deliberate, and trying to anticipate any action by careless drivers. It was a very painful journey, but one of the safest drives I had ever undertaken. Upon entering the parking lot at my apartment, I searched for a parking space that did not provide an opportunity for another accident. I finally found it and pulled into the space. Safe at home, at last. But the original cause of the damage to my car was still a mystery. And what about the woman I was dating? Was I in over my head on this one? I often wonder, would Nancy have accepted delivery of my Cadillac from my USAF friend if the car had showed signs of having already been involved in an accident? We may never know!

(25.1) Quincy, Chip, Chuck and Nancy

(25.2) Chip, Nancy & Chuck petting camel statues

26
The Marriage and the Honeymoon

Wiesbaden, Germany is a very picturesque and romantic place. There is a very good reason for that. During WWII, General Eisenhower decided that Wiesbaden would become the headquarters for the Supreme Allied Group when Europe was invaded, and the Allied Forces needed a central Headquarters to manage the ending of the war. Not one single bomb was to be dropped there by our forces so the elegant presence of the city was preserved.

Mainz, sitting right beside Wiesbaden, was completely destroyed, so a Heaven and Hell type comparison was easy to envision. Nothing was left standing in Mainz, but in Wiesbaden businesses and boutiques flourished along with hotels, spas and wonderful restaurants.

This was a playground for romantics and Nancy, my fiancée, and I succumbed to the clarion calls we heard and the *Love Potion # 9* mood that we created. For the moment, I forgot all the concerns that Nancy had fostered and I fell into the spell! This Fighter Pilot was about to ask the question that changes men's lives! Her answer was yes, so the planning began.

I asked Gen. and Mrs. Everest to play the role of my parents since there was no way of getting them to Germany for my wedding. They agreed. Now Nancy had to interact with Mrs. Everest to set dates and times and all the normal details of a wedding event; but now it also involved the Commander-In-Chief of Air Forces in Europe and all the protocol that goes with it. It was like the Bride and the show are the big deals. I became a mere passenger on this bus in the carnival. I really was not completely comfortable in this position, but as they say, "The Show Must Go On!" And it did.

Parties and gifts, gifts and parties, night and day, day and night—a steady stream of sentiment and thoughtfulness to the point that marriage seemed like a *sentence* of the court! Now second thoughts began to appear, and questions about some of the disturbing events that had happened during our courtship.

I recall that on a visit to the Headquarters of the US Commander of the Army in Europe at Heidelberg, I met his Aide—Major George Patton, the old warrior's son. We hit it off quite well and we decided to talk later about the honeymoon. I needed his help to line up hotels, restaurants, etc. for the big event. On the ride back to Wiesbaden, Gen. Everest asked how the wedding plans were going. I told him of some of my concerns, answered a few questions he posed to me and then listened to his advice. He reminded me that it was much better to call off a questionable commitment now, than to forge ahead and make a mistake that would bring regrets for years to come. Spoken like a true Father! Then he added, "Quince, when I hired you I advertised for a bachelor. If you want me to, I will tell you that is still the case and if you marry, your job as my Aide is over!"

Damn! This wasn't exactly what I had in mind. I loved my job and I really wanted some discussion that might show me the way through these doubts I had. Besides, I now had George Patton to help me arrange the honeymoon since the Army controlled all the Armed Forces recreational hotels in Europe. George could get me in anywhere. I left General Everest with a renewed spirit. He had caused me to re-evaluate my situation on my own and it worked. That sly old fox did just what my own father would do.

The plan began to take shape and it went something like this. We would have a civil ceremony at Toul Rosiere, the little village in France just off base where we first met. The French mayor would conduct the ceremony. We would then return to Wiesbaden where the official church wedding would take place one week later. The reception would be held in the Von Steuben Hotel in Wiesbaden, and we would leave for Munich, Germany, and a ten-day honeymoon immediately thereafter. My often-painted baby blue Cadillac convertible would be our mode of transportation. The plan was set, it was executed, and everything came off without a hitch. The date was April 25th, 1959.

It was a beautiful ceremony with many of my fighter pilot friends in attendance. They held sabers in an arch for my bride and me to transverse after a reception that would please a King. All cares and concerns were put away, at least for the time being. There was a Mrs. Collins now, and time would deal us some interesting hands. The events of the immediate past were still lingering, and our future was overcast with question marks. May God help us!

We drove on the autobahn over to Munich and tried hard to follow the driving instructions George Patton had given us. He had booked us at one of the famous German hotels in Munich, one with much history and a very high price tag. Driving up in front was an experience. The grounds were magnificent. The name of this hotel must have included every letter in the German alphabet and to this day I cannot recall the name. I do recall that it was the most expensive hotel I had ever visited.

After being escorted to our accommodations, a tuxedo-clad house-boy appeared to explain everything to us including the pre-ordered dinner. George had arranged for us to be served in our suite dining room, complete with the best Champagne my lips had ever tasted.

The next morning a waiter appeared dressed in a white tux and served a breakfast fit for a King! We finally checked out of the hotel, but not before we ordered a picnic lunch to have on the road to Garmisch, Germany. About one hour out of Munich we spotted a beautiful stream flowing through a green pasture and pulled over to have a glass of wine and check out our picnic lunch. This was a heavenly scene, but we hastened on because Schiswhigstein Castle was close by and that is spectacular.

After so many unbelievable scenes, we drove into Lucerne, Switzerland, and found our hotel. The lake there is so beautiful and the people so friendly that this was a great place to spend the rest of our honeymoon. The views from some of the mountaintops in the area took our breaths away. I was more than impressed with God's creation! This trip wiped away any concerns I had over our relationship because beauty, romance and life itself were so prevalent to enjoy and cherish. It could not have been better!

Mrs. Blackburn Whisnant requests the honour of your presence at the marriage of her daughter

Nancy Jane

to

James Quincy Collins, junior Captain United States Air Force Saturday, the twenty-fifth of April at two o'clock Hainerberg Chapel Weisbaden, Germany and afterwards at the reception General von Steuben Hotel

(26.1) Wedding invitation

(26.2) Photo of Neuschwanstein seen on honeymoon

(26.3) Photos of wedding in Wiesbaden

27
Sachmo at the Swim Meet

Everything was wonderful at Langley AFB, VA. and the weather was delightful. My boss, General Everest, was in good spirits and his programs for Tactical Air Command were all working out quite well. There was a battle going on within the USAF to determine who would become our next Air Force Chief of Staff. The two finalists were Gen. Curtis Lemay, head of the Strategic Air Command, and my boss, Gen. Frank Everest, Commander of the Tactical Air Command. They had known each other for a number of years, but were not close personal friends. They were definitely not going to bomb each other's headquarters or try to sabotage their operations, but anything else was fair game.

This particular morning I was at my office awaiting the arrival of the General and getting my orders for the day. Suddenly my private telephone rang as loudly as I had ever heard it ring. It was the general's wife, and I could tell that she had been crying.

"What's wrong?" I asked.

"Hank has had a stroke or a heart attack. We don't know which yet, but he wants you to come over here as quickly as possible. And don't say a word to anyone about this!"

My heart sank as I considered all the ramifications of the information

I had just received. I immediately thought of my visit to his headquarters in Wiesbaden, Germany, and my interview with him at the hospital there.

At that time he said he had a major case of indigestion and wrote it off as being just that. I assumed that he would take a similar path on this event, but I had better get my fanny in gear and show up by his bedside ASAP! I entered the back door and bumped into Mrs. Everest, who was waiting for me, hugged her and said something of a positive nature and then headed to the general's room.

My God, it looked like a camp-out! There was a breathing tent around my boss! He looked worn out and as down as I had ever seen him. He motioned for me to get under the tent with him so that he could give me some instructions in secret. These were personal messages to close friends. He wanted to inform them of his present status and future plans. He also asked that I take good care of Mrs. Everest.

As I was leaving, she introduced me to the two doctors who were treating the General. Dr. John was a handsome young cardiovascular specialist and Carroll, his male assistant, was equally well qualified in the treatment of heart problems. I could tell immediately that the three of us would quickly become close friends.

As the weeks passed by, the general became a little restless and impatient with the progress of his treatment. His doctors also complained that General Everest was trying to be too active in the running of TAC. As a result, the general asked me to evaluate several locations for him to recuperate and rehab. The two top sites were Hickam AFB, Honolulu, and Ramey AFB in Puerto Rico. We finally selected Ramey, AFB. And with my two new doctor friends, I began the task of making arrangements for housing, medical facilities, etc. for the needs of our 4-star patient.

There were fresh water fishing trips, golf, and trips to observe the whales. The weather was terrific and the General made a rapid recovery. A month later we arrived back at Langley AFB to resume normal operations.

Several weeks later, General Everest called me into his office and said he and Mrs. Everest wanted to attend a big party at the Officers Club Pool, and the great Satchmo Armstrong was to be playing that evening.

The general wanted me to work with Mrs. Everest on the Invitation list and said it should include my new friends—the doctors, and their wives.

Well, this sounded just great to me, so I met with Mrs. Everest to plan everything. Then I went to the Club Officer to firm up all the arrangements we needed.

The event was well advertised and it appeared that it would be a sell-out. This was a cocktail party only and dinner was not included. I reserved the south side of the pool for General Everest and his party. I took the area at the top of the pool where the diving boards were located for my new doctor friends, along with a doctor couple who lived and worked in the Hampton Roads area near by and were close friends of Dr. John.

On the evening of the party, I checked that all was OK with the general's group, then went to the bar to meet the doctors' group and take them to our place by the diving boards. Satchmo was on a platform at the other end of the pool and that gave us a great view of everything going on. The music was outstanding, the drinks were delicious, and the evening was one of the best I can ever recall.

Our wives were really enjoying the festivities and the general's group was getting louder with each round of drinks. As the evening was about to close and Brother Armstrong announced that the next song he played would be the last of the evening, I challenged John to dive into the pool and swim to the other end for a $20 bill I was holding.

He squirmed around a bit while his wife scolded him for even considering my challenge. Our other guests were advising John to do it and get my $20 bill. I had no idea John would seriously consider it, but as Satchmo played the final note, John gave me his wallet to hold and he got on the diving board fully dressed. His wife became wild with frustration and made a move to get to me. In her way, unfortunately, was the wife of the friend they had invited. The friend plopped into the pool in her new outfit—including new shoes, which floated to the top as she came up the ladder.

Meanwhile, John was playing Johnny Weissmuller in the pool and made it to the other end with great applause from the crowd. He headed straight for the bar where he was met by General and Mrs. Everest. John's wife escorted the wet friend to her car. I think that relationship came to an abrupt end. John was standing at the bar in a pool of water, but was being congratulated by everyone there. I gave John his $20 bill.

This little event became the talk of Langley AFB for weeks to come. John's wife and I have never spoken to each other to this day! Some people just don't have a sense of humor!

(27.1) Photo of Louis Armstrong

28
Fatherhood

There is no better feeling than to look down and see your own flesh and blood, newly born and moving around like a Mexican jumping bean inside a blue blanket. This has got to be better than winning the Lottery, especially when you begin to think of the future and what a wonderful addition this little human being is programmed to be. Now let's see—he has 2 feet, 2 arms, five toes on each foot and 5 fingers on each hand and, oh yes, the correct plumbing which appears to turn on every five minutes. There is no doubt—being a new father is a wonderful experience!

James Quincy Collins, III, was born at Langley AFB, Virginia, on May 28, 1961, to Captain and Mrs. James Quincy Collins, Jr. The entire Collins clan and Nancy's mother, Marjorie, were on Cloud Nine and asking the most repeated question of the year, "When will we get to see him?" We were probably super sensitive with this little guy since Nancy had a miscarriage during her first pregnancy and we were walking around on eggshells. My first question was, "Does he look like me?" I could visualize the resemblance in putting together my future legacy.

This was great and I enjoyed every minute of it. Whatever disagreements Nancy and I had seemed to disappear in love and admiration for this little bundle of joy that God had delivered to us. It was like Christmas and Bethlehem and a new life in our care and we loved it. The future was bright and life was good. I loved my father role. We nicknamed our son Chip. That gave me an even closer tie to my new son as I longed for him to truly be a chip off the old block. On top of all this, our little boy was good-looking, cute, photogenic, and a pleasure to look at. I was one lucky Dad!

I had received some training in being a father from being the owner of a miniature Dachshund we named Wee Willie Wilhelm. This little guy ran the house and was, indeed, a *child* that required complete supervision. One of Nancy's family friends had provided this bundle of joy right after we were married, and he had taken complete charge of our home.

Once, at Langley before JQ the Third arrived, we were having a cocktail party with many of Gen. Everest's staff and close friends invited. Nancy and I were running around getting everything set for their arrival when I noticed that Willie was not with us. I walked into the living room where I had just taken a tray of hors d'oeuvres and placed them on our lovely cocktail table. I saw Willie on top of the coffee table straddling the food while licking every piece of meat and cheese on the tray. He made not one effort to jump down or quit his hunting expedition until I yelled his name with all the volume I could muster. Nancy ran in just as our baby monster jumped down. We looked at each other and I said, "I won't tell if you won't!" We laughed, agreed, petted our wonderful canine friend and continued preparing for our guests. Ain't love wonderful!

It was time for one of our mothers to come visit us and render their judgment on our new addition. My Mom was selected and she arrived amidst much acclaim. Grandparents are prone to spoil their grandkids and this visit was no different. She loved to hold Chip while making all kinds of strange noises like birds cooing.

I noticed that she seemed to be having a problem with her mouth while doing this. I took her to a dentist friend of mine and she really had a problem that required pulling all her teeth. During the healing process Chip became fascinated with Mom's mouth and lips, much to her embarrassment. On the very day that she received her new dentures, we were invited to dinner at Major Margaret Barry's home about 20 minutes from the base. Margaret was about 6 feet tall, had a brilliant mind, and operated as General Everest's Executive Officer and Speechwriter. She had a great sense of humor and loved a good joke so I thought that she and my Mom would be a good match. They were!

On the drive to Margaret's, Nancy was in the back seat feeding Chip his bottle of milk. When I parked in front of Margaret's house, I took Chip and started up the first of three groups of steps to get to the front porch. Just as I hugged Margaret, Chip started gushing up the milk he had already consumed. Margaret threw open the front door and yelled that the kitchen sink was straight ahead. I spotted it and homed in with my little gusher still gushing. He filled the sink and I about fainted looking at what had come out of this little tyke's tummy. It was amazing!

By this time Nancy and Mom had made it up the steps and went into the living room. I cleaned up Chip, gave him to his mother and then started cleaning up the floor which was covered with you know what. All of a sudden laughter erupted in the living room. Not just a ha-ha—but also a belly-busting laugh that had the ladies bent over and crying.

Margaret had been explaining what she had observed of Chip and me when Mom started to make some comments. In the middle of this her new dentures fell out on the floor and Margaret yelled, "They're still moving!" I walked into the room and all three ladies were holding their sides while tears flowed down their cheeks. The evening was getting off to a great start and Chip was grinning from ear to ear!

General Everest, my boss, announced that he was going to retire because General LeMay had been selected to become the new USAF Chief of Staff and a whole series of changes began to occur. First, I had to find a new assignment. That would mean we had to pack up and move somewhere else. After several meetings with General Everest, we jointly decided that my best move was to get into the USAF Command and Staff School at Maxwell AFB in Montgomery, Alabama. This would be a really large step in my USAF professional education ladder and also put me in line for future promotions. Our move came off without a hitch and we rented a wonderful home about 20 minutes from the base. Our two children, Willie and Chip, seemed to really like their new surroundings and it was fun to come home and get on the floor with both of them and wrestle.

One day, while I was in class, I received an emergency call from Nancy for me to come home at once. Chip had rolled off our bed and fallen on his head. I asked if he were drowsy or lethargic and she said no. So I assumed he would be okay, but I launched off for the trip home. We took him to the base hospital. After a thorough examination he was pronounced fit as a fiddle, and we took him home to love and cuddle him while I chastised Nancy for being so reckless with Chip. I came to realize that with children, especially boys, things are going to happen no matter how careful you are.

I had made friends with a great guy named Hank. He and his wife became two of our closest friends. That only adds to the pain of telling another part of our story at Montgomery. Hank's wife was having a luncheon for some of the wives in our class. She had called Nancy to see if she might borrow a card table to add to her seating arrangement. Like any good husband, Hank was asked to drive over and pick up the card table, which he did. As Hank was backing out of my drive, Willie broke loose from his fenced confinement and ran under his car. It was the end of Willie and the beginning of a mourning time that lasted for weeks. My first "child" was no more!

Chip and I really missed our little playmate. I spent a lot of time telling my real son why Willie was not with us. It was a humbling experience for a Dad. Over time the hurt and empty feelings subsided and we all moved on.

Graduation finally arrived and I got the fighter assignment I wanted—F-104s at George AFB, California. This was the fastest fighter plane known to man and I could not have been happier. In order to properly celebrate this new move, we decided to drive through Yosemite Park up to Seattle then down to George AFB. We set Chip up in his crib in the back seat of our car and padded it with blankets and beach towels and set sail in our baby blue Cadillac convertible. Nancy was in charge of making reservations for our stays along the road. We arrived at the Lodge in Yosemite Park for a one-week stay. Our room was in an out-building with no bathroom facilities. There was a communal facility about 30 yards away. Neither was there a crib or baby bed for Chip, so we made one out of the bottom drawer in the dresser in our room.

The next morning was a disaster. Chip had been eaten alive by bugs or mosquitoes. He looked like one big whelp. I took Chip with me to visit the Lodge Manager and he was as interested as if I had brought him a bucket of elephant doo-doo. I raised hell, asked for a refund on the days not yet used, got it and checked out. Just as we walked out the front door of our cabin, a hoard of mosquitoes descended upon us and started biting and sucking blood. I was really concerned for Chip so we got in the car as quickly as possible, shut the doors and started killing this death squad that followed us. Finally, we beat the bastards, put lotion on our bites and started driving out of the park.

Before we left Montgomery, Nancy's mother had given us a bunch of her favorite plants—African Violets—to take to our new home at George AFB, California. It was my job to nurse these floral ladies through all the pitfalls of travel including watering and seeing to their safety. By the time we approached the California state line I was ready to urinate on the whole batch and throw them into the road to dry up and disappear.

As we approached the main inspection gate, a big sign appeared stating that it was illegal to carry any other type plant into California. Nancy saw it and began to cry from frustration. I could hardly wait to get the back door open, expose the plants, and watch the inspector throw them into a trash basket to dispose of them. The next 50 miles of driving into California was quiet, deathly quiet, as Nancy tried to deal with a lot of emotions concerning the violets, her mother, and her husband's obvious pleasure at their destruction. By nighttime, all was quiet on the western front.

We sat up housekeeping on base at George AFB. The base was almost empty. The Cuban Crisis was on. Several days earlier the entire Wing had deployed to Florida to provide air superiority in case war broke out. Tense times for the base as wives tried to keep things in line at home. I found myself to be the ranking officer in my squadron because everyone else was gone. Chip and I had more time to spend together wrestling and walking around the area. We still missed Wee Willie.

Living in the desert wasn't bad at all because there was no humidity. Most times a light breeze provided just enough fanning motion to be comfortable. I was fortunate in that several operational staff officers were left to be the primary contacts with the deployed units. They were all Instructor Pilots in the F-104 Star Fighter made by Lockheed. I quickly checked out in the airplane and then began to build time in the machine so that when the deployed units returned, I was also an Instructor Pilot.

During this time, Chip was growing at a rapid clip and was a joy to play with and read to. Nancy soon informed us that another little Collins was on the way. We watched her baby factory expand for us to feel the movements inside. Chip was fascinated by all this, as was I too, frankly!

It became my task to teach Chip how to go to the bathroom for #1 and #2. I decided that teaching Willie to do this was a lot easier. Standing up to pee evidently is not a natural feeling for a very young stud. I kept at it until my Squadron was selected to deploy to Moron, Spain (outside Seville). We were prepared to be gone 4 to 6 months so Nancy and I had to plan what to do about the next little Collins arrival. Chip had to be designated the next in command, and he really seemed to enjoy that thought.

As time progressed, we decided to fly Chip and Nancy back to Charlotte so that her Uncle, Dr. Newton, could deliver our next addition while she stayed in Charlotte with her mother. I put them on an airplane in Los Angeles and flew with my squadron to Moron. The very day I arrived at Moron Air Base, Dec. 17, 1964, Charles Lowell Collins was born in Charlotte. Chip's monarchy was over and we had other adjustments to make too. My kingdom was becoming overpopulated and life was getting a little more complicated. But at least we had two boys. All we needed now was a bigger cage!

(28.1) Photo of "Father" Quincy in front of F104.

(28.2) Photo of Chip standing with Steiff bear

(28.3) Three generations of James QuincyCollinses

(28.4) Collins family plus Wee Willie - Christmas card

(28.5) Quincy seeing Chuck for 1st time; reunion with Chip at Myrtle Beach, SC 1964   *(28.6) Chip and Chuck on Steiff bear*   *(28.7) Quincy, Chip, Chuck and Nancy*

(28.8) Quincy with Chip & Chuck-(3 photos)

29
The Orient Express

Several months after returning to George AFB from Moron, Spain, my Overseas Return Date caught up with me. I had last been assigned overseas in 1957, and here it was 1964.

As a fighter pilot I had two choices. The first was to be assigned to an F-105 squadron in Itazuki, Japan. This would require a stay at Nellis AFB Nevada to check out in the aircraft and weapons systems. My wife and two sons could also be with me during this time, but could not join me in Japan until I had procured a home for us to live in. I estimated this would take three to four months.

The second choice was a real loser—being a forward air controller directing air strikes from the floor of the jungle and living with all the snakes and animals that resided there. There were no family quarters so it would be a solo assignment for a year, at least. The decision was easy—*F-105 here I come!* Itazuki was to be our new home.

Nancy and our two sons would stay with her mother in Charlotte while I trotted off to Japan. After my family was settled in Charlotte, I boarded a plane in San Francisco for the flight to Japan. A new friend, Captain Jack Sterling, was boarding at the same time and our destinations were identical, so the new journey began on a happy note.

Itazuki was a well-known base from WWII and the Korean War. It was the subject of a number of old fighter pilot songs that were favorites at every stag bar at USAF bases throughout the world. Jack and I were being introduced to history at its source, and we were excited to become a part of it.

After checking into the VOQ (Visiting Officers Quarters) Jack and I headed to the bar at the Officers' Club. We met a bunch of people we already knew from other assignments, and the Wives Club was rehearsing for a show they were to present in the next few weeks. Some of the ladies knew that I sang and insisted that I join their merry group—and so I did!

That must have been a Saturday, because I attended Base Chapel the next day and sang in the choir. I was much welcomed as basses were few and far between. I also attended choir rehearsal the next Wednesday evening, as they were rehearsing Dubois' *Seven Last Words* for their Easter Cantata. I knew this selection quite well as I had sung it with several choirs through the years. Plus I had been the first Protestant Choir Director at the new air Force Academy in Denver.

That first rehearsal I attended at Itazuki Air Base was a musical disaster. The choir director became so frustrated with the slow progress of the choir that she threw up her hands and announced she was quitting.

Immediately, the Protestant minister who had been sitting in the back came forward as if on cue, and slowly and softly announced that we would have to cancel the Cantata for this Easter. The choir, in unison, said, "Oh no!"—and they dropped their heads in disbelief.

I raised my hand and said that I felt confident I could complete this task and lead this group of singers to perform the Cantata.

The minister wanted to know of my qualifications, and when I mentioned I had been the first Protestant Choir Director at the Air Force Academy, the deal was done and a new excitement took over. In the weeks ahead I understood the frustration of the old director. But by rehearsing like mad and taking over the tenor and baritone solos myself, we were able to put together a very nice program.

Thank You, Lord, for giving me the talents You did! Amen!

Shortly after Easter, our units received orders that we were leaving Itazuki for Yokota Air Base outside Tokyo, Japan. In military terms, this was a BIG MOVE! Everyone was excited and looking forward to our new assignment. Obviously the future was laden with many question marks.

What lay ahead for Quincy Collins? Is he ready? God, I hope so!

(29.1) F-105 Aircraft - dubbed "The Thud"

30
On the Way Into Battle!

Every military man secretly looks forward to the day that he officially becomes a Warrior and is put into a position to use the techniques of the trade he has selected to pursue in defending his country. As a Fighter Pilot, I was chomping at the bit to enter the fray evolving and escalating in Southeast Asia. The US was a member of SEATO, the South East Asia Treaty Organization. This group was not originally sanctioned to be a fighting unit, but rather a support group providing supplies, weapons, transportation, etc. But we guys sitting on the sidelines were training to bomb, strafe and patrol the skies, and believe me, we were poised to leap into our act when called upon to do so.

During 1964 I had checked out in the F-105 at Nellis AFB, Nevada, been transferred to Itazuke Air Base, Japan, and welcomed my wife, Nancy and two sons to the Orient. The base finally closed and we all moved to Yokota Air Base, Japan, right outside Tokyo. We rented a nice home off base, and Mount Fuji was in full view from our front yard. During this time our military mission increased tremendously.

One of our main tasks was to pull nuclear alert at Osan Air Base, Korea. I am not allowed to divulge the targets we covered. But needless to say, having a nuclear mission along with a conventional mission kept us on our toes, and let us know that we were important in defending ourselves and our allies in that part of the world. To be living in the same area that Gen. Jimmy Doolittle and his B-25 crews bombed right after WWII started was also thrilling and an enticement to travel and see the countryside.

And then it happened! Nancy became pregnant with William Robey Collins just as the tempo of preparations for war began to increase. Fortunately for us our home was large enough to accommodate a live-in maid, so I felt very comfortable in facing a possible military move for me. At any rate, this possibility kept increasing and looming in front of me.

In the middle of all this, I had an audition at a Japanese movie studio to play a French dope peddler in a movie they were about to film. The wife of a friend had an agent who booked her for several extra parts and she mentioned my name to him as a possible hire. I did go down to the studio for an interview and audition. I actually read some French (thanks to my Concord High School French teacher), posed for several shots and was pleased with the results. Unfortunately, I received orders to fly to Korat, Thailand, and never heard anything from my audition.

Nancy was bulging with son #3 when I received her call to take her to the Tachikawa hospital that was fairly close to Yokota Air Base. As we entered the front area and began the walk down the long hall, Nancy suddenly stopped. "It's too late!" She flooded the hall with amniotic fluid, and that alerted every nurse within a half a mile to come to the rescue. She was placed in a wheelchair and rolled quickly into an area already filled with expectant mothers moaning and groaning with labor pains. This was not the place for an expectant father—or a mother, for that matter. Nancy was administered to by several nurses and I was ushered out of the hospital with instructions to stand by, or at least call in every ten minutes for the latest development.

By this time it was dark and I needed a drink! I went to the Officer's Club, had one or two, and slipped into the performance center for a bite of dinner and to see the show. Julie London was performing, so I knew the show would be good. The lights dimmed, the band played the lead-in song, and the curtain opened. There stood the star holding on to the stand-up mike like it was her last chance before sinking on the Titanic. It was terrible! She sang off key, struggled to stand erect because she was so drunk, and finally just sat down in the middle of the stage. The curtain closed and the star disappeared.

I went back to the hospital to check on my wife. She was well except in pain, so I went home (nurses' instructions). The big HE was born the next day. Now this wee wiggly fellow is about 6 feet 3-4 inches—a really big guy and better looking than I. So goes life!

About four months later the clarion call blasted, and my Squadron deployed to Korat, Thailand. We now had a mission and tasks to perform in addition to our continued training flights. The days were really hot and the evenings cold. A lot of our enlisted men started hunting cobras on the runways at night, putting them in cages as they caught them. One thing we were warned about—empty your boots in the morning before slipping your foot inside. The very first morning I was in Korat I did as instructed and out swirled a good-sized Coral snake. Beautiful, but deadly!

Christmas was approaching and the air battles had become quite active. Gen. Joe Moore was in charge of all aviation activities for Gen. Westmoreland. I had been stationed with Gen. Joe at Langley AFB when I was Aide to the 4-star commander there. Later, I was sent to Saigon to head up the Plans Section under Gen. Moore, and do whatever else was required from the F-105's in the theater. My first assigned task was to plan a schedule of F-105 flights to try to fool the Russian Ambassador, who was visiting Laos, into thinking that the US had a much bigger force of aircraft in the theater than we admitted to having. I was given his driving route, and planned for my single F-105 to fly over him at low level in as many places as possible to make the charade appear real. This was a fun project, but alas—the Russians changed their plans and the mission was canceled. I took pride in the work I had done and I looked forward to the next assignment.

Within a week or two it happened. Gen. Moore called me to his office to explain a mission that President Johnson had personally authorized.

This was to be the first US bombing mission into North Vietnam, and all the Air Force brass wanted it to be a huge success. I was the guy running the mission and planning the entire operation. "TOP SECRET" was stamped on all documents having to do with this mission. Man, I took that seriously!

That first night in Saigon I was nervous as a cat. I decided to go across the street from my hotel (The Imperial) and listen to a French guitarist I had heard once before while having a martini and a bite of dinner. After being seated, I asked him to play my favorite song, *My Funny Valentine*. I also asked if I might sing along with him. He agreed and off we went. Therein followed some of the most magnificent chords and chord progressions I had ever heard anywhere! I felt like Robert Goulet, and the words and music flowed so easily from my throat. It was magic! We both recognized that something special had just been created. I returned to my hotel, relaxed and happy as a lark. That night's wonderful sleep portended good things ahead for yours truly.

Over the next week I selected the pilots I wanted from my old Squadron, decided on the routes in and out of the target area, set the dates and times for the mission, arranged air refueling possibilities, and took care of a ton of details that would make this a very successful mission. Gen. Moore approved my plan, and sent it to the President for his approval. I have no idea if LBJ by-passed his Joint Chiefs in the approval process, but I would guess that he did. At any rate, everything was approved and the mission was set for Christmas Eve, 1964.

There were six aircraft and six pilots involved, and I met them at an undisclosed airfield on the East coast of South Vietnam. In addition, we had two Intelligence officers and one weather specialist available to brief the crews. I was in charge of briefing for the overall mission, and I spent a good two hours doing that. We had four primary aircraft with two spares available in the event any of the primary aircraft had to drop out. As we ended the briefings and were ready to go to the aircraft, I led our little group in a prayer for a successful mission and the safety of all involved.

No one uttered a word as we all walked outside and the pilots climbed into their assigned F-105s.

I had asked the two spare pilots to hang back with me as I had special instructions for them. All aircraft cranked up perfectly and all six taxied out for take-off. As I surveyed the group taking off in single file, I prayed, "Oh Lord, please let everything go as planned!" They all rose into the sky and disappeared into the horizon. Damn, I wanted to be with them. I guess in a way I was.

About an hour later the two spares checked in as I had instructed them. They asked the tower for permission to drop their unused ordinance at sea rather than land with it on board, since they were the spares. This is standard operating procedure and is for safety reasons. Shortly after, the two spares taxied in and I met them with a big smile on my face. We high-fived and went into operations to await the arrival of the main strike force.

Within about thirty minutes all six of us were sitting around a table in the Ops room talking about the mission. No refueling had been necessary, so that was not an issue or a topic of conversation. I had required the two spares to remain silent on my instructions to them, so that part of the mission was also not discussed. The four primary aircraft had done their job convincingly, and the targeted small building housing weapons and supplies was no more. The mission was a smashing success. As soon as they had all refueled, the six took off and headed to Korat. I began writing my Operations report on the mission.

After filing the report, I flew back to Saigon and hitched a ride in the back of a pick-up truck to my hotel. I sensed that something was wrong. It was! When I opened the door to my room, window glass was everywhere. At least two of my windows had been blown out from the explosion at the NCO hotel next door. The VC had parked a jeep loaded with explosives under the hotel, and blew it up on Christmas Eve. Several military personnel were killed and injured. The hotel arranged for me to have another room on the other side of the hotel, so I moved quickly, went to the bar for a drink and a sandwich, and retired for the evening. I slept like a bear getting ready for a long winter's nap.

I awakened the next morning because my telephone was ringing off the hook. It was Gen. Moore, talking a mile a minute. He ended up with, "Come to my office ASAP! I need to talk to you!"

On my way to his office I wondered what was up. Had I screwed up in some way, were some of my personal decisions involving the mission to blame for the *right now*? We would soon know. I knocked on his door and was invited in.

He was smiling, and extended his hand for a good welcoming shake as he patted me on the shoulder and offered me a seat. He began, "Quince, we have analyzed the results of the mission you planned, and there is more damage and more bomb craters than our four aircraft could produce. How did this happen? Can you explain this?"

"Yes sir," I replied. "May I speak honestly to you, and off record?"

He looked at me in an unusual way with a questionable grin on his face and replied, "Of course. Go ahead!"

Then began my dissertation that could either get me fired and court-marshaled—or perhaps promoted! At any rate, I told him that since we had six aircraft and all six had to launch, and the target was fairly close to our launching base, I reasoned that it was completely useless for the two spares to fly back and drop their bombs and rockets at sea. In order to have them go by the usual procedures I instructed them to call in for permission to drop their ordnance even though they had already dropped their bombs and fired their rockets on our assigned target. I wanted everything to look and sound normal.

I looked up at the general just as he uttered, "Damn! No wonder we obliterated that target! Great job Quince! Let's have a drink!" And so we did! About a month later, back at Yokota Air Base, I was awarded a Commendation Medal for that mission, courtesy of my friend, the General.

It feels great to be recognized for doing the right thing!

(30.1) Chip holding one-week-old Corky, with assistance from Chuck.

(30.2) My family in early 1965.

(30.3) Last photo of Quincy and his "crew," Yakota Air Base, Japan (three weeks before shoot down).

(30.4) Kazuko, live-in maid, with the boys.

(30.5) The boys back in the U.S., after Quincy's shoot down

(30.6) The boys in the snow.

(30.7) At Myrtle Beach in May 1967.

(30.8) In the "Big Apple," 1975.

(30.9) Christmas 1989, with Mimi (Nancy's mother).

(30.10) My three sons, in 1997.

31
The Unexpected

It is difficult to explain to your wife that, as a fighter pilot flying in a War Zone, there is a possibility that you may be injured, shot down, captured or even killed.

Hell, I don't even like to think about it myself, so I wondered—how do I relay this concern to her?

The reality so far was that every pilot shot down in our wing had been rescued. That is a terrific record and to be envied by every squadron and wing in the theater.

I recall very vividly when Bill, my Squadron Mate and close friend, was shot down over North Vietnam. The news spread quickly, and everyone was standing by for the latest development. I knew his wife and kids at Yakota Air Base in Japan, our home base. I wondered how they would be notified that he was downed.

I also knew my wife, Nancy, would be knocking on their door as soon as she was made aware of the situation. Believe me, the wives were well-connected because the Squadron Commander's wife had a duty, as equally designated as that of her husband—to take care of every family in that unit.

This was especially true when a unit headed out to fly combat in the jungles of Southeast Asia. Our specific base was Tahkli, Thailand. All three squadrons from Yakota AB rotated through there. I had been recently assigned the duty as Wing Weapons Officer, and had attended the advanced F-105 program at Nellis AFB in Las Vegas. I was at Tahkli to fly missions to determine what type training program was needed to develop the best program for our pilots and prepare them for combat in that theater of operations.

I had not asked for the job, but because of a relationship I had with a senior officer, I was offered the position. I took it, knowing full well of the trials and tribulations that might lie ahead. My family was important to me. But my obligation to my country and the importance of training my pilots to be the best prompted me to accept this responsibility and head to the front. It was time to move to a higher level of involvement, and I was ready. Man, was I ready!

Nancy and I had been married about six years when I was shot down on September 2, 1965. Our three super kids were as cute as they come, all guys, and we nicknamed them Chip, Chuck and Corky. We lived in a home that had originally been two units off base at Yakota, and were finally joined into one large single-family dwelling. In general, life had been good for us. But there were some critical areas that later began to cause problems, primarily because we would not face the music and try to solve them before they really got to be bigger problems.

 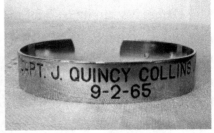

(31.1) Two POW bracelets. Every POW in Vietnam had his name and shoot down date on a bracelet. Bracelets were a fund-raising activity of wives & families to publicize POW conditions.

32
The Citadel Ring and The Beginning of The End!

Do you know how to tell if The World's Greatest Fighter Pilot is in the same room with you? Just listen—he'll tell you!

Couple that with the fact that a Citadel grad's ring hangs like an Orangutan's arm with a 50-pound weight on it—well, you get the idea. It is one heavy load to carry around. But best of all, it makes you aware that you have something no one else has—a Citadel Ring! And your swagger comes to life and you walk like no other person in the room.

At least that's how I see it. I was always told that our rings were the heaviest all-gold rings in the American College and University system. That fact made me feel even more distinguished! Especially when I was around other grads from West Point, Annapolis or the Air Force Academy. Those guys also got free tuition. I didn't!

Damn! My family paid for me to take this crap and man, am I glad they did. Coming to The Citadel saved my life—if for no other reason than I learned how to survive, on my own terms. The 4th class system, the disciplinary regimen, and the isolation from people who did things in a normal way—and finally, you had to be in total control of your emotions. Not doing so would be disastrous and you would stand out like a naked guy at a Nun's convention. But I am getting ahead of myself.

On September the 2nd, 1965, I trotted out to my F-105 at Tahkli, Thailand, for my 3rd mission of the day. I had just been appointed the Wing Weapons Officer. My job was to plan and develop the very best training program possible for our combat crews, not only in nuclear and conventional weapons delivery, but also air-to-air combat and air-to-ground strafing operations.

I had left my family at Yokota Air Base, right outside Tokyo, and had come down TDY to get as much experience as I could in the mission we had in Southeast Asia, primarily dropping bombs/rockets on selected targets and providing air coverage against enemy aircraft trying to sneak in and hit our bombing aircraft. This was my 13th mission, and we were a flight of 4. *No reported flak* that day on this bridge target, and that was music to my ears.

So, as the song says, *off we go* heading to a remote spot between Laos and North Vietnam. It was a beautiful day with no cloud formations. As I hit my afterburner on the runway to get rolling, I was aware of my ring because my glove fit so tightly that it was like a surgical glove, but comfortable, and this fighting machine was ready to go.

The weather was CAFB—clear as a frapping bell! That was great because it was the time of the year for big billowing clouds that would go up to forty or fifty thousand feet and knock you around like a tennis ball in a professional tennis match. The description from the intelligence officer as to what kind of opposition or resistance we might encounter on this mission was "No reported flak!" Man, that was the best news my ears could have heard, because in the last targets we hit we had experienced a lot of flak. That was threatening to us as pilots and to our aircraft. To tell the truth, it was scary as hell!

As a kid growing up in Concord, North Carolina, I remember seeing newsreels in the local theaters that showed our bombers flying over Germany during WWII delivering weapons on the German manufacturing complex. I always felt that these little white puffy balls that were popping up around the aircraft were kind of pretty, but little did I realize how dangerous these little puff balls really were—because as the white smoke appears in the explosion, thousands of pieces of shrapnel are being projected at a very high rate out from that center. That is what brought down the airplanes in WWII, and also the airplanes that we were flying to bomb North Vietnam.

If we were diving into an area to deliver weapons and saw the white fluffy balls, you can be certain that we would be shaking in our boots. Because the next thing would be tremendous vibrations of the aircraft as we came near that explosion. You just held your breath that the shrapnel would miss you! This little distraction, along with following your instruments, plus arming your weapons and watching your delivery systems kept you busy as hell in the cockpit. There was not time to be thinking of other things.

The final part of our flight briefing was a description of the armament we were carrying, and a brief of exactly how we were to deliver these weapons. Today the target was a bridge over a small river at a point where Laos and North Vietnam came together. I had already flown missions that day using the same delivery techniques, so I was not concerned at all about that part of the mission. Plus there was no reported flak and the weather was clear. What more could a fighter pilot ask for?

Our four F-105s lined up in formation on the runway. A nod of the Lead's head indicated that we should push the throttle up while holding the brakes and check our engine operating gauges. We had been briefed on a single ship take-off because we were carrying a lot of 750 lb. bombs under each wing, rockets, and a full load of fuel, so safety was our #1 concern.

Finally Lead released his brakes, went into afterburner, and accelerated down the runway. The afterburner coming on was a real kick in the pants as it pushed you back into your seat and the aircraft immediately accelerated. Eight seconds later each of us, in turn, would do the exact same thing until we were all airborne and climbing out to our established altitude. We kept in a very loose formation until the Lead motioned for us to get in closer formation so that we could check each other's aircraft and weapons. After that was completed, we slid out again. All was well, and now we could think about our ETA (estimated time of arrival) at the target.

I had set up my Doppler Navigation system after I started my engine (the F-105 is a single-engine aircraft for a single pilot), so my home base was now set, plus our first Check Point (where we crossed the Mekong River), and then the target. The Doppler system was very accurate. We needed it because the jungles below hid any way of telling where you were. An arrow in the cockpit pointed directly to the target, and another window showed the mileage to go. My airplane was a "Cadillac in the sky."

But about fifty miles out from the target I saw something that tied my stomach in a knot and caused my heart to begin pounding. I spotted newly uncovered ground close to the target, and that really concerned me. Why was this grading necessary? If there were no antiaircraft weapons in that area (remember, "No reported flak") then why do they need earthmoving machines there? My first thought was that the enemy was preparing to defend this site—and I was their target. My answer came very shortly!

It was time to get into position to start a bombing run. So I clicked the mic in the throttle to let my flight know that I was rolling in. We would not use voice on the mic because using that electronic device would give away our exact position in the airspace over the target. So I banked my trusty steed, put the nose down to accelerate, and rolled into a dive to begin my run. Just as I did this, my world came apart.

WHAM-BANG! I was hit! Immediately every instrument in the cockpit showed that everything that could go wrong was going wrong. Fire and smoke filled the cockpit. I was in trouble. DEEP TROUBLE! I felt another explosion. I wasn't sure if I was hit again by antiaircraft fire, or my own bombs were going off.

I went through my emergency procedures without even having to think about them because I had rehearsed them so many times. I couldn't see outside or see any of my instruments at this time. Was I upside down, nose up, or on my back? I didn't know. I gave myself an order that was tough to take: "Get the hell out of here!"

BOOM! The aircraft shook like I had been hit again. I was sitting in an ejection seat so I reached for the handles that were on either armrest. Pulling these handles would blow the canopy off and expose triggers on each armrest that, when fired, would launch me in my rocket seat to safety in the airspace above the aircraft. I recall quite clearly that all my actions seemed to be reduced to *s..l..o..w....m..o..t..i..o..n,* but I never remembered whether I left the airplane by ejecting or because the plane exploded. I do know one thing. I had to have been doing over 700 knots when I ejected and hit the air stream because my body later looked like I had been dumped into a cement mixer and dropped from Mt. Everest.

When I finally opened my eyes after regaining consciousness, I was sitting, leaning against a tree with nothing on but my shorts. Across from me were 4 ancient mariners—old militiamen protecting their part of Vietnam. There was no parachute, no ejection seat, no flight suit, no boots, no pistol or survival map. God! I was just about naked in the jungles of Laos or North Vietnam—and I was alone. No rescue aircraft circling. No choppers hovering close by. So I took stock of myself. I had two arms but could only see one leg. Damn! My left leg was bent grotesquely out to the left. I could clearly see that it was broken in several places above the knee. It made me sick to see that I did not have the means to escape—I wasn't going anywhere!

I guess every nerve ending in my body was on alert because I hurt— God, I hurt! And I only had my mind to throw up against it. I looked down again at my right arm and hand and my ring was gone. One of those old bastards had my Citadel ring and my watch and they were gone forever.

I pointed to my leg and my captors came over to see more closely. They conversed excitedly and then began to move my left leg back to its normal position. I became unglued at this point because the pain was more than I could bear. In fact, it was so intense I could not concentrate on what they were doing. Eventually they wrapped vine around my entire left leg, put me in a net with poles on their shoulders, and carried me to a Russian jeep-type vehicle and literally threw me into the rear compartment. I was holding onto my left leg because I thought it might tear off. I felt the vehicle crank up and start to drive away.

Where were we going? What would they do to me? What kind of

enemy had captured me? One thing I did know—I was in a world of hurt and these guys were in control. My life was in their hands.

God help me!

As soon as my captors threw me into the rear compartment of their Russian Jeep, all of my bodily functions erupted all at once. You name it, I did it, and the stench was strong and foul and sickening. It was as if the whole world stunk and I couldn't get away from it. My face was in it. The shorts I had on were caked with it. I tasted it. All I could do was YELL, and I mean loudly. "HOSPITAL! HOSPITAL! HOSPITAL!" And my captors responded, "OK! OK!" The thought came to me that maybe, just maybe, I was not the first American this bunch had ever captured, but what the hell could I do about it?

Soon the jeep began to slow. I couldn't tell if it was because darkness was about to envelop us and it was more difficult to see where we were going—or if we were actually getting closer to our destination and a slower speed was warranted. At any rate, we finally came to a complete stop and my captors began to jabber in Gook as if discussing how to unload me without touching this stinking passenger, and it made me more than a little uncomfortable.

My moans and groans were not loud enough to deaden the sound coming from a very high waterfall hitting big rocks and boulders not far from where my aching body lay. Eventually they slid me out of the Jeep, wrapped more vines around me and hoisted me onto their shoulders and began to descend towards the powerful sound I had been hearing.

Immediately I envisioned this as being my last seconds alive, and my entire life began flicking in front of me like an old hand-turned movie film. It was truly amazing that this could be happening. I had heard of this phenomenon, but had never experienced it. The selection of visions that appeared to me was also amazing. My earliest years, something from yesterday or earlier today, people I had not thought about in years, on and on they came. And what about how I was about to die?

As if on cue, my burial train took a right turn, I got a second breath, the visions ceased, and they carried me into a small building. The sound of water falling on rocks did not end, but now there might be a different ending to this part of the story. Yes, I was still hurting more than ever and my captors gave me another shot of morphine. I wasn't the least bit concerned about becoming an addict at this point. All I wanted was to rid myself of the physical hurting and mental devastation I was experiencing.

Now the enemy wanted to get down to business. They wanted me to operate my emergency radio to lead rescuers to our site so that they could be destroyed! Fortunately I didn't remain conscious long enough for my goons to complete their plan. I guess they thought, "Well, tomorrow is another day!"

It came too soon for me as I sank into unconsciousness again with more vivid visions, but this time they were of my beloved family.

(32.1) A U.S. Air Force Republic F-105D Thunderchief shot down over North Vietnam by Soviet S-75 Dvina surface-to-air missile.

(32.2) The Republic F-105 Thunderchief, was a supersonic fighter-bomber used by the United States Air Force. The Mach 2 capable F-105 bore the brunt of strike bombing over North Vietnam during the early years of the Vietnam War.

(32.3) The Front and sides of a Cadet Citadel Ring display the symbols and traditions of The Military College of South Carolina Corp of Cadets.

33
On the Way to Hanoi!

My captors had spent that morning and afternoon trying to lure my rescuers into attempting to pick me up. Along about midday they gave me a rice ball to eat, but no water. I took a bite and puked it right up. I tried another bite, and up it came too. Couldn't keep it down without water. I was in so much pain that the mere movement of puking caused me to fade in and out. It was going to be a "Long Hot Summer!"

My personal Jeep finally drove up and the enemy again threw me into the back with all the puke, urine, and pain I had endured there. By now it was really dark, and the driver stopped to get instructions from someone on the side of the road. I was getting sick from all the motions of the vehicle.

I had had this feeling many times while flying at night or in weather where you could not see a horizon. My inner ear would keep indicating that I was in a descending right turn, or maybe in a steep climb to the left. The only thing I could do was to look at my attitude indicator and check it against my airspeed and turn indicator, then force myself to believe what my instruments were indicating. Every time this happened I would break out in a sweat and try hard to overcome this feeling I had. Eventually it would go away, but I always knew it was standing by to jump on me again when I least expected it. This phenomenon is called Vertigo, and many a pilot has become so disoriented because of it that he had to eject and sometimes crash as a result of losing control of the aircraft. Thank God I was in a Jeep. But the sickening feeling brought back memories of other times.

Being in the back compartment of this vehicle allowed me to be able to pull a canvas flap to one side and peer out. What I saw led me to conclude that I was probably heading north on the infamous Ho Chi Minh Trail. This was the route used by the North Vietnamese to resupply the Viet Cong in the south with troops and equipment. There really wasn't a trail or even a road, just thousands of people in a line carrying flashlights, lanterns, or anything that was illuminating.

It was like a Ground Control approach (GCA) at any modern airport except that everything was on the ground. Troops and vehicles just had to put their right flank or fender beside the line of lights and that would take them down the proper path.

Of course the USAF was aware that all this was happening. But at night we could do little because of the enemy's very sophisticated warning system. This consisted of a piece of metal hanging from a tree limb being struck by another piece of metal. The sound would carry at least 50 miles. Ingenious, isn't it? When the local natives would hear the clang, they extinguished all the lights and the aircraft overhead could see nothing. So much for technical advancement!

It is interesting that within the next 12 to 18 months the good guys (USAF) came up with the infrared system which would reflect off metal and other substances on the ground and produce a penetrating heat source so that the enemy's supply line showed up like gangbusters on our aircraft radar screens—and we could wipe them out handily. We could be ingenious too!

My kidneys were responding to every bump and crash of the vehicle, so I was soaked with urine again and beginning to hurt—since my last morphine shot was beginning to fade on me. I had a feeling that I was not going to be pleased with our destination, so I began to pray about it. The pain was intensifying to such a degree that I had trouble with my own spiritual policy of, "May Your will be done, not my own." I wanted the pain to stop now, not later, right this second!

I was to confront this issue many times over the next seven years, and it would become harder to accept. God was in control, it certainly wasn't me, and I needed a lot of outside encouragement. Pain has a tendency to distort one's reasoning power, and also to cause one to question one's belief system. Thank God that pain is a temporary condition. At least we hope it is, and normalcy returns in time.

Good Lord! It was daylight and we were on a paved road. I pulled the flap open. No more people with flashlights and lanterns. A Vietnamese village appeared with people riding bikes and kids scurrying around. Where the hell was I?

Down a dirt road we go. And then we stop. I don't know why I thought of this at this particular time—but I recalled taking an oath or pledge during an operational briefing at Takhli Air Base in Thailand, my home base. I remember it well.

"As an American fighting man, if captured, I will only give my name, rank, serial number and date of birth."

So far I had not been asked any of these questions. Only one question had come out of the mouths of my captors, and that was this.

"What is your blood type?" I couldn't believe it. I had lost a lot of blood, was weak and a bit faint, so I gave it to them.

"O Positive," I replied.

I had just been captured a few hours earlier, but looking back, I had 7 ½ years ahead of me, and they hadn't gotten to the good questions yet! Things like:

"What base did you take off from?"

"How many were in your flight?"

"What was your target?"

So is this the place where my being captured takes a turn for the worse and the crap hits the fan? Our driving into this area must have been like a mobile urinal coming through the gate. A sign stating that "This Ugly American Smells" might also have been appropriate.

It seemed like hours had passed, but eventually the driver returned, cranked up and out we drove into a small village and then down a well-traveled paved road. I somehow conjured up the idea that finally they were taking me to a hospital. We drove up to a nice building and sure enough, it was a hospital. I was still dressed in my best vine and net wrapped outfit with my shorts on and smelled like a stopped-up sewer.

"My captors deserve this," I thought. Revenge is sweet!

34
"Cheers and Tears"

The following synopsis is from his book *Cheers and Tears* by Lt. Gen. Charles Cooper, USMC (Ret.). The events described took place about the time of my being shot down on September 2, 1965. I believe it adds a lot of color, context, and character to those who sealed the destiny of themselves and those who followed during the years I served in North Vietnam. I will use quotation marks when relating precise words from his book.

"The President will see you at two o'clock."

That was the message received by the Chairman of the Joint Chiefs on a gorgeous fall day in November of 1965. I was probably already in the hospital in Hanoi wondering what would become of Captain James Quincy Collins, Jr. Little did I know that my fate was being decided by some guys in a room in Washington, D.C. The generals and admirals had been calling this meeting "The Day of Reckoning." As it turned out, it really was!

The Vietnam War was in its first year, and the Joint Chiefs had already had a number of head-on collisions with Secretary of Defense Robert McNamara over strategy and how to conduct the war. The Chiefs had requested a private meeting with the Commander-in-Chief many times previously—but to no avail. Now, McNamara had finally arranged the meeting to determine whether the U.S. Military would continue its seemingly directionless buildup or take bold steps to bring the war to an early and victorious end. The Chiefs wanted to apply massive air power to Hanoi and close North Vietnam's harbors by mining them.

The big worry to the Chiefs was the reaction of the Chinese and the Russians to any aggressive movements by the U.S. Our enemies had pledged support to North Vietnam to try to reunite the now divided Vietnam. The Joint Chiefs had asked the CIA for answers and estimates to assist them in their decision-making. But the CIA had only produced reams of text, summaries, and briefs that said nothing about what the Chinese and Russians might do.

The Chiefs had to make their own unanimous decision—which they did—and McNamara and his "Whiz Kids" fought it tooth and nail. All of this wrangling had caused the Chiefs to request the seldom-used private audience with the President in order to present their military recommendations directly to him. Mr. McNamara had finally granted their request.

Here is the lineup of professionals who had already served in three wars:

- General Earle Wheeler, U.S. Army—Chairman
- General Harold Johnson, Army Chief of Staff and former prisoner of the Japanese
- General John McConnell, head of the USAF
- General Wallace Greene, Commandant of the Marine Corps.
- Admiral McDonald, Chief of Naval Operations

This group was going to push for Naval Operations as the primary force to blockade the port of Haiphong. Therefore, the Navy was to take the lead in preparing maps, etc., for the briefing of the President. This is why now Admiral (Lieutenant General) Cooper was in charge of the briefing map that weighed about thirty pounds.

The Military Office at the White House had agreed to set up an easel for the Presidential briefing in the Oval Office. Charles Cooper was scheduled to accompany the group to the White House with the map he had assembled and put the map in place when the meeting started. Then he was to get out, vamoose, and get lost so there would be no trap hangers at the big military summit with President Lyndon Johnson.

Admiral Cooper says he and the Chiefs arrived about twenty minutes early. They were led into a big room across the hall from the President's office. Cooper placed the big map on a fancy chair where all could view it, and then stepped out into the corridor. One of the star officers closed the door while they conferred in private. About fifteen minutes later someone from the White House staff interrupted them. When they filed out, Cooper retrieved the map and joined them in the corridor to await the President.

Right at two o'clock the President emerged from his office and greeted the Chiefs with all the charm he could muster. The Chiefs had not expected this. They knew that Secretary of Defense McNamara had informed the President of their mission, and President Johnson was very much opposed to their position. He was also a much bigger man than any of the Chiefs—several inches taller and thirty pounds heavier.

Cooper scanned the Oval Office to locate the easel. The President sensed that something was missing, invited Cooper in, and pointed out exactly where Cooper was to stand. He had suddenly become the human easel—one with eyes and ears!

President Johnson arranged the Chiefs in a semicircle in front of Cooper and the map. He did not offer them seats so they all stood, uncomfortably looking at each other and their trainer, the President.

The Chiefs believed that unless they could convince the President to change his strategy this war—now one year old—would become the longest, most divisive and least conclusive war in our nation's history. They believed this war was already tearing our nation apart.

General Wheeler started the presentation. In about five minutes he summarized and thanked President Johnson for giving his senior military advisors the opportunity to give the President their opinions and recommendations—even though McNamara did not support their views. McNamara did, however, agree that a presidential-level decision was required.

As General Wheeler spoke, he proposed a bold course of action that would isolate the major port of Haiphong through naval mining; blockade the rest of the North Vietnamese coastline; and simultaneously start bombing Hanoi with B-52s. All of the Chiefs chimed in on how all of this would work.

President Johnson seemed to be paying very close attention, communicating with an occasional nod.

Finally, General Wheeler asked the President if he had any questions.

The President paced over to one side of the room and turned to two Chiefs who had not said too much at this point. "Do you fully support this proposal that General Wheeler has made?"

Both indicated their full support of the proposal.

The President turned his back on the group for what seemed like several minutes then suddenly whirled to face them and exploded! Cooper almost dropped the map. President Johnson screamed obscenities, cursed them personally, ridiculed them for coming to his office with their military advice! He yelled at them, noting that it was he who was carrying the weight of the free world on his shoulders, not them. He called them filthy names like *shitheads, dumbshits, pompous assholes,* and used the *f---word* more freely than a marine in boot camp.

The President continued to degrade his Chief Military Advisors, telling them that they were naïve, and that their advice would cause WW-WIII. He concluded the conference by shouting an order for them to "get the hell out of my office."

What a meaningful conclusion for a political dumbass to have been exposed to the final decision that was used by President Nixon ten years later to stop the bleeding and bring the crisis to a close.

The best part was that I—James Quincy Collins, Jr.—got to return to America and become a human being again!

God Bless America!

35
How We Communicated

Several years later, one of my new friends, shot down just like I was, told me that he had carried a small Bible with him on every mission. It had belonged to his Dad who was an Army Platoon commander in WW II. This Word of God had a hole in it made by a bullet aimed at his Dad. The Bible stopped it and kept his Father from being wounded. Our enemy took his Bible just like they took my ring. At our release in 1973, they returned his Bible to him. I guess *the Lord giveth and the Lord taketh away*. Amen!

The first five years were a time of lots of isolation. I needed a lot of help since the operation they performed on me made me dependent on someone else to help feed me, wash me—when allowed—and just take care of my normal body functions. My recovery was slow and painful, and every day was a battle against medical incompetence and just plain hatred for Americans by the enemy.

When I finally graduated to crutches, they moved me into a small cell. I was alone again. I could take 3 crutch-steps from the back wall to the front wall. A slab of concrete I lovingly called my Beauty Rest, took up the rest of the cell. At the foot of my cell was a pair of leg irons and chains with a small porthole so that the guards could lock my ankles without having to come into my cell. All the modern conveniences! And a bare light bulb hung down from the ceiling. It burned 24 hours a day.

When they handcuffed my wrists behind my back, I prayed that I could suddenly turn in to a contortionist. But no such luck. I often looked at my ring finger and wondered what Vietnamese soldier had it, and what story he had concocted to explain how he got it. I visualized many times that I had become a casualty of the war and that some smuck had painted himself as a hero, and he had my ring to prove it.

War is hell and no fun to endure!

Will I ever get out of this cesspool?

If you happened to have a cellmate, the Camp rules stated no talking above a whisper. And there was to be NO communication with other *Piratical Airmen*, the formal name given to those of us who were guests at the infamous Hanoi Hotel. One thing I learned—you must communicate in order for Leadership and Chain of Command to function and be successful. The punishment was too severe to get caught yelling under your door to your fellow prisoners so what could we do?

Several POW's had been taught a tap code used in American prisons so they passed it on to the rest of us. How they did that is also a very interesting and creative story. Basically you put 12345 across the top of a square, and 12345 down the left side. ABCDE are the letters at the top and the 2nd line is FGHIJ, and so on.

When you tap, the first tap or taps indicates which horizontal line you are working with. The second tap or taps shows which letter in that line you are transmitting. For example, here is a tap sequence: BUMP-silence-bump-bump- bump means you are in the top horizontal line. The 3 bumps indicate it is the 3rd letter in that line—C—and so on.

When we started using this code, it sounded as though monster termites were at work in the buildings. The guards caught on and whitewashed our walls, and then would check our knuckles to see if we were tapping. So we started using our rubber-tire foot sandals to tap. We really became innovative and had the confidence that there was no way the enemy could keep us from communicating! We were survivors! And Professional Survivors at that!

36
Lunch Through The Wall

The second prison camp I was assigned to was a place out from the uptown area of Hanoi that had been a French movie colony before the North Vietnam Dien Bien Phu victory over the French in 1954. Obviously, it was not constructed to be a prison. It even had a pool near the entrance that had been turned into a garbage dump and housed fish after it became a prison. We called the site the Zoo, and it didn't take us long to give names to every building on the site.

The Zoo had a front gate and the building closest to the entrance was called the Carriage House. That became my first cell at the Zoo—a hard dirt floor in a small building with no ventilation and no way for outside light to penetrate the darkness, except for the slither of light that stole into the room from under the locked cell door.

Yes, this was indeed a prison. But change was coming as Christmas, 1965, approached. On Christmas Eve my cellmate, AJ Meyer, and I rolled up our very thin tatomi mats and single small blankets and shuffled across the courtyard. This was not an easy process as both of us were using crutches.

We finally made it into our new home, the Office. I have no idea how the building got this name because the floors were tiled like a barbershop or some type salon, and a bare light bulb hung from the ceiling by its own electric wire. Welcome to modern day North Vietnam!

The Office became a very busy place. Most of its inhabitants had moved there in late 1965 when I had first arrived. But after several months our prison routine had become a part of our lives—even though we fought it at every turn. The most important aspect of being a prisoner was that we had developed a method of communicating by a tapping code. (This code is fully explained in Chapter Thirty-five, How We Communicated.) Once you got this code and its matrix in your mind then it was easy to construct sentences to communicate ideas and pass orders from the senior level of command.

Our first meal of the day generally came after dawn, so you knew that the last meal of the day was a long way out. After my cellmate and I were separated and thrown into other cells, I ended up in a cell in that same building. My new cell in the Office had three walls behind the front cell door partition. So I had three other American prisoners available with whom I could communicate.

Everyday about noontime, when my stomach was growling and churning and beginning to call for more food, I got into the habit of picking one wall (and the guy on the other side who went with that wall) and swapping stories about our favorite lunches and where we had them.

Man! I could hardly wait to hear about some of the delicious sandwiches and salads and French dips that would penetrate our walls. Of course, we had to be careful not to be discovered tapping—but that was a given every time we got on the wall. In addition to the main courses there was always a drink. My fondest recollections were of a Coca-Cola stand several of my teenaged friends had built and operated down the street from my home on Hillcrest Drive in Concord.

As I sat on my concrete bed in prison while tapping away, I could taste the very first sip of that ice-cold Coke I had experienced in Concord as a kid. I would take a small swallow of water from my hot water teapot in my cell, but even that could not diminish the taste of Coke I was remembering from my childhood.

Then I would try to communicate the taste of the grilled ham and cheese sandwich I used to order when in the Concord Hotel Soda Shop on the Square in uptown Concord. The rich odor of hot cheese and mayonnaise dressing along with the searing of the whole wheat bread—damn, I could hardly wait to get back there to live that part of my life again.

By this time I would be slobbering all over myself, and hoping that my compatriot on the other side of the wall was caught up in this as much as I was. I would have traded my right arm for a taste of that Coke and a bite of that grilled ham and cheese.

God, please take me back to that Soda Shop!

SUNDAY, MARCH 25, 1973   Yo

WELCOME HOME! — Lt. Col. Quincy Collins gets a hug from one of the more than 5,000 persons who attended a homecoming Friday in Concord for the Air Force officer who was held prisoner in North Vietnam for more than seven years. Collins grew up in Concord and attended Concord High School where he was drum major of the band and played football. He was shot down over North Vietnam in 1965.

—Staff Photo By Marvin Eury

(36.1) Fast forward 7½ years: Homecoming parade for Quincy stops at Hotel Concord Soda Shop.

(36.2) An illustration of the Hotel Concord from a vintage postcard.

(36.3) An interior of old-fashioned soda shop, reminiscent of the one at the Hotel Concord.

(36.4) A more recent exterior shot of the Hotel Concord.

37
Interesting Events That Happened in Prison

The Snake

While at the Zoo, my cellmate, AJ Meyer, and I were banished to a building at the very back of the camp. For what reason, neither of us knew. If you needed a picture of an isolated building—this was it. There was no other building close enough to make some kind of communications contact, and rarely did any other humans beings, friendly or otherwise, appear in this area. We were alone and that was it.

Occasionally the primitive sewage line would stop up, and the guards would force one of the POWs to "deep sea dive" into it to pull out whatever was impeding the flow. This was a crappy job to say the least, but it did bring other prisoners close by.

Our building was laid out in three sections. AJ and I had our sawhorse beds with mosquito nets closest to the main door in the front of the building. There was a smaller space behind us, and a much larger room adjoined ours. It is ridiculous to say they were unfinished, because everything was unfinished. But those were really just bare, empty, uninhabitable spaces. That summer the heat was atrocious, and just thinking made us sweat.

Supersaturated air should have told us that horrible weather was headed our way, and its name was Typhoon. I have never seen so much rain, wind, and lightning. It came like a flood, further isolating us from the rest of the camp. Our single light bulb hanging from the ceiling was the only thing working, and it kept us from being blacked out. Meanwhile, the outside water level kept rising until it was slapping at the bottom of our door.

Are they evacuating the rest of the camp and forgetting about AJ and me isolated in our own private ark out back?

We could neither hear nor see anything that would erase this possibility. We were a bit frightened and a lot concerned about the situation as the storm intensity heightened. Late that evening it had blown itself out and calm was restored

We both were under our mosquito nets talking and looking at the door when a movement caught my eye. I refocused quickly to see a huge snake sliding under our door. The damned thing had to have been at least six feet long and as thick as my leg. It wiggled past me and went into the empty room adjoining ours. AJ and I agreed that we had to call for help, so I screamed "Bao Cao" (which means, *Come quickly, we need help!*).

Finally three guards waded through the pond out front to open our door. One spoke English, so we explained about the snake. Another guard left hurriedly and quickly returned with several flashlights and an additional guard. They entered our room very cautiously, and shined flashlights into the darkness of the other room. These guys were scared, and that big snake was the reason.

A guard with a machete worked with the flashlight holder to spotlight the head of the snake—which stood up like a cobra. Swish! That head was gone, but the body was twisting and wiggling on its own. Finally it stopped. The English speaker identified the snake as being the most poisonous in North Vietnam—a tiger snake!

What a story that would have been: to make it through years of imprisonment, then have it end with a snakebite.

Thank You, Lord!

~~

A Touch Of Compassion

I may have lost count of the days, but I believe I arrived in Hanoi within four days of being shot down and captured. I was taken to a fairly large facility that I concluded was the main hospital in Hanoi. Several doctors appeared, along with some nurses, to bear witness to the fact that they had captured a "live one."

As they milled around talking and planning my medical future, I observed an old Vietnamese gentleman just watching in the background. I reached the conclusion that he was to be my nurse attendant and tend to my needs, since I was so badly banged up that I could do little for myself. Let's call him Nguyen. That is a name in Vietnamese that is as common as Jim is in English.

It was early September of 1965, and the temperature was in the 95-105 degrees range. There was no tropical breeze in sight, and the hospital air-conditioning system was yet to be installed. Nguyen saw to it that I had a cup of steaming hot water. No. That is not the correct adjective. *Scalding* is closer to being the right word. I was already sweating, but just seeing the steam coming out of the pot made things even worse.

When everyone had left except Nguyen, I got his attention, pointed to the pot and said, "Glace," the French word for ice. I guessed that he had learned French from his former captors. I was right. He shook his head from side to side as he muttered, "No, no." Soon he locked me in and disappeared.

The next day after all the morning blood-letting, temperature taking and pill swallowing, Nguyen opened my door, looked around as if casing the joint, and came over by my bed. He opened his shirt and there, wrapped in paper, were five to six ice cubes. He poured about a third of a cup of water and put the ice cubes in the cup. I stirred it a moment, and then took it all down with one big gulp.

He smiled as I looked him straight in the eye and said, "Merci beaucoup," as honestly and lovingly as I could.

Later that afternoon, I came up with another idea. I wondered if he had access to beer. What the hell! *Ask and you shall receive.*

At the appropriate time, I again got his attention and, while going through a drinking maneuver said, "Beer, beer!" Again he said no, finished his chores and slipped out the door after locking me in.

I did my best!

The next afternoon Nguyen slipped in the door, locked it from the inside, and then pulled out two cold beers with a straw hanging on each one. He opened one and put the other between my mattresses. Man, I had a friend and did I appreciate him! He smiled again and then resumed his stoic posture.

It is amazing to me that the love of God shows up where you least expect it. Bless the life of this dear man.

~

Who's In Command?

AJ Meyer and I were at the Zoo in a building by the main entrance to that camp. Our cell was closest to the main gate, so there was a lot of movement and noise associated with that location. We were both on crutches, still struggling to get our broken bones to heal. But this was a slow process, especially when you consider the lousy food we were fed, and the dirty and unhealthy conditions we lived in.

I think there were four to five other cells on the other side of us, and everyone knew the tap code, so we went at it all day long. The cell adjoining ours was inhabited by George Hall, another USAF guy and an incredible golfer. His reputation in that sport was well known throughout the Air Force. He created another miracle of sorts by playing at least nine holes a day while in prison—mentally, of course, as the Hanoi Country Club was not open to us unwelcomed guests.

Protocol dictates that each building has a senior American officer as support for the normal chain of command. George was a major and I was a captain. The rules governing rank, etc., state that POWS will keep the rank they had at time of shoot-down. I was shot down as senior captain about to make major, but it had not yet happened, so for 7 ½ years in prison, I was a captain. Immediately after our release in 1973 I became a senior lieutenant colonel about to make full colonel. And so goes life!

One day the guard pushed open our cell door and the Rabbit strolled in. As required, AJ and I gave a perfunctory bow to honor his highness. The Rabbit took his time looking around and making needling type comments, then he got in my face and shouted, "You have been issuing orders to the other criminals in this building to disobey the orders of the military camp commander. You will be punished for this."

I denied the accusation, because I knew that I was not the ranking man. But I didn't want to identify George as being the man he sought. After much bantering back and forth, the Rabbit ordered me to put on my cotton shirt and follow the guard. I did as he ordered, but took my own time to get moving.

"Hurry up! Hurry up!" the Rabbit shouted. He walked on ahead as my escort, and I slowly followed. He stopped at an entrance to a room and gave instructions in Vietnamese to the guard, turned threateningly to me and said, "Follow the guard and do exactly as he tells you." With that, he walked away and out of sight.

My escort spoke no English and seemed rather dull and dumb. But he had the gun and he had me. What else could he want?

Dumbo motioned me to enter the room. I did. Then he made me put down my crutches and get on my knees.

I was wondering, *What the hell is about to happen?* The first thing I thought of was that I was about to be beheaded! Just for being the senior ranking man in the building? Boy, that didn't make sense.

Finally the guard stood his rifle against the wall and walked over in front of me. He had me look up, and then it came. A right and a left just like Mike Tyson! Each blow lifted me off the floor, but didn't bloody my face.

I was dazed for a minute, then he motioned for me to get up, get my crutches, and start back to my cell. My face must have been blood red, because it was hot. I knew I was going to be plenty sore shortly. I was a bit slower in returning and for good reason. I was not too steady on my feet.

When I got into the cell, AJ stared. "Man, you look like you have been run over by a truck. Are you OK?"

I told him yes, but not with a lot of certainty. Had I known what lay ahead, I would have been even more concerned. Each day, for ten days, I went through the same routine—walk down, kneel, get zapped with a left and a right and drag myself back to my cell.

By that time George knew what was happening and said he was going to tell them the truth—that he was the senior officer. I convinced him that was not the best idea, as the gooks would go ape because of their mistake. I could take it, and surely it would not last much longer. George finally agreed.

There was just one bright spot in all this. A new guard appeared to lead me through the daily ritual. When I was on my knees, I noticed him clearing outside as he put his rifle down. He stepped in front of me for the knockout, but instead slapped his hands together to produce a loud hitting noise, smiled, and picked up his gun. He rubbed my face to make it red, and back to the cell we went.

That angel must have been Joe Louis. What a champion!

38
July 6, 1966

It was a hot day in Hanoi. Sweat rolled down our faces, backs and stomachs. With no wind and no ventilation in our cells sweat made my skin sting and feel sticky. Back in the USA, St. Louis was at 105 degrees, Chicago 90 degrees, and Washington, DC reached 96 degrees.

In the World Series the hot issue was between Baltimore and the LA Dodgers, and Billie Jean King was warming up at Wimbledon. *The Sound of Music* was proclaimed best picture of 1966, and America mourned the deaths of Walt Disney and Montgomery Clift. Yes, life was moving along in the good ole USA—but not for those of us imprisoned in Hanoi.

We prisoners did not know it yet, but change was on the horizon—change for the better!

On July 4, 1966, I spent the day in solitary confinement, where I celebrated my beloved country's birthday and my own 35th birthday. I was recovering from a day or two of feeling sorry for myself as I wondered when in hell my stay in Hanoi would end and I'd no longer be at the mercy of those sadistic animals—our prison guards!

"Lord," I prayed, "please deliver me!"

Two days later, morning of July 6, 1966, the door to my cell burst open and a guard I had never seen before motioned for me to give him my extra prisoner's shirt and pants. His gun pointed at my midsection, indicating that I should respond quickly and not protest. I did as ordered and he slammed my cell door shut, locked it from the outside, and evidently moved on to other cells with the same request. Now what was this all about?

A few minutes later the sound of trucks driving into the camp led me to believe that a lot of people were either being brought in or taken away. This was an intriguing situation, and I was on the edge of my concrete bed waiting for another clue.

That clue came quickly as other cell doors were opened and POWs were gathered and loaded into the trucks. From what I could hear, the guards seemed deadly serious. They sounded like Al Capone's gang members, barking orders at my compatriots. I listened from my solitary confinement, wondering if I would be next. When the guards did not come for me, I figured it was perhaps because I was confined to crutches.

Were they taking a select group somewhere to be released? Or was this the execution the enemy kept promising us? Since I could not see what was going on, I had to depend on sounds. Confused and afraid, I was unable to identify any reason for this unexpected occurrence.

I could not hear even the slightest noise coming from my buddies. What I could hear indicated that they were being loaded into trucks and apparently would be taken away from this camp.

What was in store for them? And what was in store for me? My whole body quaked and shivered. Fear of the unknown had taken hold of me.

The world now knows what the communists were planning—the total humiliation of the American POWs. The communists forced 52 guys (from both the Briarpatch and the Zoo) to march manacled together in two lines through the streets of Hanoi. It is estimated that over 100,000 North Vietnamese took part in this demonstration.

Communist agitators with bullhorns in hand were dispersed throughout the mob to incite and stir up the people—which they did quite successfully. At times, the mob broke through to kick and slug the POWs and punch them with sharpened bamboo sticks.

As the prisoners were marched past the Soviet and Chinese embassies and into Hanoi's main avenue, the mob went wild and the military guards lost control of the crowd. POWs were knocked to the ground, spit on, and humiliated in many ways. The crowd was keyed up, ready to injure or kill the prisoners. The world saw the scene on international television networks.

Because the scene aired on TV, the Americans handily won this round of play between nations. Ho Chi Minh was forced to change his strategy in how American prisoners were treated. This one horrible event of July 6, 1966, ended up of tremendous importance, because before then the American government and press had overlooked the plight of our prisoners.

Within several months, those of us who were prisoners began receiving better treatment. For one thing, the commies quit emphasizing that we were common criminals and would be tried in their courts.

But on that July 6, the way the guards treated prisoners had not changed. I was still locked in solitary, living the agony of wondering what was going on. In the evening the trucks came blasting their way back into camp like they were in a mad dash for the finish line. The English-speaking officers yelled at the captives to do this and do that. I could hear rubber straps slapping against the bodies of my compatriots. Many were tied to trees and posts where they were beaten, as guards tried to get them to confess their transgressions against the North Vietnamese people.

Inhumane beatings. I listened. What else could I do? And then, as if on cue, things began to calm down. Most of the POWs were returned to their cells to recover. A few hard resisters were left tied up. Throughout the night their moans and groans echoed. By dawn all prisoners were back in their cells. And the usual routine of prison life resumed.

From then until our release in February of 1973, positive results ensued from that terrible event of July 6, 1966—because now the world knew how the North Vietnamese had been treating prisoners. Regardless of what the treasonous Jane Fonda had to say, the world now knew the truth.

May we *never* forget those who fight for our Freedoms!

(38.1) Prisoners were paraded before angry crowds in Hanoi, where loudspeakers blared insults and encouraged the crowd's abuse. Many in the crowd attacked the POWs. Front row (l-r): Richard Kiern and Kile Berg; second row Robert Shumaker and "Smitty" Harris; third row Ronald Byrne and Lawrence Guarino. (U.S. Air Force photo)

40 years after release, POWs at Hanoi Hilton reflect on experience

By WYATT OLSON | STARS AND STRIPES   Originally published: February 10, 2013

HANOI — Little remains downtown of the prison known as Hoa Lo, a name loosely translated as "hell hole."

Most of the French colonial-era complex was razed to make way for a luxury apartment high rise. The Vietnamese government turned what was left into a museum exhibiting a few of the dank cells where Vietnamese revolutionaries were held and sometimes executed by the French in the mid-20th century.

There is one small room near the back devoted to a different group of inmates who languished for years: American prisoners of the Vietnam War.

To those POWs this was the Hanoi Hilton, a nickname that oozed irony and defiance, the kind of petty "thumb in your eye" that provided some small pride in a place designed to strip dignity away.

Forty years ago on Feb. 12, the first of those long-held POWs were released as part of the Paris Peace Accords that ended America's decadelong war with Vietnam.

They boarded a waiting plane and landed free men at Clark Air Base in the Philippines. They flew on to Hawaii, then to their families at home.

"Forty years later as I look back on that experience, believe it or not, I have somewhat mixed emotions in that it was a very difficult period," said Sen. John McCain, shot down and captured in 1967. "But at the same time the bonds of friendship and love for my fellow prisoners will be the most enduring memory of my five and half years of incarceration."

The POW experience at Hoa Lo — and in the archipelago of other prison camps in North Vietnam — was unlike anything American prisoners had encountered before or since.

POWs had faced brutality before in camps during World War II and the Korean War, but America's involvement in those wars was relatively short compared with the Vietnam War. Few GIs have been taken prisoner in Afghanistan — despite the war's length.

"We had only the slightest inkling that the Age of Aquarius had happened in this country," said

(38.2) The entry to the Hoa Lo prison museum is adorned with a banner celebrating Tet, the nation's lunar new year. Some American POWs spent up to seven years behind this wall during the Vietnam War.

David Gray, an Air Force fighter pilot shot down and captured in January 1967. "We didn't have an appreciation for how widespread and pervasive the antiwar sentiment had become."

Indeed, the longest-held prisoner at Hoa Lo, Navy pilot Everett Alvarez, was shot down and captured in August 1964, a few months after the Beatles first toured America. His release in February 1973 came three years after the breakup of the band that defined that era's youth culture.

If POWs were unaware of what was happening in the U.S., Americans remained mindful of them. A student group in California created silver POW bracelets in 1970, asking Americans to wear them until POWs returned home. Millions were sold.

"There was a sense of unity, togetherness, shared adversity," said Gerald Coffee, a Navy aviator who was imprisoned for seven years and was among the first group released. "We came home and our release kind of symbolized the end of a very painful chapter in our nation's history.

"We got the homecoming that every Vietnam War veteran should have had when he or she came home. We didn't take that for granted."

Named Operation Homecoming, the series of releases returned 591 POWs to freedom.

The Hoa Lo POW exhibit doesn't provide many hints as to what prisoners such as Gray and Coffee experienced during those years. Much of it is given over to chiding the U.S. for aligning itself with the government of South Vietnam and its aerial bombardment of North Vietnam from 1965 to 1968 and then again in late 1972. McCain's flight suit hangs eerily behind a glass case, along with the parachute that saved him.

The thing is, it's not real. "Of course it's not, of course it's not," said McCain when asked about it. "They cut my flight suit off of me when I was taken into the prison ... The 'museum' is an excellent propaganda establishment with very little connection with the actual events that took place inside those walls." He's visited the museum a number of times for the sake of normalizing relations between the two countries, he said.

McCain said he has "great respect and affection for the Vietnamese people," but added with an acid laugh that "there are individuals who are still around Hanoi that I would, umm, look forward to seeing again on a level playing field.

"It wasn't so much for what they did to me but what they did to some of my fellow prisoners who did not return with us."

Behind another case is what are claimed to be belongings of downed Navy pilot Everett Alvarez, which include a pack of Winston cigarettes and box of Vicks cough drops. Prominent is what's labeled a "begging flag," which is a multi-language message printed on cloth and used by downed U.S. pilots to ask assistance from locals.

Nothing here captures what Gray described as "23 hours of boredom a day and one hour of terror."

Gray, who is 71 and lives in Fort Walton Beach, Fla., was on only his fourth mission over Hanoi when he was shot down. He fractured vertebrae and cut his face upon ejecting. Farmers quickly took him prisoner.

He was taken to Hoa Lo, where he was interrogated and tortured, sometimes by having his arms tied behind his back and then hoisted into the air. Mostly his interrogators wanted to know about upcoming planned missions.

"You make up stories as you go," Gray said in a matter-of-fact style of the torture sessions. "That's an unfortunate part about breaking in an interrogation. If you lie, they're going to ask you again and again and again. You have to remember

(38.3) This undated photo is an aerial view of Hoa Lo prison and hangs in the museum entry. Most of the prison has been torn down.

what you said. And there were a bunch of us who screwed up and somehow managed to stupidly change our stories.

"Before you come to the realization that it's important to remember your lies, which happens about the second time they catch you ..." Gray left the thought unfinished.

"The thing you learn about torture, particularly if you're not tortured to incapacitation and death, the kind of very painful torture that we went through, it leaves a mark on you and you find that over time, emotionally, the fear of torture gets worse than torture."

He remained isolated initially, but by the fifth or sixth day he made contact with another GI by talking under the door.

"Until then you think of yourself as some kind of traitor because they've bested you physically," he said. But by talking to the others "you get brought into the game of trying to frustrate" the guards as much as possible. "It's the only combativeness allowed to us in that circumstance. As different people I shared a cell with pointed out, you do things like that for the lack of anything better to do.

If they want something, then you don't want them to have it."

He would soon be taught the "tap code" for communicating through walls.

Over the next six years he would live in camps nicknamed New Guy Village, Little Vegas, Faith, Hope, Dogpatch, Dirty Bird and Trolly Tracks.

"They tried initially to keep people in solitary, but they got so many of us that they couldn't do that," he said. "Cellmates are a godsend. You'd share every tidbit of knowledge your cellmates had."

They passed the time by describing in detail books they read and movies they had watched.

After U.S. forces raided Son Tay camp in an attempt to rescue POWs, the Vietnamese moved many prisoners in outlying camps into Hoa Lo. That benefited the POWs because they were able to more easily socialize.

Gray said that he, like many others, never thought they'd be held in prison for so long.

"A thought widely shared by a lot of the American POWs was six months to a year," he said. "Your mind does that to you. It forces you into some kind of overly optimistic state."

That sense of optimism didn't just help them survive imprisonment. It is likely what helped some of the released prisoners leave such extreme trauma behind them and live productive lives, according to the findings of a study published last year in the Journal of Traumatic Stress by the Robert E. Mitchell Center for Prisoner of War Studies in Pensacola, Fla.

The center has evaluated more than 400 of the Vietnam POWs since their release.

"By knowing them and having them as patients coming up on 40 years now, what we can do is focus on the type of person who had the experience," said Dr. Jeffrey L. Moore, the center's director and a co-author of the study.

"The results indicate that among this group, it was not merely the type of trauma that occurred which explained how one fared afterwards, but in addition, what type of person who experienced the trauma," the study concluded.

Optimism was, in fact, a stronger predictor of resilience than the level of trauma, such as type and severity of torture, a prisoner received, the study found.

Gray said that he and many others were highly attuned to optimistic "signs" that release was somewhat near, whether that was an increase in the quantity and quality of food, more frequent visits by a dentist or doctor, or more humane treatment in general.

In early 1973, the search for signs ended.

One day in January they were ushered out of their cells at Hoa Lo and ordered to stand in two long lines. A movie camera was off to the side, but not hidden so well that the men weren't aware of it, Gray said.

The peace accords required that a notice of their imminent release be read to the men.

"They read this thing. Zero reaction," recalled Gray. So it was read again. "No reaction."

"And so we just wandered away. We ruined their evening news shot." It was part of POW code of behavior years in the making.

Coffee recalled a celebratory atmosphere the night he and about 60 others were scheduled for release the next day.

The next day he boarded a C-141 plane and was greeted by a crew that included "four beautiful Air Force nurses," he said.

"The pilot cranked up the engines and taxied out to the end of the runway. It really got quiet because we were all sitting there thinking, God, is this really going to be it? Are we really going home? Am I dreaming?"

The plane rattled down the rough runway, arched into the sky and smoothed out.

"The pilot came on and said, 'Congratulations, men, we just left North Vietnam.' And that's when we cheered. That's when we believed it."

Gray's release came a few weeks later in March. He was led to the open rear-cargo door of another C-141 plane.

"Alongside the ramp is a medical orderly wearing whites," Gray recalled. "He's asking, 'Who are you?' When he gets to me, I say, Captain Gray — because I knew I was a captain by then.

"What does he say to me?"

"A-y or e-y?"

It was at that moment he felt a free man.

Read more on the Hanoi March at **https://en.wikipedia.org/wiki/Hanoi_March**

39
Control Your Future!

The longer I stared at the walls and floor and ceiling, the more I feared the future. It is the unknown that makes men tremble. If you have knowledge of what's coming, at least you can prepare for it. But here I was in a situation where I had no control over anything. I couldn't even control my bowels! Dysentery was my biggest motivator, and I had that stuff for the first 3 years I was in prison. Uncomfortable—yes! Always with me—yes! And the worst part—the stench! And the longer it fermented in your bucket (called Bou), the worse it became.

Eating the lousy food they gave me became a system of in it goes and out it comes. What a way to lose weight! I went down to approximately 122 pounds. Now how do I know that? There was a cistern in the courtyard, sort of like a big horse trough filled with water. A faucet on the cistern provided the water.

We had what looked like pee pots to dip into the trough then pour the water over ourselves to bathe. Some guys managed to estimate the weight of a pot full of water. So when we wanted to weigh someone, he scrubbed down good, washed off completely, then we filled the tub up to the top with water. The guy climbed into the trough, and water displaced to the tune of how much he weighed. We then filled up the pool by counting how many pot loads it took to fill the trough back up to the top. Then we multiplied the number of pots it took times the estimated weight of each pot full. *VOILA!* We had his weight. The old Greek Archimedes principle of specific gravity worked…even in prison.

Back into the unknown. I became convinced that if a person wanted to live, he or she could be made to do anything. But if that person lost control of his/her faculties and lost the element of judgment, they could die or be badly maimed by a torturer.

My idea must have made sense to our senior officers as they issued specific instructions regarding torture. It went something like this: If the enemy wants you to do something you know you shouldn't do, resist or try a song and dance routine to get out of it. If that doesn't work, then you will probably be faced with some type of pain-inducing technique to force you to give in. Our instructions were to hang in there as long as you could. But plan on trying to stop their actions before you lost control, or don't know what you are doing, or end up giving the enemy what he wants—plus injuring yourself, perhaps permanently.

On paper this probably looks easy enough. But it is tough as hell and tries your will power and your entire body to the limit. Remember that we all took an oath when we joined the US military regarding being a POW. It went something like this: I am an American fighting man. If I am captured, I will only give the enemy my name, rank, serial number and date of birth.

The very first question my enemy asked me was, "What is your blood type?"

I started to reply, *"You dumb ass! That's not the right question you should be asking."* Of course, I didn't say that. I gave them my blood type. I didn't know it then, but I had 7 ½ more years ahead of me, and as I said earlier, they hadn't even gotten to the really good questions yet!

Well, our Senior Officers had the right idea. Fight off what is in front of you; do what you can to lessen the impact of information you might have to provide them; get them off your back, and come out in the next round to WIN! Did the enemy ever break any of us? Sure! But they had to work for what little they got from us. Our motto was—*To Return Home With Honor!*

Under the superior leadership of our Senior Officers, we accomplished this. And we were able to look every American citizen in the eye and say, "I did my very best. God Bless America."

Yes, The Citadel saved my life because it gave me the mettle to survive. It gave me the tools I needed to overcome adversity, and to always see that light at the end of a dark, dark tunnel. Inside my ring is this quote: "A gift of The Citadel- May 27, 1973."

Yes. My Alma Mater replaced my ring, but it did so much more in the process. I have taken my place in The Long Gray Line, with honor and humility and service to my country and to my fellow man. May each of you seek to do the same, and make your days worthwhile in the sight of God!

40
The Man Who Never Was

It was the fall of 1966 and we POWs were still praying for our release each and every day.

Meanwhile, our captors were still trying to extract information from us about our military plans and strategies, about our personal lives before capture, and how we were organized and communicated with each other in our present situation. They changed their technique of obtaining this information by switching to a written biography-type form rather than by torturing us into admitting or confessing our mission at the time of capture.

This involved our writing a basic biography of our entire life, especially about our military history. We called this the "Blue Book," and tried to avoid having to write this narrative at any cost.

The procedure was to bring us in before some senior gook, listen to him tell us what bad people we were, then have him explain what he wanted and when he wanted it. For the first year of this system, our answer was always "No." This answer always led to some type of punishment—from outright torture to deprivations by taking away mosquito nets, water, food, and finding yourself in solitary confinement.

If we refused to cooperate with the enemy, then those of us who had the privilege of writing to and receiving letters from home suddenly got nothing. Since I had never been allowed to write or receive mail, that wasn't an issue for me. I didn't get any communications from home—or wrote anything to home for the first five years I was imprisoned. Finally, my time came to face the music. I was hustled off to sit on a three-legged stool before the mighty "Rabbit."

This bastard was mean as a snake, spoke good English, and hated us American "Piratical Airmen." The Rabbit was a master at creating ways to hurt us, and devised the most uncomfortable things to do to us so that we might provide information we would not ordinarily give them. He was, indeed, cunning in his efforts to trick you, threaten you, and coerce you into betraying your loyalty to America and its citizens. The Rabbit was one Bad Ass!

As I sat there, every glance from his beady eyes skewered me with the meanest look he could muster up. I fixed my countenance to show complete distain for and hate of this pseudo human being. He criticized my past behavior and reminded me of all the difficulties I had caused him and the Camp Commander. These remarks were the best part of that day. I felt rewarded for having accomplished so much.

Finally he came to the issue at hand—the Blue Book. I had not written my background, and he wanted to know why.

I replied, "In the first place no one has asked me. Secondly, you don't need to have it!"

I thought he was coming across the table to choke me as he yelled obscenities in Vietnamese.

His face turned blood red. "You do not have the right to talk to me like that because you are my prisoner, and I can do with you what I want!"

I made the decision to remain silent, to say and do nothing more to irritate this cobra. On several other face-to-face meetings, he warned me that even if I ever returned home, his sources could locate me to follow up on making my life miserable. I believed him!

He paced up and down in front of me before calling the guard to take me back to my cell to get my mat and the items I had left there. He had me stand at attention before yelling, "Bow, Pig!" He walked out while I was bent over bowing with the help of my crutches.

His parting words were, "I will see you later!"

I wasn't looking forward to that time.

On the way back to my cell the guard kept poking me in the back with his rifle butt and yelling at me in Vietnamese. I guessed he was preparing me for what lay ahead. I came up with a name for this person—Numb Nuts. This seemed like a perfect fit to me so a new star was born!

Numb Nuts took me back to my cell to pack up my belongings and carry my crap bucket and tatomi mat about twenty-five yards away to a small solitary building I called the Outhouse. It had a couple of boards lying across two sawhorses to form a bed. I put my tatomi mat on it and folded my thin blanket to act as a pillow. This beauty rest platform was to be my dream maker matrix for how long? I didn't really know.

Every day Numb Nuts would visit me to remove or reduce the amount of some item I really needed. First, it was the mosquito net. Little did I realize how critical this net was to my survival and well-being. Then the amounts of food and water they brought to me diminished by the week. My crap bucket was almost full, although I didn't have enough intake of food and water to declare the bucket an emergency. I killed mosquitoes by the hundreds because the single bare light bulb hanging from the ceiling illuminated them like they had headlights on.

The Rabbit softened me up with this treatment for about two weeks before having Numb Nuts bring me before him again. I was a bit slower and weaker by this time, and he knew it. The Rabbit started smiling and asked me, "How do you like your new home?"

"It's probably the best that you can provide—so I accept it," I replied.

The expression on the Rabbit's face showed me that I had not replied in a favorable manner. I was not concerned because a day earlier a fellow POW managed to get close enough to the Outhouse to get my attention. He told me that our senior POW had sent out the word that we should not take any more torture from the gooks over writing in the Blue Book.

"Be creative and make up stuff," was his final word. For this reason I wasn't sweating my meeting with the Rabbit.

I could see that the Rabbit was still not pleased with my answer, but he wanted to move on. He shoved a book with a blue cover in front of me. All the pages were blank.

I asked, "Do you want me to read this?"

He thundered, "No! I want you to write about you and your life—with special attention to your military career."

I saw nothing to lose by bargaining a bit to regain all the things I had lost in the move, so I asked if things could return to normal if I agreed to write.

He evidently hadn't expected me to ask this, so he stood up and paced a bit to show that he was considering my request. Then he called Numb Nuts to return me to my cell.

As I hobbled away on my crutches he said, "We shall see." This technique was in line with his normal routine of never responding immediately to a request from us POWs.

Shortly, my cell door opened and Numb Nuts threw my mosquito net on the floor, put a new crap bucket in my cell, and replenished my water supply. Now, all I had to do was create a brand new Quincy Collins to fill in the squares for my captors. I looked forward to the challenge.

I began to mentally list the items I didn't want the gooks to know about me:

#1: I didn't want them to know that I was my Wing's weapons officer, and was in charge of training our pilots to deliver both nuclear and conventional weapons on enemy targets. I also knew how they operated in the F105s, the primary aircraft used against the enemy.

#2: I didn't want them to know I had been Aide-de-Camp to the Commander in Chief of all USAF forces in Europe, and later I was his Aide when he took command of The Tactical Air Command at Langley AF Base.

#3: And finally, I didn't want our enemy to know that I had a personal relationship with Gen. Westmoreland who commanded all American forces in Southeast Asia. If I could keep these things in mind, I felt I would have clear sailing on anything else I might say.

I didn't know it then, but I would have to remember what I wrote in the Blue Book for the next seven and a half years in case the enemy challenged the information that I had provided them. It has been fifty years since I wrote about myself in prison, but the following description is an example of the fictitious facts I gave them. Enjoy!

THE LIFE OF JAMES QUINCY COLLINS, JR.

I was born on a hot July day in South Carolina because I wanted to be near my Mother. My Mother and Father were married, and it was quite normal for parents to have children. I had a good time playing with the other kids. I have a sister who is some years younger than I. When I was about one year old the family moved to North Carolina and I was allowed to go with them. That is where I grew up and finished Grammar School before I could attend High School. If a child is normal he or she enters Grammar School in the first grade at age six. I was slow as a snail so I entered at age seven.

High School was a blast and usually takes about six years to complete. I managed to take eight years to finish. That was really good for me because I didn't have to rush through school.

When I finished High School I could sing and play an instrument, so that was good for me. I sang off-key so most of the time I was singing solos by myself.

The College I selected was William and Veronica, a good Liberal Arts school up in the mountains. It had a lot of raccoons and hound dogs and I really felt good with all the animals. I did a lot of Snipe hunting and bagged a lot of those boogers while I was there. One time I had to climb up in a tree to capture one of them and I fell out of the tree. The trip to the ground was really exciting, and from that time on I wanted to be a pilot.

I talked to a lot of people about flying, and from what I could gather the Air Force was my best bet. The worst thing was that you had to pass a lot of tests and things like that, and I was never any good doing that.

At any rate, I finally graduated, (or maybe it was they quit teaching me) because Dad stopped paying my college bill. Whatever it was, Dad bought me a diploma and I signed up for pilot training.

I couldn't believe that these machines could get off the ground and fly as if I were Superman. As you might imagine, I had a little difficulty with the academics—that's the reading and studying part—but I finally was able to take off by myself and land without hurting either me or my machine. I was one proud boy when somebody pinned wings on me and I became a real live officer in the Air Force.

I had heard that there was a war going on overseas and you know what? I got asked to prepare myself for combat and to fly them jets" I had always thought that they were too fast for me, but after awhile I got used to it. I never was really good at flying or hitting a target on the ground, but they needed pilots real bad and real bad described me to a T.

Every now and then, I would write to my wife and three sons and they liked for me to tell them how, and what, I was doing. I thought it was kinda secret so I didn't tell them much.

One day my Flight Commander said for me to suit up and get ready to go on a mission. They was three other guys going too, so I felt OK about going with them. I did everything they told me to do so I thought I would be just fine.

We had some bombs hanging off the wings and they had showed me what to do to drop them on a bridge or something. I am flying along and all of a sudden I heard an explosion and my airplane started doing weird things. One of my guys told me that I was on fire and to get out ASAP.

I had practiced this many times so I knew what to do to eject. I pulled the handle and the next thing I knew I was falling in a chute. I knew I was in trouble when I hit the ground and my left leg was broke and

there sat four old Vietnamese militiamen to capture me. I wasn't going
anywhere so I was easy to capture and haul away. Man, this was scary
to me, but I was still alive!
I hope that I can soon go home and see my family again. I hope they
miss me as much as I miss them. God take care of them for me!

Quincy Collins

I couldn't believe that I wrote the above junk. Even more unbelievable was that my Dumbass Captors never questioned me about what I
had written. I seriously doubt they ever read it. Sometimes you have to
play the game even if you don't know what the rules are.

Fighter Pilots have all the fun!

(40.1) North Vietnamese officer in charge of all POWs in N. Vietnam, nicknamed "The Rabbit."

41
Singing in the Rain

"Who amongst you pirantical airmen is the Music Man?" This question was thrown at the Senior Captured American held at the Zoo in the fall of 1967. The Colonel hesitated to answer because another American would be involved if he responded with a name. The requested information would be used to identify another POW and provide additional information to the camp authorities about this person. This might not be in anyone's best interest, so he did not respond.

At the Zoo, as well as at other POW camps in North Vietnam, the camp commander was God, and was not to be denied anything, especially from us captured airmen, so silence on the part of the Colonel was not acceptable. The situation demanded an escalation in pressure to obtain an answer. So "the goon squad" was ordered to get an answer from this criminal. Who knows what these applied pressures were? I was not there, but eventually a name was mumbled, so noted by the camp commander, and the Colonel was returned to his cell to recover. Captain Quincy Collins was the name on the commander's pad, and my involvement was imminent.

It is hard for me to realize that my interest in music during the 1938 timeframe at Clara Harris Grammar School in Concord, North Carolina, was going to weave a web of intrigue in Hanoi in 1967. Of course I had studied music and played instruments all through high school, college, and even later while in the USAF.

By this time, the Colonel had sent me word that I would be called upon by the Vietnamese commander to put a group of singers together for some type of Christmas program. My mind went wild with these fragments of information, so I had to cool it and wait for the camp commander to act. If I acknowledged knowing about the situation before the camp authority informed me himself, I would be exposing our communications system to the enemy—so I sat tight!

During the first five years of our incarceration, we found ourselves either in solitary confinement or with one other person. My cellmate was AJ Meyers from Medford, Oregon. He was an F-4 pilot, and had been shot down on June 1, 1966. His left ankle was broken upon landing, and the enemy associate doctors (one step above a Red Cross volunteer) had reset his ankle so that it was not in alignment with his leg. His entire foot and leg up to his knee was in a cast and he walked with the aid of crutches. Blood had soaked through the cast, and the decaying odor was sickening. We had a lot of wood in our cell because I was also on crutches from a broken left femur.

These cells had no windows or openings to the outside. A big heavy door was the only opening available, and it was always locked as tight as a submarine latch. A bare light bulb hung from the ceiling, and it shed its light over the 7' X 7' tomb we were encased in. Indoor plumbing was still several centuries away, so we had to use a bucket called a Bou (pronounced Bo). Motel 6 would have been a palace compared to this place!

Eventually, we heard the jangling of keys coming down the hall. The guard stopped at our door, opened it, and called my Vietnamese name—Kong (like in King Kong). He motioned with his gun for me to step out into the hall, then he locked the door again. Down the hall I hobbled on my crutches, then outside and into another building where the camp commander had his office. We had names for all the camp officers—like

Rabbit, Fox, Owl, Eagle, and a few other names I am too embarrassed to mention.

A regulation they forced on us was that we had to bow to any and all Vietnamese people—to include dogs and chickens—if the guards so indicated. They wanted a full 90-degrees bow, not a small nod. This irritated the hell out of me, not just because I was on crutches, but because I did not want to acknowledge that these slimy bastards even existed. I also add inhuman to my descriptive list of adjectives for my captors.

In a moment the camp commander entered the room yelling, "Bow!" so that I would know that his royal highness had arrived. I am already pissed off, and he hasn't asked me to do anything yet. Being a POW ain't fun! He finally told me to sit down, and then made some small talk about my health.

I kept thinking, *OK Adolph, get to the point so I can get out of here.*

He then asked me about my musical background, and did I realize that Christmas was about a month away?

I told him that I was trying not to think about it because it was such a joyful season back home, but not here! I don't think the commander got my point. At least his expression never changed.

He came right to the point and said that one of my friends had told him of my musical talents, and he wanted to discuss it with me.

I asked, "What is there to discuss?"

At this point he went into a long dissertation on all the traditions of an American Christmas and how we, together, might bring a little more festive mood to the camp.

"How?" I quipped.

"Through some Christmas music that we will record then play back over the camp PA system," he said.

I was rather caught off guard by this proposal and asked for more details.

Then he brought up the big item—forming a choir to accomplish this! Apparently he was willing to allow me to assemble a choir through our own POW communications system. In effect, he was acknowledging that I could get to the men in any building in order to form a singing group. The very system that our captors wanted to snuff out, that they would punish us severely if we were caught communicating—now it might be OK?

Now I am on the spot to reply, and am not certain if he will allow me to return to my cell without giving him an answer. I am hanging onto my crutches like Gen. Custer did with his pistol, except there are no Indians dashing around me. But there is one mean bastard facing me who could bring a lot of misery to my existence with just one motion of his hand.

I needed time to discuss my decision, because I quickly realized the propaganda value to the enemy on something like this. There were a few positives also, but the negatives were strangling me at that moment. I just wanted to get out of there to discuss it with my Senior Officer and hear some other opinions on the issue. I could have done a pull-up on the icy bar resulting from the most intense stare between us that I had ever experienced.

What the hell is he going to do next?

Without another word, he stood up and asked me to think about it. He would talk to me later about my answer. Then he walked out. In a few minutes a guard came to escort me back to my call. The immediate crisis was over. I had avoided a confrontation and possible torture this time! What about tomorrow?

"What about tomorrow" is a life-long search that causes stress, turns dark hair silver, and leaves you in a cold sweat. I turned on the tapping machine and started sending out messages asking for advice and counsel. The response was immediate. I knew that I was going to have to make this decision based on the situation as it presently existed, not as it might be some weeks down the road. Some of my friends were hardliners. I knew this. I also knew what their response would be. "Screw the Camp Commander! They want to use you and a bunch of singers as fodder for their political purposes. This amounts to aiding the enemy. Don't do it!" That was an easy conclusion to reach. Another said, "What's the harm? Singing

Christmas Carols is not a bad thing. At least all of us can enjoy a touch of Christmas."

While filing away all the responses, I had begun to develop a plan that might be of assistance to all of us in the POW world. What if I could get one volunteer from each building in camp to be in the choir? I especially would be seeking a guy from our Senior Officer's building. That guy could be our messenger from our senior man, could deliver any instructions to the rest of us, and we would not have to bridge the gaps between buildings.

I concluded that I would have to get one concession from the camp commander—that they would record our carols and other Christmas songs and play them over the camp PA system for all of us to hear! Of course, I had no way of forcing or compelling the enemy to do anything, but it might be worth a try.

There was one voice I was missing, so immediately I sent a message to our Senior Officer explaining the various considerations involved. The next morning I received an answer that went something like this:

"Yes, they will use a recording for propaganda purposes.

"Yes, I believe we will get a morale boost if they play it for us.

"Yes, your communications plan could work.

"Yes, no matter what good comes from forming a choir, there will be some POWs who will adamantly oppose you.

"You are authorized to form this group for the good of the camp. You make the decision!"

The ball was in my court, and all I was waiting for was for the whistle to blow and the game to begin. It came the next day.

(41.1) The POW "music man" being congratulated by President Richard Nixon after singing "The POW Hymn" at a dinner at The White House, May, 1973

42
Sunday Book Club

We spent a lot of time together—Norman McDaniel, Mike Kerr and me. I estimate that we lived in the same cell probably three years total. We got to know one another quite well, as you might imagine!

Norm was from Fayetteville, NC and graduated from North Carolina A&T in the Greensboro, NC area. He majored in electronics, so it was a natural for him to be assigned to a crew whose mission was in that field—searching for enemy radar signals from SAM missiles, pin-pointing signals from pilots and crew members who were shot down, etc.

I was a fighter pilot who had been shot down early on in the war with North Vietnam (September, 1965) and did not have the benefit of rescue operations to pick me up and return me to my home base. Bad timing on my part!

Mike Kerr had majored in some type of psychology that prepared him for police work in civilian life. Under the circumstances, I would have to say that the three of us were a pretty good fit to be POWs together for as long as we were incarcerated. Our personalities were compatible and we could carry on conversations that were interesting and informative. We never figured out how the gooks decided to put the three of us in the same cell.

Even stranger was the fact that we were put under the control of a Cuban guy we called Fidel. He tried to convince us that he was from Hungary, but his Cuban accent gave him away. He was a vicious man who could change his stripes at the drop of a hat.

At any rate, this describes our situation at that time and Fidel was in charge of 6 or 7 more POWs who were in an adjoining cell to ours. We could hear the beatings and punishment he inflicted on his charges, and we were not surprised to learn that one of the POWs had died from the bad treatment by this Cuban monster. Fortunately, the 3 of us did not get the kind of treatment I have just described, but we knew that it could happen to us in an instant.

We decided that we would make each Sunday "story telling" time to help pass the dreary days. The format was always the same. One of us would draw a straw to see who would be first to set the scene, describe the list of characters, and set up the beginning plot. We also drew straws to determine who was second and who would end the story. I would guess that the time involved would stretch from one hour to two hours, depending on how the plot progressed.

Because Norm was a black man, one might assume that all of his characters would resemble him, but that was not the case. Norm was a fine Christian and all of his characters were too. Mike and I liked to insert shady characters to juice up the plot and add mystery to the story. Sometimes feelings got hurt because one man might add a human trait to a character that otherwise might make him be out of character from how he originally started. Looking back, I think this was good for us and might have caused the 3 of us to be a little more flexible than normally might be expected.

You can imagine how our stories went if a character was established as "holier than thou" and then in a sentence or two, one of us made him into a villain with all the human frailties one can imagine. Tempers would flair, and sometimes one of us would have to change the story in order to "mend the fences" so to speak. This little exercise kept our minds moving and made us realize that by changing a character's actions, a satisfactory conclusion could be reached that would allow the story to perhaps end on a more positive note.

Most of the time we would just laugh at where our story had taken us. Other times it might take a day or two for feelings to subside and everything to get back to normal. Overall, I think this technique gave each of us room to express ourselves without creating a big stir with a lot of hurt feelings.

Our Congress might learn a lesson from this!

43
The First Christmas Service—1967

The camp commander approved my plan to rehearse hymns and Christmas songs to be replayed over the camp public address system for all the POWs to hear in a camp we called The Zoo. It was right outside the city of Hanoi and had been built as a movie lot by the French years earlier. It had a concrete pool in the middle with streets running around it. Our captors were using the pool as a garbage dump, throwing leftover food into it. They also raised fish in it, but I am certain that a scum grew on those fish—the pool had to be contaminated! Other buildings were used originally as offices and storage structures. We rehearsed in one of those buildings.

A hymnbook in English showed up at one of our initial meetings. We used it to select the songs we wanted to sing. I could never get our captors to acknowledge that there was a Christian hymnal in all of North Vietnam nor tell how they got this one. The enemy also came forth with a small pump organ that our resident organist, Glen Perkins, played to make our singing sound better. I was amazed that we had so much talent amongst our American captives.

I spent a great amount of time teaching the group to sing the four-part harmonies basically written for piano or organ. Little by little our choir became a solid singing chorus and a pleasure to direct. All during rehearsals we would exchange information that had been passed through the walls by tapping. Talking to each other face to face was certainly a lot easier and quicker, and we didn't have to be concerned with getting caught by the guards. This also gave us the opportunity to get away from the bare walls and burning light bulb that was a staple for every cell—not to mention the ghastly smell coming from our s--- cans. We could actually talk and interact with other Americans. Life became a bit more tolerable.

We met twice a week for about a month. Then the Rabbit brought in a recording device. This gave us the chance to hear how we really sounded. Our Christian holiday was drawing nigh, but we continued to meet.

On the eve of Christmas, when the sun had set and the night was dark, my cell door opened and the guard indicated that I was to get into my best clothes. In other words, put on the pajama-looking outfit that was our normal uniform. I had a folded pair that I pressed by sleeping on them under my mat. The guard left and returned in a few minutes to blindfold and handcuff me (hands behind my back). I could tell that other prisoners were already there, but we were not allowed to speak. This is one hell of a way to go to a Christmas service, and I would expect the service to be packed with a lot of American sinners!

After taking a seat inside the bus, I was chained to other prisoners. We all knew the tap code and were very proficient in using the system to communicate. I did not know who was sitting next to me, so I tapped my name on his arm that was touching me. He came right back with his name. My legs were stretched under the seat in front of me, so I found an ankle and tapped away. He replied, and suddenly I felt that I was among friends. Everyone started doing the same thing, so soon we knew who was on board for the jolly, jolly Christmas program.

Soon the bus pulled up to a building and stopped. The guards started unloading us worshippers. With all the handcuffs and chains rattling, it sounded like silver bells coming from a dungeon. The guys who were not choir members were ushered into the big room while my choir waited outside. Blindfolds came off, and handcuffs too. Then the doors opened like we were the star attraction. My jaw fell as I looked in and saw over a hundred captured Americans, a lot of whom I recognized. Some old friends looked at me as if I were a ghost. The guards hurried us along and seated us at the front, just where you would expect to see the choir. Right beside us was a beautifully decorated Christmas tree. How did these bums know what to do with that tree?

I quickly assigned areas to members of the choir to communicate with and exchange information. Some tapped on their faces, while others who were quite close just talked out loud.

While all this was happening, the Communist who was decked out in a red regal gown (the minister or "Pope", whatever he was known as) began reading scripture and the Rabbit translated it. Then we would sing a Christmas hymn and the Pope would make remarks, translated by the Rabbit. I got one message loud and clear. This Pope compared Herod to Lyndon B. Johnson. I thought this was a valid point, and gave a thumbs-up to the Pope for comparing the two.

It seemed that this service would never end, although we still had a lot of information to exchange. We wanted to know camp names; how many POWs were in each area; who was the ranking American; if torture was prevalent; the general esprit of the troops; and any other bit of information that might be of interest to our group. We were so busy communicating that I almost forgot that I was to sing "O Holy Night" as a solo.

By this time I had become convinced that the Rabbit and his troops were not paying much attention to what we were doing. So I told Glen Perkins to not fall out of his chair when he heard the lyrics I was going to use in the next song. He said something about pushing my luck and getting shot, but what the heck, this was Christmas Eve. So Glen began the song we all know so well, and all ears seemed to perk up as I began:

"Oh, Holy Night, we're over at the Zoo
A hundred and seventy-five guys just like you.
Jim Stockdale leads us with Denton, Risner too.
Please keep the faith and be loyal and true!"

I don't remember precisely the lyrics I sang, but they were similar to these. The audience came to life, punched each other to pay attention, and smiled approval that we were trying to pull one over on the Gooks. I frankly didn't care if they were aware of what just happened. It felt good, and I was happy as hell to be an American fighter pilot. Screw Ho Chi Minh!

And best of all, when we returned to our home camps, they played our recorded Christmas music for all to hear, not just once, but four or five times. God's Christmas message was being delivered to guys in prison in North Vietnam along with a touch of freedom. Amen!

(43.2) Blurred photo of POW choir rehearsing.

(43.1) Quincy singing message to assembled POWs. The tune was "O Holy Night" but the lyrics described our treatment, numbers of POWs in our Camp, our ranking officer's name and other pertinent information.

44
A Dream That Became Real

It is Monday, September 2, 1968. I have been in this damned hole for three years. Not only that, but I have had no contact with the outside world. Why is that? God—I can think of a million reasons, but I don't want to accept any of them.

All I know is that I am lonely and feel forgotten. Forgotten by my family, my country, my government, and maybe by my God. I really wish this damnable enemy would forget that I was here. But I guess this is asking too much.

From time to time some of my POW mates will be called over to an enemy officer's office to receive mail from family back home. As soon as they return to their cells and the guards have left, the banging of the code on the walls leaves no doubt that information will soon be passed on to the rest of us. Why the hell can't that be happening to me so that I can be the source of information from home?

Looking back, I can now tell you that on September 2, 1968, Lyndon Johnson was still President, and still trying to run the war from the Oval Office without benefit of recommendations from his Joint Chiefs—or anyone else for that matter. The Rascals had a hit song, *People Got To Be Free*. And in the UK, the Beatles had a top-five song—*Hey Jude*. The temperature in Charlotte, NC, was ranging from 64 to 84 degrees and the sky was clear.

On that same date Britain was stunned by the birth of sextuplets and they all lived. And yet here I am sweating and hurting in weather that is scorching, a cell that is suffocating, and a future that looks dismal, to say the least.

In spite of all these distractions, that night I slept like a baby. It was as if a heavy burden had been lifted from my shoulders and I was able to see into a future that had great appeal. This appeared in the form of a dream, a dream based on the assumption that my wife would not be waiting for me whenever I returned home. My three sons were not a part of this image. I guess that's why I didn't feel guilty over this apparition during or after this dream.

The fact that I had received word from new "shoot downs" that a memorial service had already been held in the base chapel at Yokota Air Base, Japan, to honor my life, gave even more credence to the notion that my wife wasn't expecting me to appear at her door to give her a big hug, pick up the pieces after a 7 ½ year absence, and launch off again, together.

But there was something different about this daydream. I can even say that I was looking forward to the experience. Who would I be meeting to replace my current wife? What was she going to look like? Maybe more importantly—what did I *want* her to look like? Would she be a knockout type, a blonde, maybe a brunette; an all-American type or a sophisticated beauty?

I felt a little excited about the situation because I could paint the portrait of this woman, just like I wanted: sparkling eyes, slightly puffy lips, a figure second to none, and hair flowing over her shoulders and breasts. And a walk that would turn every head wherever she went. I couldn't wait to begin the selection process. Keep the dream moving!

I must have fallen into a deep sleep because the noises—and this prison had plenty of them—did not disturb me in the slightest. Snow White had nothing on me, and a long sleep was evidently in store for this lonely fighter pilot.

I don't know how this came about, but in my dream I saw women with no faces—only bodies and hairstyles. It was a parade of manikins without clothes. This was not what I wanted because my horny level was already too high for me to ignore—even as I slept!

My God, there were some fantastic shapes, but none that looked real. I wanted a real woman with skin, hair, and beautiful clothes. Most of all, I wanted someone who wanted me! That was the key—this dream person had to desire this bald-headed warrior!

Slowly and almost in slow motion, these figures started becoming real women with makeup and personalized hairstyles. *Now we're getting somewhere,* I thought. Eventually the girl of my dreams took shape, and I filed her away in the hope that when I was back in the real world I might have a chance to meet this damsel. For some reason, I didn't dwell on this dream or think about having it again. *Damn! Am I weird or losing my manhood? What the hell is happening to me?*

Little did I realize that it would be five years before I revisited this illusion and became engrossed in trying to determine what was real and what was the dream. Was this whole thing a premonition of my life after prison?

At this point I realized it was completely up to me as to what I wanted my dream and the reality to be. After all, I thought, this is my life and it will evolve like God and I want it to be.

If I can ever get out of this stinking prison!

45
Another Wasted Day!

Let's see. What day is it? Have I lost count again? It was a hell of a lot easier when I had a cellmate to help keep up with these important bits of information. Not that it made that much of a difference, but why am I in solitary confinement to start with? What did I do this time to merit being pulled out of my normal imprisonment and shoved into this miserable cell alone?

Was it music or choir rehearsal singing, or was it because the Rabbit just loved to stick it to me whenever he got into that mood? Perhaps he read my eyes and felt the true meanings of my stares at interrogations, or heard the inflections of hate that pervaded my speech whenever I answered one of his prying questions. This slime ball made me want to puke any time he spoke to me. I suppose, over time, he became able to read my very being and responses and inner feelings and, believe me, they were not flattering—at least not to him! For whatever reason, here I was, and I guess I should try to make the best of it.

This accommodation was somewhat smaller than others I had been in. The electrical wire that held the sole light bulb that hung from the ceiling was longer than normal. "Aha!" I mused. "The gooks are giving us more rope to hang ourselves." I quickly dismissed any thoughts of doing that. Besides, the omnipresent light piercing from that bare light bulb would be extinguished and a new one would have to be installed.

I wondered how many guards it would take to do that job? It probably would shut down the camp for at least a month.

I also noticed that the Beauty-Rest concrete bed that was to be mine had some unique gadgets at one end—leg irons. I had been fitted for and worn them before, so I knew what lay ahead. Just beyond them was a small trap door to allow the guards to open it so that they could strap you in without having to come into your smelly cell. Smelly does not adequately describe the odor emanating from the open bucket used to hold all the elements being thrown off by a human POW body—especially after having eaten some of the garbage we were fed. That in itself was punishment befitting the crime!

Looking around the approximately 7' X 7' cell, I noted that the old windows had been boarded up so that no light or ventilation could penetrate the room space. Nor was there a transom to allow air circulation. At least I wouldn't spoil—because you can't do that in a vacuum. Spoiling was not the problem to solve on this miserable day, but sweating your life away was! My guess was that the temperature in my cell had to be in triple digits—maybe 110 degrees plus. There was nothing that you could do to lower the temperature or cause a breeze.

One phenomenon that always accompanied these hot conditions was the appearance of "alligator skin." Over several days of this stifling weather condition, the skin on my upper body, hands, arms, and belly would erupt like a volcano, causing craters on top of the big bumps that rose, and it looked very much like the skin of an alligator.

But that was not the bad part, although it did provide some frightening thoughts as to when it would go away or what I will look like in the future. The really bad part was the stinging and aches and pain caused by the heavy perspiration. It felt like pouring iodine into an open sore. Wow! It just would not end!

The only way to lessen its effect was to pour cold water over the affected areas and hang on, because the initial application of water added more pain until the mass cooled down. At that time the alligator skin suddenly disappeared and life became normal again.

The big problem was that this wonderful antidote could not be applied until or unless a guard opened my cell and allowed me to go to the place outside where we bathed. A big trough held water running from a spigot, and what looked like a kid's pee-pot was available to dip into the trough and pour water over my body. Of course, this was a temporary fix because as soon as I was put back into my cell, the process regenerated itself and I soon became an alligator again.

The walls and ceiling of this cell were plaster. They dried with uneven formations of plaster that many time left impressions of faces, animals, the sky, or other weird cyberspace illusions. I searched for hours to identify something or someone I recognized. Finally I hit one. Churchill! I could even make out a cigar in his mouth, although some days it appeared that he had stopped smoking. How much time I spent on this exercise I do not know, But it certainly helped pass the time—time I would never be able to recover.

(45.1) Standing at the foot of his bed made of boards, an unidentified prisoner defiantly turns his back to the camera.

46
The Widowmaker, F-104s, Cuba and Spain

One day while in solitary confinement, I abruptly woke from a weird and disturbing dream to find that the wind was howling from a storm outside, and the building shook with each bomb explosion from an F-105 attack on the area around our prison camp in Hanoi. Talk about noisy! The cord of the single bare illuminated light bulb hanging from the ceiling was probably two feet long and kept swaying back and forth, casting an erratic pattern around my cell. Even though the light burned continuously, the blackness from outside seemed to penetrate the walls of my prison and snuff out all evidence of outside light. This freakish condition caused me to remember a previous time when I was stationed at George Air Force Base, California, in 1961.

Rather than get up and try to see if I could determine if any damage was done in the F-105 attack that had just occurred, I decided to lie back and recount those first days on my new Fighter Base.

～～

I HAD BEEN ATTENDING the Air Force Command and Staff College at Maxwell Air Force Base, Alabama, when I received orders to report to George AFB after graduation to fly the F-104 Starfighter made by Lockheed. This assignment was exactly what I had wanted, and what I had requested for my next assignment out of Command and Staff.

At that time, this airplane was the fastest in the world, and was unique in many ways. First, it was a single-engine, high-performance, supersonic interceptor originally developed for the US Air Force. It was a relatively new aircraft, having been introduced into the Air Force in 1958. It was a "Honey" of an airplane designed by the fabulous aviator, Kelly Johnson, of Lockheed Aviation. In order to maximize its speed, Kelly introduced the "Coke Bottle" design for the fuselage to attain the desired airspeed.

I was in heaven! Every fighter pilot I knew wanted to fly this machine, and I was the envy of the class. It was affectionately known as "the missile with a man in it," and it started a flying category called "High Fasty." I could hardly wait. I counted the days until I would be sitting in the cockpit, raring to go.

My family and I drove from Montgomery, home of Maxwell AFB, to Yellowstone National Park, and on up to Seattle. We came down the coast to San Francisco, and then over the mountains to Victorville, California—home of George AFB and the F-104.

We drove onto the base and went down to the flight line so I could show my wife and son, Chip, what Daddy was going to be flying. There was not an airplane in sight. Where the hell did they keep my new airplane? I finally saw a human being in uniform and asked about what I wasn't seeing.

He laughed and said, "The wing is in Florida getting ready in case Russia and Cuba start pointing missiles at us." Now it all made sense. The Cuban missile crisis was responsible. Every F-104 America owned was somewhere in Florida just waiting for the word from President Kennedy to launch an attack on missile sites in Cuba. This was serious stuff!

At least we had a home to live in and could start setting it up. I began to feel better.

I didn't realize until later that during this period of time the U.S. and the Soviet Union came closer to Nuclear War than at any other time in our history. I am convinced that most Americans do not yet realize

the seriousness of the situation. The truth surfaced on this event only after years of analysis by scholars and government officials. The five points
below are a synopsis reported by Jessica Sleight of Ploughshares Fund in
October 2012.

1. A Soviet submarine was forced to surface by American destroyers
   using depth charges. The sub was carrying a nuclear-tipped tor-
   pedo. The Soviet sub commander believed that war had already
   started and was prepared to fire it. Fortunately, authorization
   from three other officers on board the sub was required. Two were
   in favor—one was not. This is what I would call a "close call!"

2. In order to gain support for an invasion of Cuba by the U.S., recommended actions included the sinking of a ship near the entrance
   of Guantanamo Bay, then conducting funerals for mock-victims,
   plus blowing up an American ship in the bay and blaming Cuba.
   These possibilities were discussed by the Joint Chiefs in Washington. This was hard for me to believe. Deceit should not be an
   answer!

3. The Bay of Pigs invasion of Cuba (planned for 1961) led the Soviets to conclude that Kennedy was determined to get rid of Castro.
   Khrushchev then sent nuclear weapons to Cuba to protect Castro,
   his ally. This should have been predictable!

4. On October 27th, the Soviets deployed Nuclear Cruise Missiles
   within fifteen miles of the U.S. base at Guantanamo Bay. President Kennedy was never told that this was happening, so no action was taken. Why was he not notified immediately?

5. A U.S. spy plane (U-2) accidently entered Soviet airspace during
   this crisis. MIG fighters were sent to shoot it down with nuclear
   missiles. U.S. nuclear-armed fighters were sent to escort the plane
   home. It took one hour and a half for Kennedy and McNamara
   to learn of this event. (Wow! How close could we come?)

Over time some F-104 aircraft returned to our base, and other "birds"
had been in inspections and were being prepared to go to Florida. Since

I was not checked out in the F-104, I was like the Pope in a House of Ill Repute. I knew the routine, but was not yet cleared for action!

Finally, I went to ground school and took all the academics on the airplane and spent hours in the F-104 simulator. Before long I was actually flying the machine and building up hours. The guys in Florida were not getting much flying time, if any, because their aircraft were on alert, so I was gaining ground on them. When the F-104s started returning to home base, I was already checked out in the machine. I was now an official Instructor Pilot (IP), was assigned as a Flight Leader, and settled in a nice home on base. Oh, by the way—Nancy was pregnant again!

I was also flight-testing aircraft after they had been through the maintenance process. Part of our training program was to use the "moon suit" and the "head bubble" in a maneuver named the "Zoom." The idea was to fly over two times the speed of sound, then pull up with afterburner on and turn your aircraft into a missile as you coasted to an altitude over 80,000 feet.

At this altitude, if you had to eject, your blood would boil and all body fluids would evaporate. Thus, the moon suit and head bubble would sustain the pilot until he fell to a lower atmosphere. Of course, in a real war situation the pilot and his aircraft would be vectored towards the enemy bogey approaching so that, at the right time, the heat-seeking missile being carried could be fired to bring down the enemy.

The altitude chamber, built on the ground, was used to give you a "real" feeling for the altitude you would be in and also let you respond to things not working properly. At altitudes over 50,000 feet, the human body falls apart very quickly, and you have only a few seconds to respond with the right procedures.

This is enough to draw your attention away from your primary job of bringing down an enemy aircraft, but there are other things that get your attention too. The higher you fly, the less oxygen there is, and your engine must have oxygen if it is to drive you through the sky.

At around 50,000 feet, explosions knock your feet off the floor of the cockpit, and it seems that the aircraft is just prior to exploding. Air and fuel are being forced into the engine and the igniting of that mass is what is exploding. The next thing you notice is that you have "flamed out." You have no more "juice in your tomato." Now, you really are a missile and you look around to see what you can see. The answer is—nothing! Instead of a bright sunny day like you had a few minutes ago, everything is as black as the ace of spades and you have no control of the aircraft. It is falling, and you now try to read your instruments to determine your altitude so that you can restart your engine when there is enough oxygen to support burning the fuel.

Also, at that high altitude your aircraft controls are useless. The air is too thin for your airfoils to get any traction, so you wait and pray that everything will come together soon. The nose of your aircraft has now dropped below the horizon and the world is light again. The ailerons take effect and you feel the elevators working, so it is time to start the engine.

"Please start, please start! So I don't have to eject to get back home!"

I push the start button and some noises I have never heard before just about knock me out of the cockpit. Suddenly it smoothes out and I feel the power of my engine pushing me ahead. Now things are normal again, and I can land this tiger and get out of this Moon outfit and go buy a beer. Wow! What a day! I wonder what the rest of the world has been doing while I have been "Flying High?"

As you might imagine, the F-104 was not the safest aircraft in the Air Force inventory. Initially it had a downward ejection seat that played hell with pilots having to eject at take-off or landing. Thus, it came to be known as "The Widowmaker." By the time I arrived on the scene the seat system had changed to an upward ejection.

The F-104 needed a lot of speed—around 219 mph—in order to get airborne, and landing was in the 207 mph range. After landing, a drag chute was deployed to help slow the plane so that normal taxi speeds were possible. This magnificent bird could go past Mach1 going straight up. Man! That is moving out!

It was about then that our squadron was notified of our pending deployment to Moron, Spain, in an Air Defense capacity. The base was outside Seville and we were all ecstatic. Dancing on the ceiling is closer to the truth!

During these type deployments, the family must make arrangements to be without their Fighter Pilot Sponsor for up to six months, so we had some planning to do. We decided that Nancy and Chip should go to Charlotte, NC (Nancy's home town) to stay with her mother. Her Uncle, Lowell Newton, a well-known Charlotte doctor, would deliver our child.

The squadron was to leave George AFB in about a month and a half, and getting Nancy on an airliner by then was going to be questionable—so we decided to send her off to Charlotte before she became too pregnant. I bought her an extra-large coat to try to hide nature's doings and got them on a flight out of Los Angeles. With all the toys and baby stuff they were going to need, we looked like a circus going down the aisle of the plane. After seating them I drove back to the base to become a bachelor and learn to cook for myself. (It was a little lonely.)

Our squadron began practicing air-to-air intercepts as this is what we would be doing while in Spain. Getting close enough to a "bogey" to identify him as friendly or hostile was not an easy task to perform, and it took a lot of practice to perfect it.

Our aircraft were already at Moron as our sister squadron had flown them there over three or four months earlier. We packed our gear, boarded a transport plane, and headed to Spain like normal travelers on a slow boat to China.

On December 17, 1962, we touched down at Moron, and began unpacking our gear and setting up our rooms. Before we had departed George AFB, I had won a magnum of Bourbon at a Bingo game at the Officers' Club, so I stashed it away in my baggage to celebrate the birth of my baby in Charlotte when it happened. I had made arrangements with an old friend at Myrtle Beach AFB in SC for Nancy to call when our child was born. My friend would then call Moron AFB to let me know of the event.

As soon as I had put all my belongings away I walked over to the Operations Center and called my friend in Myrtle Beach to tell him I had arrived and asked if Nancy had called yet. The answer was a big *NO*, so we talked a few minutes before I signed off and hung up. About thirty seconds later the Operations phone rang. It was my friend in Myrtle Beach saying Charles Lowell Collins had been born at 10:42 that morning and weighed in at 6 lbs. 10 ½ ozs.

I hit the ceiling and ran for that big bottle of Bourbon I had won! We celebrated all night, and a huge hangover greeted us the next day. Two boys! Can you believe that? This was one proud Fighter Pilot, and I already had future plans for both of them. Fathers act so silly when kids come along, but this was a huge "Joy Of Life," and I treasured every moment of it!

The squadron went through a short training period where we were exposed to all the different functions of our mission—and how we were going to handle it. Most of us had been on alert before at other bases and other aircraft. But that was for nuclear alert in the F-100, and the line was drawn as to how far you could taxi the aircraft with a fully loaded nuclear weapon hanging on the aircraft after the alert horn sounded. The F-104 was different!

In the F-100 or F-105, when that alert sounded, you had three minutes to get to your aircraft and crank it up to taxi. In this F-104 alert posture in Moron, we had three minutes from the alert horn to be at 30,000 feet to intercept a "bogey." Can you imagine being asleep in the hanger (sleeping in your flight suit) and this blaring horn goes off? You get your boots on and head for your aircraft while this damned horn keeps blaring to urge you on your way. It is in the black of night and two crew chiefs greet you as you climb up the metal ladder to slip into the cockpit. One starts the engine and the other straps you into your parachute. The engine winds up with its own sounds blotting out the Klaxon horn, and the cockpit "comes alive" with all the lights showing that all systems are cranking up.

Thank God, there is no monitoring of a nuclear weapon required in this intercept format. What a relief! Three sets of eyes are checking all the gauges. When the crew chiefs are satisfied that all is well at this point, they slap you on the shoulder and disappear down the ladder.

Now, you are all alone except for the instructions being broadcast to you through your helmet. You push the throttle forward to get this monster moving and head for the runway. The direction of the wind is of no consequence in this exercise. Your job is to go full throttle, hit afterburner, get airborne ASAP, and follow headings as you head towards 30,000 feet. This is a single-seat fighter plane so there is no one else to talk to or check with or hear breathing—just little ole' YOU!

The nights are really coal-black in Spain! There are few big cities with streetlights and road lights to give you some balance as to your relative position to the ground. Vertigo tries to interfere with your normal brainwaves, and heavy sweating may result as you fight your inner ear feelings about what is really happening to the aircraft and to you.

Using your instruments is the only answer. Check all of your instruments to see if you are turning. Are you gaining airspeed? Is the altimeter unwinding or are you climbing? (Wow!) So much to do to regain your confidence and establish the instrument readings that indicate you are doing what you need to be doing. Sometimes I wish I had wanted to be a truck driver rather than an all-weather fighter pilot!

OK! The radar man on the ground says turn left 5 degrees and the bogey you are to identify is 30 miles out at 35,000 feet altitude. He says the ground speed of the bogey is 485 knots. I pick him up on my own radar set and estimate that my closing speed on this foreign aircraft is over 1,000 mph. In other words, I will only have a few seconds to compute what to do to intercept this other aircraft in such a way that I can identify him accurately while doing all the other things I must do to fly my own machine.

My radar has locked on to the bogey, so between what that shows me, and what my radar guy is telling me, I should be in a good position to identify this aircraft. I hold steady while decreasing my airspeed, so that I don't zoom by without really identifying the other aircraft. I want to be beside and behind him in case he is an unfriendly and I have to take action against him.

Fortunately this is an airliner that has failed to turn on his transponder and is ignoring all the procedures established to eliminate the necessity for an intercept. Being an aggressive Fighter Jock, I have got to show this high altitude bus driver that we are on to him. So I zoom up in front of him, hopefully to wake him up or startle him into being a bit more professional about flying into restricted areas.

My personal sense of accomplishment is soaring as I request information for returning to Moron Air Base. I pick up the runway lights in my descent into the area, and ask the Ground Control Approach to lead me to touchdown as I elect to practice a weather approach. I taxi into the hanger, get the thumbs-up from my crew chief, shut down the engine, and crawl out to become a human being again.

Mission accomplished!

My euphoria fades and I am again in a dark prison cell thinking about an airplane I used to fly. Most of the time it flew me, but at least I could escape the strife of the present by returning to the past.

Being a fighter pilot ain't all bad!

(46.1) High-altitude pressure helmet.

Sky High in a Starfighter— My climb to the top in the F-104.

By George J. Marrett, excerpted from *Air & Space Magazine*, November 2002

The Lockheed F-104 Starfighter looked more like a rocket than an airplane. Out in front was a sharply pointed nose with a long pitot tube. The airplane's straight, stubby wings were canted downward, and they were so thin and small, like fins, that you wondered how it could fly. Lockheed press releases even described the airplane as "the missile with a man in it." For pilots, its tiny cross-section made it the kind of aircraft you put on like a glove. The cockpit was small but comfortable, and the pilot sat reclined with legs extended, the way you sit in a sports car.

Early versions were designed with an ejection seat that fired downward, and to prevent injuries the pilot wore metal spurs attached to his flight boots, cowboy style. The spurs were connected to cables that would automatically pull his feet against the ejection seat during an ejection. Later, the seat was redesigned to fire upward, but the spurs stayed. Most pilots put their spurs on just before they boarded and took them off immediately after deplaning; others wore them around to show off. When I was a second lieutenant attending flying school, I saw an Air Force colonel wearing an orange flying suit and a dress military hat with "scrambled eggs" on the visor. His spurs were clinking and clanking as he walked. Then and there I knew I wanted to fly the Starfighter.

I got my chance in December 1963, when I was selected to attend the U.S. Air Force Test Pilot School at Edwards Air Force Base in California. At the time, the grand old man of supersonic flight, Colonel Charles E. "Chuck" Yeager, was the commandant of the school, and he was guiding the Air Force toward the new frontier of spaceflight.

Our class had 10 Air Force pilots, two Navy pilots, two NASA pilots, and one pilot each from Canada and the Netherlands. We all wanted to be part of the Space Age even though our very presence here put us in competition with NASA. The Air Force had initiated its own manned space program with the Boeing X-20 Dyna-Soar, a single-seat space

(46.2) Zoom climbs in the rocket-boosted NF-104 could top out at 120,000 fet in zero gravity. (photo courtesy George J Marrett)

vehicle scheduled to make its first flight in 1966, just three years away.

All X-20 pilots would be graduates of Yeager's school and actually fly their spacecraft from liftoff to an unpowered landing on Edwards' Rogers Dry Lake. NASA astronauts, on the other hand, returned to Earth in a capsule suspended from a parachute and landed in the ocean.

Yeager was instrumental in changing the curriculum of the test pilot school to include spaceflight training. The name of the school was also changed to Aerospace Research Pilot School, though it was commonly referred to as Yeager's Charm School. He still had the golden touch: Yeager seemed to have a credit card enabling him to tap into the Air Force budget, and there seemed to be no limit to what he could spend. His motto appeared to be "Follow me. I will put the Air Force in space."

To give his students a real taste of space, Yeager contracted with Lockheed to modify three production F-104s for high-altitude flight. Designated NF-104s, they were inexpensive trainers that would expose students to altitudes above 100,000 feet. Like the X-15, the NF-104s had small directional thrusters in the nose and wingtips for attitude control up where normal controls had no effect.

Each NF-104 was equipped with a Rocketdyne liquid-fuel rocket engine that used JP-4 fuel and hydrogen peroxide as an oxidizer to produce 6,000 pounds of thrust. With the reaction control system, a student could control the NF-104 on a zero-G trajectory through the thin atmosphere at the edge of space for about 80 seconds. The pilot wore a pressure suit; without engine power at that altitude there was no cockpit pressurization.

It was widely understood that whoever first pushed the NF-104 to its maximum performance was certain to set a world record for altitude achieved by an aircraft taking off under its own power. In 1961 the Soviets had set a record of 113,890 feet with the E-66A, a rocket-powered variant of the MiG-21 fighter. Some U.S. X-planes had flown higher, but they had to be carried aloft by a Boeing B-52 (see "Mother," June/July 2001).

In 1963, Lockheed began shakedown flights on the NF-104 with company test pilot Jack Woodman. After a few months the program was turned over to Major Robert W. "Smitty" Smith at the Air Force Flight Test Center (AFFTC), flying out of the Fighter Branch of Test Operations. A year later, when I was assigned to the fighter branch, I did a little off-the-record dogfighting against Smitty. By disabling the safety system that prevented loss of control at high angles of attack and high Gs, he could fly the F-104 near its aerodynamic limits. You couldn't beat Smitty in an F-104.

To reach maximum altitude, the pilot accelerated the NF-104 at full power to maximum speed, then pulled up into a "zoom climb." In a zoom, the more energy you could build up during acceleration—and the more precisely you could maintain the optimal climb angle—the higher the airplane would climb when it coasted to the top of the zoom. Smitty reached 120,800 feet on one zoom—not an official world record because it was a test flight and the official monitors were not in place. Optimum climb angle for the aircraft turned out to be between 65 and 70 degrees, which, added to a 14-degree seat cant and a five-degree angle of attack, left the pilot reclined at an angle of about 85 degrees. You couldn't see the ground from that position, so all zoom maneuvers were made on instruments. On one flight, Smitty tried an angle of 85 degrees, but he lost control and tumbled, going over the top upside down. The aircraft entered a spin but he recovered. Smitty was fearless.

Yeager had taken the NF-104 up three times to get a feel for it, and on December 10, 1963, he was scheduled to fly two zoom flights in preparation for an all-out record attempt the next day. During the morning flight he reached 108,700 feet, but Yeager felt the Starfighter could be taken much higher.

On the afternoon flight, Yeager's test profile called for him to accelerate to Mach 1.7 at 37,000 feet, light the rocket engine to accelerate to Mach 2.2 at 40,000 feet, and then climb at 70 degrees. As the aircraft passed through 70,000 feet, ground control informed Yeager that he had less than the desired angle of climb. He applied the reaction controls to get back on the flight path, a technique he had used before. But on this flight he was at a lower altitude (101,595 feet) and the reaction controls were not yet effective. There was a higher dynamic pressure on the control surfaces, meaning the horizontal tail would have been more effective. Then, when he attempted to lower the nose at the peak of his climb, he found that neither the aerodynamic controls nor the reaction controls could reduce the angle of attack enough to prevent a spin. Soon he was gyrating in all directions, and nothing would stop it. A mile above the desert and falling like a manhole cover, he ejected.

As his parachute opened, he was struck in the face by the base of his rocket seat. His helmet's visor broke and burning residue from the rocket entered the helmet. Pure oxygen for breathing was flowing to the helmet, igniting a flame that started to fry his neck and face. As he descended, Yeager removed a glove and used his bare hand to try to put out the fire around his nose and mouth, charring two fingers and a thumb. The aircraft hit the ground in a flat attitude, and Yeager landed a short distance from the wreckage. Within a few minutes a helicopter and flight surgeon arrived. Yeager had second-degree burns on the left side of his face and neck and on his left hand, and a cut on one eyelid.

The loss of an NF-104 was not the only bad news that day: Secretary of Defense Robert S. McNamara announced the cancellation of the X-20. The Air Force lost a manned space program, Yeager was injured and wrapped in bandages, and the Air Force had put a hold on his spending.

47
Looking Through A Hole

When you are in a completely blacked out room/space, a hole will tell you where it is, how big it is, and how much light is on the other side. When you put your eye in front of the hole during daylight hours, you should be able to see outside as if you are looking through a camera lens, but with a fairly narrow focus area.

If outside is dark (like at night), you will only be able to see objects that are reflecting light. This little scientific example probably proves that I should stick to very simple explanations and leave the rest to Edison and Einstein. However, it does serve a purpose I have in mind.

In 1969 I was in solitary confinement at the Zoo and still having a lot of medical problems with infections and a pneumonia-type illness that just about knocked me out. We were still being treated badly by our captors, and morale was borderline weak. We really needed a life—and out of the blue we got one!

Hanoi Hanna came on one evening over the P.A. system and announced that the bad government of the USA had just landed two piratical airmen on the moon! They made it sound as if only America had reported this. Baby Hanna made the point that no one else had verified the happening, so the whole deal could be a P.R. stunt with no truth to it at all. Hanna did say that the two men who had landed were Neil Armstrong and Buzz Aldrin.

I just about fell in the floor as I knew both of them! Suddenly the entire event became personal. Neil and his family lived around the corner from me when I was the Aide to the Commanding General of the Tactical Air Command based at Langley AFB in 1960. All the original astronauts were stationed there, and everyone knew what they were training for. I met Neil as a result of that situation.

I also knew Buzz quite well as we both were stationed at the new US Air Force Academy in 1955. He was the Aide to the Dean of the Academy when I reported in as an Air Training Officer (ATO) to handle the first three classes of cadets reporting into the new Academy.

Buzz had been in Korea flying F-86s, and when that war subsided, he came to the Academy for the Aide assignment. There were F-86s available to us at Lowry AFB, so Buzz and I often would be flying together either locally or on cross-country flights. I recall that he was a bit haughty, perhaps slightly arrogant, but what would this bit of notoriety do to him? I had no idea as I never had the opportunity to talk to him after his big experience.

Once we were in the same hotel when I was speaking to a group in a city in another state, so I wrote him a short message inviting him to call me so that we might meet and renew old times at the academy. I had the desk clerk put my message in his room box, but I never heard from him. Some people are just too famous for us ordinary run-of-the-mill people.

I had not even seen the moon in at least a year or two, so I decided I needed to bring it into my cell. Now how the heck could I do that? My cell was like an airtight box with no way to peer outside. Only the cell door, which the guards used to enter my cell and take me in and out, could connect me with the world outside.

It seemed useless to even try, but I finally examined the wall that faced outside to see if any places existed that might lend itself to boring a hole so that I could see what treasures surrounded me. Amazingly, I found that needle in a haystack! In plain language, I discovered that a window had been boarded up and a thin coat of stucco applied to it to hide what was really there. I spent hours trying to locate the best spot to make my nail bring views to my eyes that I could only dream about.

I had "liberated " the nail weeks earlier from the medic's shack, and was hanging on to it for dear life for just this type opportunity. Now the excavation project could begin!

I felt like a New York Skyscraper Building Supervisor as I planned my moves. I also had to be a Houdini because I had to hide residue from my diggings, and always have a plug ready to hide the hole I was preparing. Of course, there were hundreds of interruptions each day. Every time I envisioned being relegated to some dark hole for breaking the camp regulations. I can't explain how stressful it was to be so bold with this project. I also learned the true meaning of vulnerability. But you know what? Being able to see something, especially the moon, was worth all the trouble I might get into. I could hardly wait for the first preview.

In about two days it happened. It was late afternoon, and the evening slop had been served to us criminals. The camp staff and guards appeared to be feeding themselves. Outside was quiet, which made my continued efforts with the peephole sound like I had a jackhammer in my room. I kept trying to get a view that would allow me to be looking up. I wanted to be able to see the sky, the moon, the stars, and the bombers coming to blow up the enemy so that my tired ass could go home.

I hadn't given much thought to timing, so I wasn't sure of the position of the moon. It had been several days since Hanoi Hanna's announcement of the moon landing, so I wasn't too sure of what I might be able to see. Several hours later I computed that the moon was going to be visible from my new viewing platform. I just didn't know when! Another hour or so went by and I became aware that the reflection from the moon was illuminating the area around that end of the building.

I cried out, "My God, there she is!"

I couldn't believe it. The moon was nearly full, and I had a full view for my unbelieving eyes. I had done it! I could see where Hanoi Hanna had been talking about.

Of course my friends had left by now and were successfully reclaimed out in the Pacific Ocean, but my personal joy and happiness were wrapped in the belief that we had indeed landed these guys on the moon. I was looking at the site where it all happened—from my prison cell in North Vietnam!

"Dear God, it is so great to be an American who has a peephole to view the world!"

(47.1) Looking at the earth from the moon. (Photo by NASA)

*(47.2) Looking at the moon from the earth—my view from
my prison cell. (Photo by Mike Petrucci on Unsplash)*

48
A Noise That Shakes Your Soul!

The noise that results from striking one piece of metal that is hanging from a tree with another metal piece will certainly get your attention—like reveille in the dark of a Communist prison camp before morning sunrise. Just the raw sound is enough to shock one's heartbeat into an abnormal cadence that stresses one's entire body. It is an introduction to another day as a captive—where the unknown rules, and you become a responder to your captor's most sinister schemes and horrific ideas.

Yes, this sound affects your entire being and is the ultimate alert for you to be prepared for the worst of circumstances. As I listened to this normal camp sound on a daily basis, my mind often recalled a similar frightening experience—the penetrating sound that a Klaxon horn produces when it announces an unidentified bogey is approaching the space your are defending. Or the bogey is already penetrating it, and your job is to launch your aircraft immediately so as to positively identify the bogey, turn him back, or shoot him down.

This is quite a list of "To Do's" for a fighter pilot to accomplish when he is awakened in the black of night in an Air Defense posture, especially in a foreign country. It is a very difficult task to train for because there are so many unknowns that have to be unmasked to expose the facts.

What kind of aircraft is this bogey?

Which country does it represent?

Is it a fighter plane or a cargo/transport type aircraft?

Is it evasive or flying straight and level?

What code is the bogey transmitting? Your ground controller should have notified you of the type signal coming from the bogey's transponder.

Finally, a decision must be made as to the action to be taken. Assuming that emergency radio channels have not provided a means to communicate with the bogey, your best course of action is to try to get the bogey to follow you to land at the nearest airport that can handle that type aircraft.

As you might imagine, during the past minutes both aircraft have been speeding along at a high rate of speed while you have been trying to determine how to handle this situation. Hopefully, ground control has made contact with the bogey's primary control to inform them that this aircraft is off course and not where he should be.

This is the type event that can happen in any area of operation. It requires cool heads and professional pilots in order to solve an otherwise complex situation. The USAF provides that kind of training and experience.

THEOLDMOTOR.COM
TYPE L PROJECTOR 9 INCH

(48.1) An illustration of a Klaxon Horn from "Motor" magazine, May 1908.

(48.2) An ad for the Klaxon Horn from "The Automobile," December 1909.

49
The Son Tay Raid

Sitting in a prison cell is boring as hell! No magazines, no newspapers, no TV—just sitting there waiting for your time to be interrogated, and the resulting treatment depending upon your answers to your captor's questions. Will it be the ropes, or will it be a gun butt to the head? Will you be relegated to silence and darkness in a solitary cell, or will you be sent back to your present cell to think about your answer? From 1965, when I was shot down, until late 1970, the norm was that you were either by yourself or with one other person. In November of 1970, all that changed.

A helicopter force, much like the Doolittle Raiders in WWII, made a night raid on a POW camp named Son Tay. Their goal was to rescue and liberate any American POWs who happened to be there. Much to their dismay, no one was there. Not even a Vietnamese guard.

The POWs who had occupied this camp some months before had named it Camp Hope because of the vast improvement in treatment and food. Interestingly, at the time of the raid a group of us were up the road from there about three or four miles at a new camp we called Camp Faith. We gave it that name because the treatment and food were much better than we had received prior to this at the Zoo.

Our conclusion was that this was our fattening-up place before being released. Wrong again! At least on that night, when we heard all the bomb and afterburner noise, we immediately felt closer to the war in that we actually heard gunfire and saw American jets going into afterburner right in front of our very eyes. Damn! There really was a war going on!

When we had arrived at Camp Faith several months earlier, we were in blindfolds and handcuffs and were in the back of trucks with canvas covers over us so that we could not see out and local citizens could not see in. The day after the big raid when we had heard lots of anti-aircraft fire and had seen a USAF jet go into afterburner—although we didn't know what had actually happened—we were physically thrown into the back of trucks and hauled into Hanoi to what we named the Hanoi Hilton. No blindfolds, no handcuffs, no cover to hide us. This was a quick and dirty move designed to further isolate us by putting us in their most heavily defended fortress.

From that moment on, all guards wore hand grenades strapped on their belts. We assumed that they were prepared to throw them into our cells if ever there was another attempt to rescue us. This new tactic made us feel more uncomfortable than ever before. We had no idea that our military actually planned this exercise to free us and also make it known to our captors that America had the capability to pull off such a far-fetched idea.

Once we understood the goal of those who volunteered to come in after us, we were even more proud to be Americans. We knew that we were on the right side, and that our enemy needed to have their butts beaten into submission! All I need now is a weapon with lots of ammo! I had not felt like this since I was captured. I realized that we must be careful as our enemy was walking on eggshells, and ready to take action against us.

I was reminded of the old saying, "Discretion is the better part of valor." Be calm, young man, and remember that your goal is to get back home alive!

After a breakneck speed trip into Hanoi, we arrived at the Hanoi Hilton to see line after line of Vietnamese prisoners being led out of their present prison cells chained together like animals. This included men, women, and children. Some of the women were still breast feeling their younger ones. The scene was very disturbing to say the least.

But into each big cell we marched. The local housekeeping squad had not yet cleaned up, and neither had the crap containers been emptied. It was a mess, and the bad odors kept reminding us of where we were. I counted 50 of us initially, then I spotted a section of the wall by the front gate that had marks indicating the last head count for that cell. It totaled 144 people.

We all had tatomi mats and a blanket and assorted clothing, so there was not a lot of space available for 50 guys to even sit down, much less lie down. We discussed what we had just witnessed and determined that this new accommodation was not a step up for us—but rather several steps backward.

The best part of this move was that it afforded us a real opportunity for the very first time to get organized and have our own chain of command work in our behalf. Senior officers were appointed in each cell, and all of us were assigned to "flights" with commanders for each. We truly were a joint cell group as Army, USAF, Navy, and Marines were in command. It didn't take but a few hours before our Senior Commander began issuing orders.

Man! This was just like being in the service and we loved it! It felt natural and very comfortable. I hoped that the next set of orders coming from on high would be, "Prepare to vacate the premises. We are going home!"

These activities took place in November of 1970. The first group of POWs was released on February 12, 1973. Time crawls on like a snail when you have no control over events. Will this ever end?

The Son Tay Raid - A 35-Year Retrospective
By Charles Tustin Kamps

On the night of 20–21 November 1970, the North Vietnamese were treated to an aggressive demonstration of Pres. Richard Nixon's concern for the welfare of US prisoners of war (POW)—the raid on the Son Tay POW camp. Although we rescued no POWs (the enemy had moved them to other facilities), the raid serves as a model of a well-planned and -executed joint special operation. Indeed, Son Tay stands in stark contrast to the dismal effort mounted to free hostages in Iran 10 years later. Marked by outstanding organization, training, and unity of effort, Operation Kingpin badly embar rassed the North Vietnamese.

Brig Gen Donald Blackburn, special assistant for counterinsurgency and special activities in Washington and an old Army hand at special war fare, came up with the idea for the raid. After a fa

(49.1) Son Tay was located about 23 miles from Hanoi. With the entire compound measuring only 140 x 185 feet, the landing zone targeted for the HH-3's crash-landing point was little more than the size oof a volley-ball court.

vorable feasibility study, meticulous planning began with the blessing of the president. Most im portantly, the operation remained directly subor dinate to the Joint Chiefs of Staff, bypassing the bu reaucracy in Southeast Asia. Brig

(49.2) Brigadier General Donald D. Blackburn

Gen Leroy Manor, commander of USAF Special Operations at Eglin AFB, Florida, and the joint task force com mander, wielded a very free hand. His deputy, Col Arthur "Bull" Simons, a long-time Army veteran of "spec ops," would go in on the ground with the raiding party.

The Central Intelligence Agency provided a scale model of the prison and surrounding buildings, and engineers constructed a life-size mock-up of wood and canvas in Florida that they could quickly disassemble before Soviet spy satellites made their twice-daily crossing over the area. The rigorous training involved dangerous dissimilar aircraft for mation flying at night. Full-dress rehearsals proceeded under operational conditions until the team felt 90–95 percent confident of mission success. Barely three months had transpired from the time Manor had been summoned to the Pentagon until the force deployed to Thailand.

The Army provided the assault force (limited to 56 men), and the Navy committed 59 aircraft to a diversion in the direction of Haiphong, drawing the attention of the North Vietnamese air-defense network. The Air Force organized its mission air craft into robust packages: (1) five HH-53 helicop ters and one HH-3 (which had to crash-land the

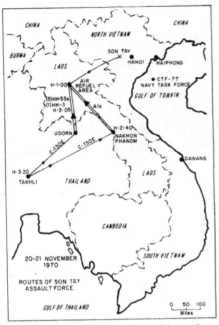

(49.3) Map showing routes of Son Tay assault force.

(49.4) Reconnaissance photos taken by SR-71 "Blackbirds" aircraft revealed that Son Tay "was active."

(49.5) Racing from the glare of a North Vietnamese surfacr-to-air missle exploding overhead, the last Kingpin HH-53 escapes the deserted POW camp moments before a demolition charge insude the HH-3 "Banana 1" explodes.

rescue team in the middle of the prison compound) carrying the assault troops and (2) five A-1E attack aircraft providing fire support. After refueling from separate HC-130Ps over Laos, each group then followed its own MC-130E Combat Talon special operations aircraft, which broke off in the target area to drop flares and diversionary ordnance. Ten F-4s flew combat air patrol in the objective area, supported by five F-105 Wild Weasels for suppressing surface-to-air missiles (SAM). Additional aircraft provided aerial refueling, radar coverage, enemy-radio monitoring, and command and control relay for General Manor, who operated from a ground station in South Vietnam.

Although Simons's helicopter landed at the wrong compound and a SAM downed one of the Wild Weasels, the force achieved surprise, com pletely overpowered the garrison, and evacuated the area one minute ahead of schedule. Only one raider sustained wounds. The effort stands as an excellent example of the masterful execution of a joint special operation. Well over a decade would pass before US special operations forces organized on a permanent basis to carry out raids like Son Tay.

(49.6) Colonel Arthur D. "Bull" Simons ansers questions about the Son Tay POW Rescue Raid from the Pentagon Press Corps.

Excerpted from the Air & Space Power Journal, Spring 2005

50
POW Choirs in Vietnam Prisons

After the failed Son Tay raid on November 21, 1970, a US planned helicopter POW rescue mission, most of us were shipped quickly to the big prison in the middle of Hanoi. We named it the *Hanoi Hilton*. Now we were in cells of 40 to 55 men. The center of the big cell was poured concrete that looked like an inverted V. We placed our heads at the top, spread our tatami mats over the concrete for a bed, and used a separate partitioned space as a latrine—with big barrels to contain excrement.

Each day the guards would open our gate and allow us to go outside for exercise or to just mill around. I still used crutches and was standing there talking with another POW when all of a sudden—WHAM! I am on the ground with 2-3 guards grabbing me as they drug me out the courtyard gate and threw me on the ground outside. My back and neck were injured during my ejection along with a severely broken left femur. I blacked out when the guards hit me. When I became conscious again, I hurt just like I did after ejecting.

Several hours later I was moved to an individual solitary confinement type cell and was put into leg irons with my hands handcuffed behind me. This was certainly not meant to be a comfortable position so that I could rest. I concluded that I am being punished for something, but I don't know what. Within several days I am removed from the leg irons and handcuffs and can move around in my 7' X 7' cell.

During the time I was experiencing the most discomfort, I reasoned that we POWs should have a special song that reflected what was happening to us on a daily basis. First, I worked on a set of lyrics that might be appropriate. I did not have paper or pencil so I had to compose and memorize. Now this sounds simple enough, but I found myself making changes several times each day. Finally the words took shape, and then I started searching for a melody line. My guess is that it took me at least 3 months to get to this point. The good news was that I did not have a deadline I was trying to meet.

I was enough of a musician to have plenty of melodies flowing through my mind. I just needed to find or create one that fit best. I also found that as I experimented with the melody, I had a tendency to modify the lyrics. I can't tell anyone how frustrating this is, but I am certain that Rodgers and Hart would understand completely.

Almost as important to professionals is the rhyming scheme. Oh, how I wanted a dictionary or some type of special book to make this task easier! But alas, it is just me, my memory, my knowledge and my ability to put it all together. A daunting task to say the least!

I suppose the fact that I had played in marching bands in high school and college led me to a melody that had a cadence to it. Hup, two, three, four type beat. This was also closely woven into the military regimen I had received at the Citadel, and my melodies seemed to flow in that direction. I kept coming back to something like "Onward Christian Soldiers" and the silent drum beat that seemed to move that melody along. I was getting close, but Christmas passed by, and finally I am back in a big cell with a lot of other "criminals." I now had an opportunity to turn my "dream" into reality!

It wasn't long before "The Music Man" was asked to put a choir together for the sole benefit of our own POW group. Our task would be to provide music for our own church services and also for our patriotic services. Even there in prison we chose to separate the two.

I suppose there are those who would say that I was a purist or perfectionist in that I just did not want a group who could only sing the melody. I wanted a real choir. In order for me to have that level of singing for my fellow mates, I was going to have to write and compose songs with at least 4 parts—like a Barber Shop Quartet.

Obviously, I could not ask our captors for paper and pencil and straight edge so I could write music for us to sing in our cell. My Dad used to say, "Necessity is the Mother of invention." I needed paper, so I got my mates to donate some of their toilet paper to my project. I needed a pen, so I found a nice "Shaffer" fish bone in my next fish dinner. Now I needed ink. I found that diarrhea pills, when mashed up into powder and water added, made great ink for my Shaffer fish bone pen! Finally, I needed a straight edge. So I found a small limb from a tree and honed it down on the cement floor until it was flat and rectangular. I am now ready to begin my music publishing business in a cell in Hanoi!

I think the very first arrangement I did was, "Lord, Guard and Guide The Men Who Fly." This was the same melody for The Air Force Hymn and also The Navy Hymn. It is also in your local Protestant Hymnal with different lyrics. I had been the first Protestant Choir Director at the new Air Force Academy when it opened at Lowery AFB in June of 1955. I had the choir memorize all the 4 parts to this hymn so I had it locked in my memory.

Musical composition was not one of my strong suits, but I knew enough about the various key signatures to determine what key a song was in. Getting this 4-part hymn on paper gave me the guide I needed to write any song.

1. Write the melody.
2. Write the tenor or harmony part.
3. Write the bass (this was easy for me because I am a bass singer and can easily hear what that part should be).
4. Give the baritone the notes that will make the harmony complete.

Now, after putting the notes on paper, with the help of a straight edge for drawing the Treble and Bass clefs and deciding what key I would use, I would write the specific notes for the melody and the other 3 parts.

Somehow, one of my cellmates had a metal cup he used for drinking water. I reasoned—when thumped—it gave off a b-flat sound. Now I had my own pitch pipe to get us started on any song—sacred music, hymns, and then into patriotic and secular music. I even tried my hand at Four Freshmen arrangements, including "Angel Eyes!" Now it was time to get our POW Hymn on paper and let the troops hear it in concert.

I had not planned on having to change it very much after listening to it in my mind for months. But putting it on paper was another dimension that caused me to have to finesse certain parts. I already had 10-12 singers to work with, and I was like a cat on a hot tin roof to teach this to the group and then perform it for the entire cell.

I had already done an arrangement of The Star Spangled Banner that even blew me away with pride and tears as we sang it one Sunday for the patriotic event. I could not keep my guys' voices down because all the pent-up emotion of being an American seemed to erupt in their voices. Other cells heard it and popped to attention amid much applause at the "Home of the Brave" ending. Wow! I could be put in prison for this.

Then I thought, *Hell, I already am in prison!*

I rehearsed my group in the latrine area because it did give some privacy, and lessened the noise factor, which was important in keeping the guards out of our hair. I could not believe that these men could sing so well and catch on so quickly to new tunes, different parts, and blend so well. The Mormon Tabernacle Choir could not out-sing this group—because their very lives were a part of every note we sang!

If you are a downed fighter pilot in a cell in Hanoi, how do you react and respond to this song, your song:

> *O God, to Thee we raise this prayer, and sing from within these foreign prison walls.*
> *We're men who wear the gold and silver wings, and proudly heed our nation's call.*

Give us strength to withstand all the harm that the hand of our enemy captors can do.

To inflict pain and strife and deprive every life of the rights they know well we are due.

We pledge unswerving faith and loyalty to our cause, America and Thee! Amen!"

I will have to admit that the response from an audience was most spectacular in 1973 at the Nixon White House Dinner. The message, the melody, the harmony, and the sincerity of the singers made this event even more wonderful that it was designed to be. I, as the writer/composer/director, could not have been more pleased and proud of the All American group standing in front of me.

This is a song about love—love of country and of your fellow mates. It is a song of remembrance—remembering how being a citizen of the greatest nation the world has ever seen is not always easy. It is a song of duty—to serve our country and our fellow citizens, and to preserve the freedom and liberty that has been passed down to us. Finally, it is a song of sacrifice—some give their very lives for it. Others pay a price that is sometimes too much to imagine, but it takes all this to keep our nation alive and well.

"To be born in freedom is an accident,
To live in freedom a struggle,
But to die in freedom is an obligation."

May we and future Americans be willing to meet this obligation.
God Bless America!

(50.1) *Quincy sings "O Holy Night" with the help of other POW Choir members (1967).*

(50.2) *The Infamous "Rabbit" peers from above as we sing a carol.*

51
Fred Astaire in Hanoi

The Fred Astaire Studio at the Hilton in Hanoi was first located at a POW camp out from the city. In "POW" land you were never quite certain who might be your cell-mate from day to day because we were never certain who might be the "bad ass" on any given day and be moved into your cell. So here I am trying to identify the date of an event that took place probably 54 years ago.

The scene was at "The Zoo", an American POW camp on the out skirts of Hanoi. There were about 175 American Airmen incarcerated there in approximately 9 buildings. At the time we knew where every-one was housed and in what cell. It was important to keep up with this kind of information even though communicating data was very difficult in this camp. In my cell were 3 of us: Norman McDaniel, a black USAF electronics officer who happened to be a fellow North Carolinian and graduated from college at NC A&T in Greensboro. Over time, Norm became a life-long friend along with his wife Carol. They now live in the Burlington, NC area. And then there was Mike Kerr, an Air Force First Lieutenant who graduated from a small college out west and had majored in Psychology. He worked in the field of Criminology until he joined an aircrew unit and was shot down like the rest of us. The three of us got along quite well considering our varied backgrounds and interests.

A heated Sunday afternoon discussion changed all that. The outside temperature and the resulting boiling hot cell sweatbox was certainly an element in the cause-and-effect of that moment. Outside must have been way over 100 degrees causing complete misery to us inside a cell with no ventilation, no windows, and no holes to the outside. It was like being inside a pan on the stove with a top on the pot. We were miserable and sweating like a tree in a rain forest. How long must we endure this hell that surrounds us every minute of every day?

Each of us was issued a cotton uniform type shirt and pants—one size fits all—and that was it! There was no decision to make as far as what to wear was concerned, and in this situation our clothing was as wet as if a bucket of water had been poured on us. If hell was this hot then I was going to try to be a nice guy for the rest of my life so as to qualify for the other place! We could take off the shirt until a guard opened the peephole in our door, then he would order us to put it back on. And so it went, day after day after day until you thought you couldn't take it anymore, but we did!

Now back to the Sunday in question. The three of us were just sitting motionless, trying not to move a muscle as we talked about home, wives, kids, anything to take our minds—and hopefully our bodies—miles away from our cell and our circumstances. Mike was interested in learning how to dance as his wife loved dancing—and he had three left feet. I loved dancing myself and explained to Mike how dancing was a vertical expression of a horizontal desire.

Mike replied "What?"

Norm knew what I meant, but said nothing.

Not knowing at that time what Mike's musical knowledge was, I quizzed him on rhythm and beat and asked if he could feel anything when listening to a song—slow or fast. He looked at me like I had just quoted Einstein's theory of relativity and asked him to respond! At least I now knew the extent of his musical background—a big zero! Talking made us perspire even more so we both shut down for a few minutes and just sat there quietly sweating.

Finally, Mike spoke up and posed a very interesting question. "Can you teach me to dance"?

The first vision that popped up in my mind was a guard opening the peephole in the door and seeing me holding Mike! From that humble beginning I guess I could become the fairy godfather for the POWs. Damn! To go from the World's Greatest Fighter Pilot to this, all because Mike wanted to learn how to dance! I'd have to do some serious thinking about this because the consequences could lead to places I would not want to go.

Norm appeared to be in another world and not connected to us at all. It was time to get him involved!

I spoke directly to Norm, summarizing the situation and telling him of Mike's great desire to learn how to dance so that he could really surprise his wife when he was released from the Hanoi Finishing School! "Norm, our cell mate is very serious about this dance project and it would mean a lot to him if he could accomplish his goal of learning how to trip the light fantastic while here in prison. Are you willing to help?"

An uncomfortable and unaccommodating look came across his face as he looked at me as if to say, *are you crazy?* I tried to be explicit about what I thought he could do to help if I agreed to handle the dance lesson part. I asked him to hum the tunes we would use to show Mike how to hold, move, dip and the other motions involved. As cool as he could be, under the circumstances, Norm said that he wanted no part of this exercise, as it was too risky from the guard's standpoint.

All three of us then entered the discussion. Finally, it was decided that I would do the teaching and also be the orchestra. Norman would just watch and comment as he felt it necessary. Because of the guards' duties and their assigned tasks, we decided that Sunday afternoon was the best time to produce our version of "Dancing With The Stars." So the next week, the show would begin.

The next Sunday was even hotter than the one we had just endured, but "the show must go on," and so it did. I played the role of the girl and explained to Mike the importance of his hands in guiding his Lady around the floor. A push here or a tug there let her know the direction they should be heading, so we tried it. I cranked up the best arrangement I had of Ray Anthony and "Man with a Horn."

Mike immediately trounced on my toes like he was stomping out a cigarette. *WOW! This deal could qualify me for a Purple Heart!* But I tried to remain calm. I sat Mike down on his board bed and asked him if he could feel a beat to the tune I was humming. It was "A Train" by Duke Ellington. I accented every single beat to that song like a pendulum swinging back and forth. Mike sat there looking at me, but not feeling anything. I tried other tunes but to no avail. Mike simply had no rhythm and his body felt nothing. I thought, "His marriage is in trouble already, and no amount of my tutoring is going to change that!"

I ordered him to stand up and put his arms around me and listen— listen— listen! I hummed "Tenderly,"—the song, not the emotion. He seemed to do better so we made some progress that Sunday. Thank God! Mike was excited that I saw some light at the end of our dance tunnel so we talked about it all week long. Sunday arrived and it was as if Mike had had both legs amputated. Not only could he not hear my tunes and beats, he was crushing my toes to the point that I just had to quit. This Ginger Rogers was worn out and needed some serious recovery time.

It was time for a new approach and I thought I had a winner this time. I had to keep going because Mike was really into the program. He dreamed about dancing with his wife, Jerri, and damn it, I was going to make it happen for him if it was the last thing I did on this earth! Unity Before Self. That was the POW motto and it rang a bell for me. We talked all week about the NEW APPROACH and actually, we all three got excited about it. Come on Sunday. Hurry up!

Sunday was somehow slow in arriving but eventually it was here, heat and all! I explained to Mike that my New Approach was to teach him a routine so that he could move without benefit of a partner, namely me. This also eliminated the risk of being discovered "in each other's arms" by a guard.

I showed Mike the steps I wanted him to learn. The "orchestra" sat down by the dance floor and began humming some of the most famous songs ever written as my student went through the steps I was showing him. *Oh, if Gene Kelly could see me now!* As Mike twisted and turned I would correct him as necessary, but one thing was certain, Mike Kerr wanted to conquer his fear of dancing and be able to sweep Jerri off her feet.

I felt so good about being a part of that dream. Music can lift one's spirits no matter where you are and dancing while holding the one you love ain't bad either, even if you do step on her toes!

When we were released and Mike went home, Jerri had left him for someone else. I'll bet the bastard can't dance worth a damn! It must run in their family!

51.1-The Charlotte Junior League Follies showed me how Mike Kerr must have felt when eight of us tried to learn to dance and sing a number from "Hair."! (Quincy pictured front row, third from left.)

Quincy Collins

From:	NAM-POWs Corp <nam-pows@nam-powscorp.ccsend.com> on behalf of NAM-POWs Corp <tomhanton@hotmail.com>
Sent:	Saturday, August 10, 2019 2:50 PM
To:	jqccid@bellsouth.net
Subject:	Mike Kerr

From Mike McGrath..,
Hi CC:

I have been in contact with Darlene Kerr, wife of Mike Kerr. Mike has been battling bladder cancer which spread to the bones and now to the brain.

He is non-communicative and only has a few days to live. He didn't want to worry any of his old friends with his own troubles so Darlene and family followed his wishes to keep his problems within.

Mike was shot down 1-16-67 in an RF4C out of Ubon. Released 3-4-73.

Darlene has now asked me to let the NAM-POW community know Mike's condition. Plans will be made for Arlington. Here are few words from Darlene.

"Now is the time to let people know what is happening, if you would be our spokesperson, we would be honored and grateful. Especially as a family member even if it is ten times removed. He got a great kick out of that.

Michael would want you and his fellow "jailbirds" to know that he was honored and proud to have been in the company of so many admirable men.

Yesterday I was again reading the poem he has always kept by his bed, "High Flight" and remembered that in spite of the constant pain caused by his choice of profession, he felt like the luckiest guy on earth to have actually been able to do that which he dreamed of as a kid and to have served the country he adores for 32 years.

I'm going to try to dwell on those things for the next few days that I have him. You guys always talk about "flying west." Knowing Michael as I do, he'll
probably go perversely in the opposite direction as fast and low as he can!"

NAM-POWs Corp, 17 Belmeade Drive, Bluffton, SC 29910

(51.2) An email from Mike McGrath to Quincy about Mike Kerr.

52
Fate

The dictionary defines FATE as "the supposed force, principle, or power that predetermines events." I assume that fate could be a positive or negative force. It could be God-driven or Devil/evil driven—or from some type spirit floating around the planet that puts various elements together to make a single event happen. No human could possibly create such a happening. It is ethereal in nature and cannot be explained. Therefore, it is a mystery.

Besides that, it is fascinating, especially when it becomes part of an ongoing story of war and survival in the jungles of Vietnam. Let's pick a starting point and follow this mystery to see who will experience my idea of FATE.

A nurse with the Maltese Aid Service in West Germany, Monica Schwinn, volunteered to go to Vietnam to offer medical assistance to both sides of the war—a tenuous spot to be in to say the least. One sunny day Monica, a dental assistant, and three German nurses were taking pictures of the Vietnam countryside, unaware that the infamous "Tet Offensive" of the Viet Cong and the North Vietnamese was about to envelope them. Out of nowhere, 12-15 armed men surrounded the women, took them prisoner, and forced them to march from one prison area to another.

Monica witnessed three of her comrades starve to death during her 1,346 days of captivity. She spent a total of 529 days in solitary confinement in one camp alone. Normally female prisoners would have been placed in civilian internment camps. For Monica and her friends to be put in regular military prisons without food and water, and to be treated so inhumanely, shows the nature of the enemy Americans were fighting.

During this time, her captors were force-marching her group up the Ho Chi Minh Trail, getting closer to Hanoi with each move, and with each step closer to starvation. Finally, Monica was repatriated on March 5, 1973, after having been released from the Hanoi Hilton. Now the "Fate" part enters the scene.

The last camp Monica was in prior to being at the Hanoi Hilton was a small punishment camp we named Skid Row. It was unique in that individual cells were built side by side in a row, but they were elevated above the adjoining walkways and camp paths. A huge bamboo partition separated this cell area from the adjoining area that consisted of a small stand-alone building that housed a solitary cell. There were two concrete beds in the cell, built so that each bed had a wall at each end. At the entrance was a banana tree that actually had fruit on it. Monica and one of her girlfriends were housed there in the early summer of 1971.

About that same time, the Rabbit and I had butted heads over something and he had me thrown into solitary confinement. After a couple weeks of harassment, a guard walked in and motioned that I was to pack up my mat, blanket, towel and soap and stand by to move out. Later, I was blindfolded, handcuffed, and led out to a vehicle. The ride was rough, and I did not have an opportunity to move the blindfold to see where I might be going because the guard was right on top of me. Eventually the vehicle stopped, and I was led into my new "home away from home," the infamous Skid Row! When my blindfold was removed, standing there in front of me was the skinniest human being I had ever seen.

Scotty Morgan was a reconnaissance pilot whose name I knew because he had been a prisoner about as long as I had. As that first day dragged on and I could see Scotty's condition, I came to the conclusion that the Gooks wanted me to be with him so that I might be a witness to his death—and be able to verify that they were doing everything they could to keep him alive. They brought him milk, meat, fruit and other special foods, but Scotty could not keep anything in his stomach. He vomited everything he ate and drank.

I encouraged him to recycle what came up, thinking that osmosis might have a positive effect. We had a pan that we used to accomplish the recycling plan. Scotty was giving it his best shot, but I could not see any change. Was I, indeed, to become a witness to his starvation?

Meanwhile I tried to make our surroundings more pleasant, but someone had beaten me to the punch! At the foot of my concrete Beauty Rest was a drawing—a *nude* drawing of a female!

Man! I had had dreams of my cell door opening, and there to join me would be a beautiful blond fighter pilot, recently shot down and needing some personal nursing services. "My girl" wasn't real, but she would have to do! She had breasts, lips, hair, hips, legs and everything else men desire. Wow! I was almost in love. At least I was in heat, and that made me feel somewhat normal again.

I had no idea as to how this came about until I heard later about the Red Cross worker from Germany who may have been in our area as a POW. My conclusion: she drew a self-portrait on the wall to bring a poor slob like me back to life!

I now have seen a photo of Monica, and have read with a lot of interest about her captivity. We have never met and never will. She died last year. This lady provided me hours of wonderful thoughts, and activated my mind to help me through some difficult times. Fate is a wonderful partner to have.

God Bless you Monica! Look forward to seeing you in the Great Beyond!

(52.1) My "lady friend" in prison—Monica Schwinn, pictured at a 1998 NAMPOW reunion in Dallas, TX.

Monica Schwinn Bio

Name: Monica Schwinn
Branch/Rank: CIVILIAN MISSIONARY
Unit:
Date of Birth:
Home City of Record: GERMANY
Date of Loss: 27-APR-69
Country of Loss: South Vietnam
Loss Coordinates:
Status (in 1973): Returnee
Category:
Aircraft/Vehicle/Ground: Jeep
Missions:
Other Personnel in Incident: Bernhard Diehl (returnee) and 3 other missionaries, Mary Louise Kerner, Rica Kortmann and Georg Bartch (killed in captivity)
Source: Compiled by P.O.W. NETWORK from one or more of the following: raw data from U.S. Government agency sources, correspondence with POW/MIA families, published sources, interviews and CACCF = Combined Action Combat Casualty File. 2019—updated with information from various sources. REMARKS:

In the Spring of 1969, the VC picked up five W. German nurses...two male, Bernhard Diehl, Georg Bartsch, and three female: Rika Kortmann, Marie Louise Kerber, and **Monika Schwinn**. They worked for an organization called The Knights of Malta, which was established as an aid organization in the Middle Ages, under the aegis of the Roman Catholic Church. The modern Knights of Malta are much like our Red Cross, rendering aid without religious overtones. These five young, idealistic nurses were working near Danang. They were helping the Vietnamese people, regardless of ideology. Monika worked on a children's ward in Danang. They went out in the countryside for a picnic and were picked up by the VC. [I always thought they were captured by mistake, because they were Caucasians and thought to be Americans. By the time the VC realized the mistake, one had died and they couldn't afford the bad PR, so they were held until the end of the war.] The VC brought them to our camp west of Tam Ky in late spring of '69. They had been walking about a month. Marie Louise Kerber died in route, and I never knew her. Bernhard told me she died of malaria. They stayed in our camp until the fall of '69, I think November and then held in NVN until the end of the war. I saw Monika and Bernhard in the Hanoi Hilton from January to March '73 when they were repatriated. In the interim between June and November 1969, I had constant daily contact with them. They lived in a hooch next to ours with a fence intervening, and we had free access to each other. They had slightly higher rations and more medicine than we did, indicating to me that the VC realized they had screwed up by taking them.

But they were sicker and less able to cope with the environment. We tried to help them. We tried to teach them the ways of the camp, gathered wood for them, carried rice, helped them with water, washing, making fires, etc. Georg Bartsch died of a sudden pulmonary embolus in mid-summer. This was a strange death for a young man, even a captive, with Beri-Beri. Bernhard told me that Georg had rheumatic heart disease, and had fudged his physical a little to be allowed to come over. Rika (I think her real name was Henrika) Kortmann died of generalized weakness and inanition. She had malaria, malnutrition, and was terribly sick. Monika lay at death's door with Bernhard for months. He got well before she did and began to nurse her, physically and psychologically. He did physical therapy on her and helped her a great deal (her dad had been in the German Army during WW II, had been captured by the Russians and never came home).

03/18/19:

.... but I thought you might be interested in that Monika Schwinn the German nurse from the Hanoi Hilton died last Monday, aged 76.   CA

Excerpted from https://www.pownetwork.org/bios/s/sx10.htm

53
A Typical Day in a North Vietnam Prison!

There are so many directions that a typical day could go that I hesitate to try to pin down what could be called a normal day. If you were in solitary confinement that brings about a completely different set of circumstances than one in which you had a cellmate or maybe two. It also depends on the time frame of your imprisonment because the first five years or so we were either alone or with one other prisoner. Injuries also played a role in our confinement because it was easier to have another American prisoner in the same cell with an injured "piratical airman" just to help take care of the injured person. Whatever your situation, the biggest problem we had to face was losing one's freedom and also coping with the unknown. Will I die here? Does my family know that I am alive? Will I be tortured? Can I survive what lies ahead? All these thoughts run through your mind and consume your time.

There is praying, crying, pleading to God to save you, and then it dawns on you. There are others here having the same thoughts that you are having. If there is another person with you then you can discuss the situation and share your personal opinions. The main idea is that you must be able to communicate with others and establish a unity that will enforce your own will to survive. That's why communication with your fellow prisoners is so critical.

In our military system, there will always be a senior officer based on rank and or date of rank. It is his responsibility to step up to the leadership plate and be our leader. Jim Stockdale was that man for us. And he was an inspiration for us all! Upon our release from prison, Jim was awarded the Congressional Medal of Honor by President Nixon—the highest award our nation can bestow upon any person. Yes, Jim was our leader, our commander, and he directed us through some very difficult times. He deserved this recognition and we POWs will always honor him and his service to us and to America.

The night is ending and a public address system is blaring a Ho Chi Minh exercise program for all the masses outside the confines of our prison walls. This program is to keep them in shape, and also to keep everyone under the control of their Master. A light bulb is hanging from the ceiling. It is on as it always is, spreading light throughout a darkened cell. The stifling odor coming from our bucket, called a "BO," permeates the cell as the guards and camp staff began moving about the camp preparing for the day's activities.

The first order of business is breakfast. The enemy feeds us twice a day—once in the early morning and again in the afternoon. Both meals look the same, taste the same, in fact they are the same—a watery soup with no meat base and maybe a piece of a green plant floating in the soup. A ubiquitous bowl of rice always presented its own unique set of problems because a system had to be devised so that you could discover if your rice serving had a rock or stone in it. My plan was to always clear the bottom of my plate. When I could verify that it was clear, I would dip my spoon in the rice then throw it into the clear area. If it sounded like "plop" then I would feel clear to eat the rice. If it went "clang" then I would hunt the rock, throw it away then eat the rice. Every meal was an adventure!

A guard opens the cell door, points to the BO and indicates who has been selected to dump it for today. The guard takes a position as far away from the bucket as is feasible. This routine takes all of a few minutes until we start refilling the bucket because most everyone has Ho Chi Minh Revenge!

Things start to settle down for an hour or so then the rattling keys begin. The guards are instructed to bring designated prisoners into the offices of some of the English-speaking Gook officers. This is not a good place to be so anxiety sets in as the noise of keys rattling presents a disturbing element to all who can hear the sound. No one wants to go through the hassle of an interrogation with the possibility of ending up in irons, handcuffs or solitary confinement.

If you are told to do something and your response is "No," then all the above punishment probably will become a reality. Yes, sounds are important and can give a glimpse into the future. A boring day is desired over a day when you must make certain decisions that expose you to some type of punishment. Hearing keys ring from a guard walking up to your cell door is not something you look forward to!

As I said earlier, communication with other prisoners is essential if you want to remain healthy both mentally and spiritually. We used a tap code to "talk" to prisoners in the cells adjoining our own because each cell was encased and had no windows or openings to see or hear what was happening outside your own space. I have covered the tap code in another chapter and how we used it. Needless to say, this system was critical to each of us and kept us in contact with our fellow prisoners and allowed our senior officers a method to pass along official orders and other information beneficial to all of us POWs.

It was through this network that I learned all the names and ranks of every prisoner who was in my specific camp. I knew what building each man was in and who his cell mate(s) were. Just having this information was a unifying factor and made me feel that I was a part of an active American military group. In fact, our country accepted the official name that we gave ourselves—The 4th Allied POW Wing, and our motto was "To Return Home With Honor!" It was important that we acknowledge that with us were other prisoners from South Vietnam and Thailand so "Allied" was appropriate in our designation.

Most of each day's tapping was about who had been to an interrogation and what it was about. Also important was what was seen or heard on the way or returning from a fellow POW's visit with an English-speaking Gook. I learned early on that if I were allowed to be outside or visit with a Vietnamese officer, it was my duty to case the joint thoroughly for items that could give us clues as to what might be happening that might have an impact on us.

Many of us were in need of medical care and treatment, and we made it our business to keep up with each man's health status. This became especially important if the enemy decided to move us around by assigning us to other buildings with different people. There was a war going on, so we had "FNGs" joining us constantly. This stands for "frapping new guys" and they always brought news on what was happening in the world, how the war was going, what sports teams were doing, etc. All news was current news for us because we had no way of getting it.

"Hanoi Hannah" might be piped into our cells to read off the latest casualty list, what aircraft were shot down that day, and any bad news from back home like a protest march, street shootings, etc. And, of course, news came to us from the most despised woman on earth, Jane Fonda, who always told us how well we were being treated, and that we should always listen to those who had captured us because they were looking out for us.

I had never really paid much attention to those people who voiced displeasure at my service to my country. But man, I began to listen and I mean, listen carefully. Why? Because it affected my well-being and had become a sledgehammer to my patriotic body. I hated it then and I hate it now, and those who don't like America and what it stands for should get the hell out and go somewhere else. Disagree? Okay. But at least discuss it before attempting to change our culture and our history!

Afternoons were more of the same, and then another meal of soup, rice, and hot water. I was always thirsty, but boiling water did not do the trick. At least we had some liquid to drink, but early on I had to wet a small piece of cloth to wash my body. That was a lot of fun, but then I had another item to stink and draw mosquitoes. Vietnam's national emblem should be a huge mosquito sucking the blood out of a person in handcuffs and leg irons.

If you want to really punish someone or torture them slowly and deliberately, then just take the guy's net away from him and expose him to the elements. No black and blue marks from beatings. Just whelps, swelling, blood stains from smashing the bastards—and itching! Three days and nights of this and I promise that you will be receptive to doing things for the enemy that otherwise you would never do.

These are just a few of the inconveniences that we faced. Some were tougher than others, but they were designed to make it more miserable for those involved. Did I want to give up and surrender my very being to this wretched enemy who had captured me? Hell no! My main goal was to make it through whatever trial and tribulation I was in so that I could return another day to beat the bastards at their own game. This is what our senior officers advised, and I think it was correct. A lot of good Americans suffered under the hands of a despicable enemy, and those memories will last a lifetime.

Being informed by a guard that you had mail was like manna from heaven! Some guys received letters shortly after they were captured, while others rarely, if ever, got mail. I was one of those. I came to the conclusion that if there were no newsmen present when you were captured, then the Gooks felt no responsibility to account for you. That's why I was listed as MIA (Missing In Action) for about three years before my status changed to POW.

The first letter I received was after spending about a year in solitary. The letter was from my Mom and was over two years old. She mentioned that my Dad had died. What a nice message to get—especially after a punishment tour! It took five years after I was captured before I was allowed to write the standard seven-line POW letter to my family.

The first time I wrote my wife I asked her to send me a glamour photo of herself. Many guys had received this type photo from their wives and I wanted one too. Sometime later a friend of mine was called up to get mail. When he returned to the large cell we were then occupying, he told me he had seen a big envelope with my name on it. "Wow!" I thought. She got my request for a special photo and here it was! A guard called my name and off I went to receive my prize. The officer handling the mail detail evidently wanted me to wait to get my "goodie," so there I sat, looking around expectantly. Finally, he threw the envelope my way and I began opening it. As I pulled the photo out of the brown envelope I could see that the lady had on a very fashionable dark gown. It has a message written across the top of the photo.

Another POW buddy sitting next to me leaned over to get a better view and yelled for all to hear. "Is that your wife?"

I, too, was surprised—as the person smiling at me from the photo was none other than Pearl Bailey, actress, singer, writer and Hollywood personality. She had written a personal message to me with all the loves and kisses possible, and telling me how much everyone missed me. My Mom and Sister, Carolyn, had evidently gone to a book signing at Rich's Department Store in Atlanta where Pearl was appearing.

I really believe that the dumb-ass Gook officer assumed that the person in the photo was my wife. He couldn't keep his eyes off her. When I returned to my cell with the photo in hand, my cellmates went berserk over Pearl. I decided to pin my new love to my mosquito net for all to see. My final words each evening were, "Good night Pearl, wherever you are!"

Life gets interesting, doesn't it?

(53.1) Hoa Lo Prison front gate

(53.2) Aerial view of Hoa Lo Prison

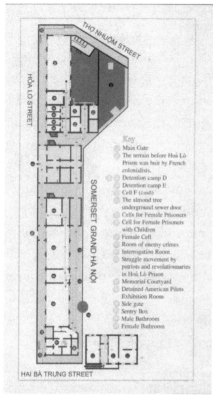

(53.3) Layout of camp

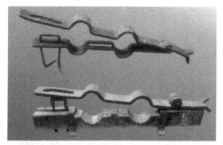

(53.5) Fetters (leg irons)

(53.4) Historic Vestige

(53.6) Head cutting machine

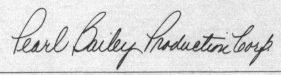

Pearl Bailey Production Corp.

P.O. BOX 52
NORTHRIDGE, CALIFORNIA 91324

PRESIDENT: PEARL BAILEY

March 14, 1973

DODI BROOKS
Executive Secretary

Dear, dear Carolyn:

Your letter so thoroughly warmed my heart – The prayers of so many people, such as yourself and your family have finally been answered – what more can be said. The poem written by your brother after he learned of the passing of your Dad is so beautiful and full of warmth.

I'm so happy your brother enjoyed the picture I had sent. Please see that he gets the enclosed books. I do hope he enjoys reading them.

My love and prayers to all of you and thank you for taking the time to write to me.

All love,

Pearl Bailey

PB/db

(53.7) Letter from Pearl Bailey to sister Carolyn

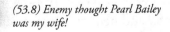

(53.8) Enemy thought Pearl Bailey was my wife!

54
Infection in Prison

Have you ever just sat around waiting for something to happen? Maybe you have put all of your ducks in a row and have made all the arrangements you can possibly make to achieve a desired result. Now you are sweating it out as time ticks away, and you seemingly have no control over when or what will happen. A lot of life seems to fall under this type scenario and all of us become spectators to activities pertinent to our own personal lives. I hate this routine as it lessens the importance of one's own individual talents and personal drives, and throws the results to the wind to blow where fate decides to take it.

As I sit in my prison cell, cowering to every prison noise that thumps on my eardrum, my life seems to be floating away without direction or purpose. How can I regain control? What can I do to enhance the predictability of my life and of being a free man again?

This may sound a bit naïve, so let's get down to real life. I am in an enemy prison with no rights of my own, and I have strange and unpredictable things happening to me and my body—health-wise. I do not know what to do. Medical treatment is on a par with Civil War medicine in the U.S., and neither Captain Marvel nor Superman are here to carry me to a medical center that can help me. Two occasions have faced me and caused me to ponder what I should or can do to alleviate the medical problem disrupting my body and mind. Let me explain.

I am at the Zoo. My cellmate is AJ Myer. We are both on crutches. AJ has a cast molded around his injured foot and ankle, and it has turned red from internal bleeding, and smells as a result of decaying tissue and blood. I am trying hard to be of help to AJ, and I suppose that I am achieving that to a small degree. But now another unknown has blown my way—pneumonia! At least that is what we think it is, as all the observable symptoms point in that direction.

Coughing out the gazoo, inflammation in my lungs and sinuses, and a heavy fever. We called for the camp medics, and they descended on me like Hitler on Poland—with about the same results. Yes, I did display all the symptoms of pneumonia, but did they have a treatment available to help me? I could tell that my lungs were filling up with mucus and that I should try with all my might to keep my breathing tract clear. AJ was doing his best to keep me upright so that my breathing would be as normal as possible. It was about time for the incompetent medical team to come to my rescue, and sure enough here they were—white robes and plenty of needles.

Several vials of a dark brown fluid appeared and the lettering on the outside of the vials indicated that the medicine was from Russia. How calming to me! The first shot was in the muscle of my right forearm, and the lady who delivered this blow looked like she could have been a Vietnamese Sumo Wrestler. But that wasn't the worst part of it. The injection was quite easy, but as soon as she put the pressure on the plunger to push that brown stuff into the muscle, I came unglued!

"My God!" I yelled. "This is so painful that I can't stand it anymore."

She stopped, stepped back a step or two and left the needle hanging there in my arm. The residual pain kept me in a grimace until my body started shaking. The nurse started talking to me in Vietnamese and using gestures that indicated if I wanted to get well there was a price to pay. With that last motion she pushed hard on the needle and plunger to get the balance of the brown stuff into my arm. By this time several medical goons were holding me in place as this medical torture was really getting to me.

Finally she withdrew the needle and stopped the flow of the medicine. It took fifteen to twenty minutes before the pain subsided and the traveling medical circus left my cell. My heart was pounding out of my chest as AJ started talking to me to soften the blow that I had just endured.

Now my thoughts settled on the big question—when would they be back? I prayed. "Oh God, please keep me safe."

It was several days later when the results really became known and visible for all to see. The site where my glorious Vietnam heavyweight nurse or doctor, or whatever she was, had stabbed me with that huge needle and forced that horrible brown stuff into my arm, was now swollen beyond belief and throbbed with every heartbeat. At the top of the swollen mass was a big pimple-looking growth complete with pus. Obviously this thing had become infected and was going to cause me a lot of pain and concern as time moved along.

By the next morning my internal alarms began going off because red lines were forming and working their way down my arm and horizontally towards my heart.

"Good God! This is serious and could kill me. Does this novice medical team understand the results of these red lines streaming from the infected area?"

My concern is showing up in the form of huge beads of sweat and a fevered brow. My body is telling me that something is wrong and I had better get help—and soon.

Evidently I began to lose consciousness as AJ began yelling for help. The Vietnamese word we were told to use is "Bao Cao." AJ's nickname was "The Bear" because he was a big guy with very broad shoulders and a deep booming voice. Once he started yelling, people started moving toward our cell. I felt so fortunate to have AJ as my cellmate and friend. Right now he might be the difference in my getting assistance, and having a horrible consequence. We had had many discussions about helping each other in times of urgent need, and man, this certainly was one of those times.

The medical people seemed to realize the seriousness of the situation, and also that they were overwhelmed with what to do. Shortly a gurney arrived and I was loaded aboard and put in the back of a Russian jeep. There appeared to be some reason for haste as everyone moved at top speed, including the trip to the hospital. I was quickly carried into a corridor as the sun began to sink in the west.

The jabbering amongst the medical workers was driving me nuts as I was constantly trying to determine what was about to happen. Eventually a calm came over the chaos. I was moved to the center of the stage, and trays on mobile tables were pushed to either side of me. I saw all the instruments that were to be used in doing whatever was to be done.

Medical people with masks started to get closer and take positions that indicated their work was about to begin. I noted one man had opened his hand and a nurse had placed a knife in it. He came closer and closer until I sat up and yelled. "No! No! I need something for pain!"

He seemed startled, but spoke to another person who stepped closer and rubbed something that smelled like ether on a gauze pad all over my swollen arm. It was cooling and seemed to lessen any feeling I had in that part of my body. I looked directly at the doctor holding the knife and he moved in closer to do his job.

He approached my arm like a golfer addressing the ball, and then motioned three of his muscle men to take their positions to hold this tiger down. He made an incision about three inches long and the infected area exploded right in his face. It sounded like a rocket firing, complete with the recoil associated with a shotgun blast. Not only that, but a big glob of pus and tissue hit the wall beyond the group gathered around me.

All of them began to wipe their faces and reach for masks to replace the ones that they were wearing. There was an odor that was sickening. The entire medical group began to move back and away from me—the originator of all this nasty infectious residue.

My yells of pain might have also helped them move back. I used every muscle in my vocal cords to relay the pain I felt. I was waiting for stitches, etc., but none came. My wide-open gash was left open to drain as it might. My American doctors informed me years later that this was the best thing they did for me. It allowed all the bad stuff to drain away and free me from further infection. I was returned to my cell at the Zoo, and AJ wanted to know what had happened—every step of the way.

We watched it heal over the ensuing weeks without any complications. God has created a magnificent machine that we call our body. Thank you Lord!

Now spring is coming. The biting cold has evolved into warmth and I find myself alone again. My friend AJ has been moved, probably so that a POW in better health than I am can take care of him and his needs. I guess they thought that I could make it on my own. Being alone is not so bad, especially if it is for a short duration. But I had no idea how that thought would play out. Several weeks later I would have a better feel for this.

In the meantime, I continued on with my daydreams and mental thrusts into the past to pass the time. I thought of my two Citadel roommates, Jim Black from Greer, SC, and Tom Peterson from Marlin, Texas. Great guys, friends, and confidants. And where are they when I need them most?

I remember a song Tom used to sing:
When the ice melts off the trees
And the wind blows through my BVDs
It's springtime in Charleston!
I chuckled over the lyrics, as they seemed to be appropriate for the time and place.

My arm is no longer a concern as it appears to be healed now. But last night was not fun. A sharp headache awakened me and I became nauseous. I had no idea as to the cause of this condition, so I decided to give it another twenty-four hours to develop or just go away. My headache came on full-time and I started vomiting. That really got my attention, so I yelled, "Bao Cao!" and asked for medical care.

One of the camp's Practice Doctors arrived and poked around my stomach area after taking my temperature and checking inside my mouth. He left for about an hour and returned with the magic potion that was to cure my malady. He showed me a bottle of huge pink pills that, again, had a Russian prescription written on the bottle.

I thought, "Oh hell! What am I about to expose myself to now?"

The doctor poured two of these King Kong torpedoes into his hand and gave them to me to swallow. Down they went with all the coughing and gagging I could muster. I admit that at this point my mental status was not very positive. So I prayed for a calm to come over me, and I also prayed for sleep. I received both, and soon drifted into the land of dreams.

During the night I awakened with a jolt that found me throwing up, and a back pain that made me cry. My lips didn't feel right, and that eternal headache was back.

"What else can go wrong?" I wondered.

My lips were swollen to an unbelievable size, and I was slobbering like a horse after a race. It was still dark, so I decided to wait until the gong went off signifying it was time to get up. Finally the gong shattered the silence of the night and our POW world started moving.

I rose up from my concrete mattress and felt that I needed to relieve myself. Little did I realize what was in store for this Fighter Pilot from Concord, NC. I lifted off the top of my Bo, dropped my PJ trousers, and began to urinate. I just about passed out because all I could see was pure blood streaming into the can.

I thought, "What the hell is going on? Could this be real blood, or is it the color of my urine from those huge pills I took?"

The back pain I was experiencing led me to conclude that this was a kidney problem. Either way, I needed help. So "Bao Cao!" again echoed from my prison cell. A brand new Practice Doctor appeared. I will have to admit that this fellow checked everything before reaching a conclusion and then treating me.

Looking back, I think he reached the same conclusion I had: my kidneys were the culprits. By this time every organ in my body hurt, and I felt I just wanted to die. How can I get some relief from all the pain I am experiencing?

My doctor seems to have an idea, and sent for his assistant to bring what he needs to help me. By this time I am open to anything that might help. My head hurts, and my back area—probably my kidneys—are about to drive me wild. I am still peeing pure blood. Finally the assistant arrives with a big needle and a vial that read Novocain.

I thought, "What the hell is he going to do with this stuff? How is he going to use this painkiller to treat my problem?"

I didn't have to wait long to discover the answer to that question. The Practice Doctor and his Practice Assistant turned me over on my stomach, pulled my clothes away from my torso, and rubbed alcohol over my back area next to my kidneys. Two other Vietnamese guards held me down as they stuck the needle full of Novocain directly into the small of my back and emptied it there. I immediately felt better, and very shortly the back pain disappeared. But it took a week for my lips to return to normal size and the blood in my urine to go away.

Damn! No matter where you are, ain't medical science wonderful? Especially if you have faith in God!

55
Mike Christian Story

Here is something I remember—vividly. At the Hanoi Hilton, we stood every morning and recited the Pledge of Allegiance to a bare prison wall. Mike Christian, a Navy jock and fellow choir member, decided we needed a real flag, so he began the task. It took him weeks and weeks to get something that looked close to the flag—but he finally did it—and we pledged to a real flag.

During a sneak inspection, the guards found the flag in Mike's space. They brutally dragged him from our cell and beat and tortured him in an adjoining cell where every scream of pain could be heard by all of us.

Finally, the next day, they dumped Mike back into our cell, and we did what we could to help him recover. He finally opened his eyes and proudly announced, "It's time for flag #2!"

My friend Mike is now deceased—the victim of drugs and a fire that took this beautiful human being away from us. But every time I see Old Glory I think of Mike—his dedication to his country, to his fellow POWs, and his love for our flag.

In honor of Mike, and in honor of a great group of men who learned about freedom the hard way and we will never, ever, forget—allow me now to speak to you as the voice of Old Glory.

I AM "OLD GLORY!"

I am the flag of the United States of America. My name is *Old Glory*. I fly atop the world's tallest buildings. I stand watch in America's Halls of Justice. I fly majestically over great institutions of learning. I stand guard with the greatest military power in the world.

Look up and see me!

I stand for peace—honor—truth and justice. I stand for freedom. I am confident—I am resolved—I am proud.

When I am flown with my fellow banners, my head is a little higher—my colors a little truer—I bow to no one!

I am recognized all over the world. I am respected—I am loved—*and I am feared!* And when attacked, my goal is victory.

I have fought in every battle of every war for more than 200 years: Gettysburg; San Juan Hill; the trenches of France; the Argonne Forest; Anzio; Rome; the beaches of Normandy; Guam; Okinawa; Japan; Korea; Vietnam; in the Persian Gulf; and a score of places long forgotten by all but those who were there with me . . . *I was there!*

I led my soldiers, sailors, airmen and marines. I followed them and watched over them. They loved me.

I was on a small hill in Iwo Jima. I was dirty, battle-worn and tired. But my soldiers cheered me! And I was proud!

I have been soiled, burned, torn, and trampled on in the streets of countries I have helped set free. But it does not hurt—*for I am invincible!*

I have flown over the rubble in New York City after a dastardly attack on America and the Free World, where thousands of my citizens perished—and that does hurt. And my men and women fighting to free Iraq are meeting resistance both on the battlefield and at home.

But I shall overcome—for I am stronger than the terrorist cowards and dictators who have now sealed their own fate—*Defeat!* And mark my word—*we will not fail.*

I have been a silent witness to all of America's finest hours, and I now see America divided as never before. But my finest hour comes when I am torn in strips to be used as bandages for my wounded comrades on the field of battle; when I fly at half-mast to honor my soldiers, my sailors, my airmen, my marines, firemen, policemen, and medical workers; and when I lie in the trembling arms of a grieving mother at the graveside of her *fallen son.*

America, I am proud to be your flag and your banner for freedom. My name is *Old Glory*. Long may I wave, dear God, long may I wave!

(55.1) Two items that impacted me the most upon my release from prison was the American Flag and the Golden Gate Bridge! Damn, it's great to be back home!

56
My Friends—My Dogs

The camp was quiet. Very quiet. No prisoner screams or guards yelling to force some American Fighter Pilot to do something like bowing to a Vietnamese chicken or another guard. These had become the standard sounds in our POW world.

But wait—what was that? Was it really a bark or a sound like a bark? I edged over by my cell door and pressed my ear close to the doorframe and listened. Damn! It *was* the bark of a dog. Wait a minute. There was more than one dog, and they were running around chasing each other. These didn't sound like big dogs that might be used by the guards to keep us prisoners in line. These barks were from smaller dogs that don't herd sheep or goats or cattle or American prisoners. My thoughts ran wild for a moment that they might even be tonight's dinner—or at least a part of the horrible soup we were being fed. That made the most sense!

I shuffled back to my concrete bunk and sat down for a moment. Some recollections started darting through my mind—recollections of dogs I had as a kid on through my current Dachshund twin miniatures back home in Japan. Of course, I had to get rid of the food idea because that was a real obstacle to the clarity of my recollections.

The first canine I can recall in our household was a fairly large Spitz named Spot, white and fluffy with a black spot between his eyes. Spot was too energetic for a kid my size to handle. We lived on Hillcrest Drive in Concord, NC, and the red hills that surrounded us came into our home as stains on our fluffy mutt. After playing with Spot for an hour, the red hue spread to every part of my body and I would look like an Indian—native that is—and it would take a good scrubbing to reveal who I really was. Spot was my buddy, and we loved each other dearly. Fortunately, I don't remember the end of our relationship. I guess it's just as well.

In about 1940-41, Dad had purchased a number of acres of farmland about ten miles east of where we lived on Hillcrest Drive. He built an eight-acre lake with a nice summer home on it. On the main road by the farm he built a big barn, stables for several horses and a pony, and all the attachments required to raise hogs, sheep, goats, chickens, and white-faced cattle. Dad was reproducing where he had grown up near Elko, SC.

That was also going to include Rex, a hunting dog that would also substitute as a four-legged companion for me. Rex and I became good friends. My primary job was to wash Rex and rid him of the ticks he would accumulate from running through the woods and thickets. I soon became tired of this relationship (and chore) and turned my attention to cars, music, and girls.

After I married Nancy, we became the owners of a dachshund we named Wee Willie Wilhelm—Willie for short. He became our best friend and did everything with us, even slept at the foot of our bed. By this time JQC III, alias Chip, had been born and Willie became his watchdog. When a babysitter had to change Chip's diaper, she had to take Chip into another room and close the door, or else Willie would have a fit and bark his head off.

During the time I was attending Command and Staff College at Maxwell AFB In Montgomery, AL, a dear friend called Nancy to borrow some chairs for bridge and had her husband Hank drive over to get them.

Yes, it really happened! He backed over Willie. Nancy put in an emergency call to me at the college to ask that I come home. I did, and took care of burying Willie. Man! That hurt!

In early 1965, we arrived at Yokota AB Japan to fly F-105s. By this time we had three little monkeys running around the house—Chip, Chuck and Corky. Everyone wanted a dog, so we brought a set of twin Dachshunds. One was named Willie, but I don't remember the name of the other one.

NOTHING HAPPENED TO THE dogs, but the "Big Dog" (me) got shot down and captured, and that sort of ended the entire story—until I returned to the USA in 1973 and eventually married Catherine!

Then life really began for me!

57
The Last Days in Prison

Hanoi Hannah announced that our Secretary Of State, Kissinger, was in Paris talking......talking......talking, but said nothing about who might be listening! B-52 bombings seemed to be hour after hour, day and night, and carpet-bombing appeared to be edging closer and closer to our cells. We had received orders from our superior POW officers to play it cool and keep a low level of response to what was happening.

What our President had ordered our Air Force and Navy to do was what should have been happening eight years ago! LBJ was a real loser, but thought he was a master planner for winning the war. President Nixon did not want to make the same mistakes, so we showed the enemy what "force" was all about.

In his writings after the war, Gen. Giap, the chief military man in North Vietnam, said that the U.S. quit too soon, as they, North Vietnam, were getting ready to throw in a white surrender towel. In other words—an unconditional surrender—which is what we really wanted in the first place. This situation could only exist when our American citizens were so tired of war that they would give away anything to end the war.

Meanwhile, back at the ranch, we POWs were as antsy as could be. One day the guards opened up all of our cells, instructed us to get into our cleanest and best POW garb and form outside in a military formation. This had never happened before, but as we gathered outside we saw lots of cameras and TV sources. The word spread quickly that this was the announcement we were all waiting to hear. THE PARIS PEACE ACCORDS HAD BEEN SIGNED and we were going to hear about how we were leaving this dirty, rotten prison and when! No one was to show excitement or real interest in this staged affair. Just be calm and listen.

His Excellency, the Rabbit, got on stage and tried to stir us up, but to no avail. He then read from a copy of the Accords, but since he was speaking in "Gook" no one batted an eye. Our Senior officers had been replaced by the most Junior officers, but the Juniors only took orders from their American Seniors.

Finally, the Rabbit said he would now speak in English and off he went. The basic information was that C-141 aircraft would fly into Gia Lam airport, outside Hanoi, over the next few weeks to pick up teams of prisoners and take them to Clark Air Base for recovery to the U.S. That was all we needed and wanted to know—*WE WERE ON THE WAY HOME!*

When the Rabbit dismissed us, evidently they thought we might be hard to handle, but there was not a single yell or exclamation made by any American. We simply walked back to our big cells, went in, they closed the big iron gates, and then *ALL HELL TORE LOOSE* as we let our pent-up feelings overflow!

We had discussed for weeks how our final release would go. Some thought a big ship full of nurses and doctors would dock close by and we would sail away for home with lots of champagne and pretty nurses. Others envisioned a meeting place like Saigon where airplanes would take us all to pre-sanctioned destinations. Some even guessed it would happen just like we were briefed. I didn't really care—a goat pulling a cart would be fine with me! Just get on with it!

Hanoi Hannah had been reporting on the progress in Paris, but most of her commentary was on whether they should have a circular table or a rectangular one. We didn't give a damn if they even had a table. Just get us out of Hanoi and back to the good old USA! The Rabbit tried to read the "Accords" like they were God's "Last Will and Testament". So that you, the reader, can get an appreciation for this document, I will reproduce it for your intellectual satisfaction. Here is The Paris Peace Accords!

(Text of the Agreement signed by the Democratic Republic of Viet Nam and the United States)

PROTOCOL
TO THE AGREEMENT OF ENDING THE WAR AND RESTORING PEACE IN VIET NAM CONCERNING
THE RETURN OF CAPTURED MILITARY PERSONNEL AND FOREIGN CIVILIANS AND CAPTURED AND DETAINED VIETNAMESE CIVILIAN PERSONNEL

The Government of the Democratic Republic of Viet Nam, with the concurrence of the Provisional Revolutionary government of the Republic of south Viet Name.

The Government of the United States of America, with the concurrence of the Government of the Republic of Viet Nam,

In Implementation of the provisions of Article 8 of the Agreement on Ending the War and Restoring Peace in Viet Nam, signed this date providing for the return of captured military personnel and foreign civilians, and captured and detained Vietnamese civilian personnel,

Have agreed as follows:

(Text of the Agreement signed by the Parties participating in the Paris Conference on Viet Nam)

PROTOCOL
TO THE AGREEMENT ON ENDING THE WAR
AND RESTORING PEACE IN VIET NAM
CONCERNING
THE RETURN OF CAPTURED MILITARY PERSONNEL
AND FOREIGN CIVILIANS AND CAPTURED AND
DETAINED VIETNAMESE CIVILIAN PERSONNEL

The Parties participating in the Paris Conference on Viet Nam,

In implementation of the provisions of Article 8 of the Agreement on ending the War and Restoring Peace in Viet Nam, signed this date providing for the return of captured military personnel and foreign civilians and captured and detained Vietnamese civilian personnel.

Have agreed as follows:

The Return of Captured Military Personnel
And Foreign Civilians

Article 1

The parties signatory to the Agreement shall return the captured military personnel of the parties mentioned in Article 8 (a) of the Agreement as follows:

-- All captured military personnel of the United States and those of the other foreign countries mentioned to in Article 3 (a) of the Agreement shall be returned to United States authorities.

-- All captured Vietnamese military personnel, whether belonging to regular or irregular armed forces, shall be returned to the two South Vietnamese parties; they shall be returned to that South Vietnamese party under whose command they served.

Article 2

All captured civilians who are nationals of the United States or of any other foreign countries mentioned to in Article 3 (a) of the Agreement shall be returned to United States authorities. All other captured foreign civilians shall be returned to the authorities of their country or nationality by any one of the parties willing and able to do so.

Article 3

The parties shall today exchange complete lists of captured persons mentioned in Articles 1 and 2 of this Protocol.

Article 4

(a) The return of all captured persons mentioned in Articles 1 and 2 of this Protocol shall be completed within sixty days of the signing of the Agreement at a rate no slower than the rate of withdrawal from South Viet Nam of United States forces and those of the other foreign countries mentioned in Article 5 of the Agreement.

(b) Persons who are seriously ill, wounded or maimed, old persons and women shall be returned first. The remainder shall be returned either by returning all from one detention place after another or in order of their dates of capture, beginning with those who have been held the longest.

Article 5

The return and reception of the persons mentioned in Articles 1 and 2 of this Protocol shall be carried out at places convenient to the concerned parties. Places of return shall be agreed upon by the Four-Party Joint Military Commission. The parties shall ensure the safety of personnel engaged in the return and reception of those persons.

Article 6

Each party shall return all captured persons mentioned in Articles 1 and 2 of this Protocol without delay and shall facilitate their return and reception. The detaining parties shall not deny or delay their return for any reason, including the fact that captured persons may, on any grounds, have been prosecuted or sentenced.

The Return of Captured and Detained Vietnamese Civilian Personnel

Article 7

(a) The question of the return of Vietnamese civilian personnel captured and detained in South Viet Nam will be resolved by the two South Vietnamese parties on the basis of the principles of Article 21 (b) of the Agreement on the Cessation of Hostilities in Viet Nam of July 20, 1954, which reads as follows:

> "The term 'civilian internees' is understood to
> mean all persons who, having in any way contrib-
> uted to the political and armed struggle between
> the two parties, have been arrested for that rea-
> son and have been kept in detention by either
> party during the period of hostilities."

(b) The two South Vietnamese parties will do so in a spirit of national reconciliation and concord with a view to ending hatred and enmity in order to ease suffering and to reunite families. The two South Vietnamese parties will do their utmost to do so within ninety days after the ceasefire comes into effect.

(c) Within fifteen days after the cease-fire comes into effect, the two South Vietnamese parties shall exchange lists of the Vietnamese civilian personnel captured and detained by each party and lists of the places at which they are held.

Treatment of Captured Persons
During Captivity

Article 8

(a) All captured military personnel of the parties and captured foreign civilians of the parties shall be treated humanely at all times, and in accordance with international practice.

They shall be protected against all violence to life and person, in particular against murder in any form, mutilation, torture and cruel treatment, and outrages upon personal dignity. These persons shall not be forced to join the armed forces of the detaining party.

They shall be given adequate food, clothing, shelter, and the medical attention required for their state of health. They shall be allowed to exchange post-cards and letters with their families and receive parcels.

(b) All Vietnamese civilian personnel captured and detained in South Viet Nam shall be treated humanely at all times, and in accordance with international practice.

They shall be protected against all violence to life, and person, in particular against murder in any form, mutilation, torture and cruel treatment, and outrages against personal dignity. The detaining parties shall not deny or delay their return for any reason, including the fact that captured persons may, on any grounds, have been prosecuted or sentenced. These persons shall not be forced to join the armed forces of the detaining party.

They shall be given adequate food, clothing, shelter, and the medical attention required for their state of health. They shall be allowed to exchange post-cards and letters with their families and receive parcels.

Article 9

(a) To contribute to improving the living conditions of the captured military personnel of the parties and foreign civilians of the parties, the parties shall, within fifteen days after the cease-fire comes into effect, agree upon the designation of two or more national Red Cross Societies to visit all places where captured military personnel and foreign civilians are held.

(b) To contribute to improving the living conditions of the captured and detained Vietnamese civilian personnel, the two South Vietnamese parties shall, within fifteen days after the cease-fire comes into effect, agree upon the designation of two or more national Red Cross Societies to visit all places where the captured and detained Vietnamese civilian personnel are held.

With Regard to Dead and Missing Persons

Article 10

(a) The Four-Party Joint Military Commission shall ensure joint action by the parties in implementing Article 8 (b) of the Agreement. When the Four-Party Joint Military Commission has ended its activities, a Four-Party Joint Military team shall be maintained to carry on this task.

(b) With regard to Vietnamese civilian personnel dead or missing in South Viet Nam, the two South Vietnamese parties shall help each other to obtain information about missing persons, determine the location and take care of the graves of the dead in a spirit of national reconciliation and concord, in keeping with the people's aspirations.

Other Provisions

Article 11

(a) The Four-Party and Two-Party Joint Military Commissions will have the responsibility of determining immediately the modalities of implementing the provisions of this Protocol consistent with – their respective responsibilities under Articles 16 (a) and 17 (a) of the Agreement. In case the military commission, when carrying out their tasks, cannot reach agreement on a matter pertaining to the return of captured personnel they shall refer to the International Commission for its Assistance.

(b) The Four-Party Joint Military Commission shall form in addition to the teams established by the Protocol concerning the ceasefire in South Viet Nam and the Joint Military Commissions, a sub-commission on captured persons, and, as required, Joint Military Teams on captured persons to assist the Commission in its tasks.

(c) From the time the ceasefire comes into force to the time when the Two Party Joint Military Commission becomes operational, the two South Vietnamese parties' delegations to the Four-Party Joint Military Commission shall form a provisional sub-commission and provisional joint military teams to carry out its tasks concerning captured and detained Vietnamese civilian personnel.

(d) The Four Party Joint Military Commission shall send Joint Military teams to observe the return of the persons mentioned in Articles 1 and 2 of this Protocol at each place in Viet Nam where such persons are being returned, and at the last detention places from which these persons will be taken to the places of return. The Two-Party Joint Military Commission shall send Joint Military teams to observe the return of Vietnamese civilian personnel captured and detained at each place in South Viet Nam where such persons are being returned, and at the last detention places from which these persons will be taken to the places of return.

Article 12

In implementation of Articles 18 (b) and 18 (c) of the Agreement the International Commission of Control and supervision shall have the responsibility to control and supervise the observance of Articles 1 through 7 of this Protocol through observation of the return of captured military personnel, foreign civilians and captured and detained Vietnamese civilian personnel at each place in Viet Nam where these persons are being returned, and at the last detention places from which these persons will be taken to the places of return, the examination of lists and the investigation of violations of the provisions of the above-mentioned Articles.

Article 13

Within five days after signature of this Protocol, each party shall publish the text of the Protocol and communicate it to all the captured persons covered by the Protocol and being detained by that party.

Article 14

The Protocol to the Paris Agreement on Ending the War and Restoring Peace in Viet Nam concerning the Return of Captured Military Personnel and Foreign Civilians and Captured and Detained Vietnamese Civilian personnel shall enter into force upon signature of this document by the Minister for Foreign Affairs of the Government of the Democratic Republic of Viet Nam and the Secretary of State of the Government of the United States of America, and upon signature of a document in the same terms by the Minister For Foreign Affairs of the Government of the Democratic Republic of Viet Nam, the Minister for Foreign Affairs of the Provisional Revolutionary Government of the Republic of South Viet Nam, the Secretary of State of the Government of the United States of America, and the Minister for foreign Affairs of the Government of the Republic of Viet Nam. This Protocol shall be strictly implemented by all the parties concerned.

Done in Paris this twenty-seventh day of January, One Thousand Nine Hundred and Seventy Three, in Vietnamese and English, The Vietnamese and English texts are official and equally authentic.

(For the Democratic Republic of Viet Nam and the
United States)

FOR THE GOVERNMENT OF THE DEMOCRATIC REPUBLIC OF VIET NAM	FOR THE GOVERNMENT OF THE UNITED STATES OF AMERICA
MINISTER FOR FOREIGN AFFAIRS	SECRETARY OF STATE

(For the Parties participating in the Paris Conference
on Viet Nam)

FOR THE GOVERNMENT OF THE DEMOCRATIC REPUBLIC OF VIET NAM	FOR THE GOVERNMENT OF THE UNITED STATES OF AMERICA
MINISTER FOR FOREIGN AFFAIRS	SECRETARY OF STATE
FOR THE PROVISIONAL REVOLUTIONARY GOVERN- MENT OF THE REPUBLIC OF SOUTH VIET NAM	FOR THE GOVERNMENT OF THE REPUBLIC OF VIET NAM
MINISTER FOR FOREIGN AFFAIRS	MINISTER FOR FOREIGN AFFAIRS

PROTOCOL

TO THE AGREEMENT ON ENDING THE WAR AND RESTORING PEACE IN VIET NAM CONCERNING THE REMOVAL, PERMANENT DEACTIVATION, OR DESTRUCTION OF MINES IN THE TERRITORIAL WATERS, PORTS, HARBORS, AND WATERWAYS OF THE DEMOCRATIC REPUBLIC OF VIETNAM

－ － － － －

The Government of the Democratic Republic of Viet Nam,

The Government of the United States of America,

In implementation of the second paragraph of Article 2 of the Agreement on Ending the War and restoring peace in Viet Nam, signed on this date,

Have agreed as follows:

Article 1

The United States shall clear all the mines it has placed in the territorial waters, ports, harbors, and waterways of the Democratic Republic of Viet Nam. This mine clearing operation shall be accomplished by rendering the mines harmless through removal, permanent deactivation, or destruction.

Article 2

With a view to ensuring lasting safety for the movement of people and watercraft and the protection of important installations, mines shall, on the request of the Democratic Republic of Viet Nam, be removed or destroyed in the indicated areas and wherever their removal or destruction is impossible mines shall be permanently deactivated and their emplacement clearly marked.

Article 3

The mine clearing operation shall begin at twenty four hundred (24.00) hours GMT on January twenty seventh, one thousand nine hundred and seventy three. The representatives of the two parties shall consult immediately on relevant factors and agree upon the earliest possible target date for the completion of the work.

Article 4

The mine clearing operation shall be conducted in accordance with priorities and timing agreed upon by the two parties. For this purpose, representatives of the two parties shall meet at an early date to reach agreement on a program and a plan of implementation. To this end:

(a) The United States shall provide its plan for mine clearing operations, including maps of the minefields and information concerning the types, numbers and properties of the mines;

(b) The Democratic Republic of Viet Nam shall provide all available maps and hydrographic charts and indicate the mined places and all other potential hazards to the mine clearing operations that the Democratic Republic of Viet Nam is aware of;

(c) The two parties shall agree on the timing of implementation of each segment of the plan and provide timely notice to the public at least forty eight hours in advance of the beginning of mine clearing operations for that segment.

Article 5

The United States shall be responsible for the mine clearance on inland waterways of the Democratic Republic of Viet Nam. The Democratic Republic of Viet Nam shall, to the full extent of its capabilities, actively participate in the mine clearance with the means of surveying, removal and destruction and technical advice supplied by the United States.

Article 6

With a view to ensuring the safe movement of people and watercraft on waterways and at sea, the United States shall in the mine clearing process supply timely information about the progress of mine clearing in each area, and about the remaining mines to be destroyed. The United States shall issue a communiqué when the operations have been concluded.

Article 7

In conducting the mine clearing operations, the US personnel engaged in these operations shall respect the sovereignty of the Democratic Republic of Viet Nam and shall engage in no activities inconsistent with the Agreement on Ending the War and Restoring Peace in Viet Nam and this Protocol. The US personnel engaged in the mine clearing operations shall be immune from the jurisdiction of the Democratic Republic of Viet Nam for the duration of the mine clearing operations.

The Democratic Republic of Viet Nam shall ensure the safety of the US personnel for the duration of their mine clearing activities on the territory of the Democratic Republic of Viet Nam, and shall provide this personnel with all possible assistance and the means needed in the Democratic Republic of Viet Nam that have been agreed upon by the two parties.

Article 8

This Protocol to the Paris Agreement on ending the War and restoring Peace in Viet Nam shall enter into force upon signature by the Minister for Foreign Affairs of the Government of the Democratic Republic of Viet Nam and the Secretary of State of the Government of the United States of America. It shall be strictly implemented by the two parties.

Done in Paris this twenty-seventh day of January, one thousand nine hundred and seventy three, in Vietnamese and English. The Vietnamese and English texts are official and equally authentic.

FOR THE GOVERNMENT
OF THE DEMOCRATIC
REPUBLIC OF VIET NAM

FOR THE GOVERNMENT
OF THE UNITED STATES
OF AMERICA

MINISTER FOR FOREIGN
AFFAIRS

SECRETARY
OF STATE

-- 11 --

Chapter VIII

THE RELATIONSHIP BETWEEN
THE DEMOCRATIC REPUBLIC OF VIET NAM
AND THE UNITED STATES

Article 21.-- The United States anticipates that this Agreement will usher in an era of reconciliation with the Democratic Republic of Viet Nam as with all the peoples of Indochina. In pursuance of its traditional policy, the United States will contribute to healing the wounds of war and to postwar reconstruction of the Democratic Republic of Viet Nam and throughout Indochina.

Article 22.-- The ending of the war, the restoration of peace in Viet Nam, and the strict implementation of this Agreement will create conditions for establishing a new, equal, and mutually beneficial relationship between the Democratic Republic of Viet Nam and the United States on the basis of respect for each other's independence and sovereignty, and non-interference in each other's internal affairs. At the same time this will ensure stable peace in Viet Nam and contribute to the preservation of lasting peace in Indochina and Southeast Asia.

(Text of the Agreement signed by the Democratic Republic
of Viet Nam and the United States)

Chapter IX

OTHER PROVISIONS

Article 23.-- The Paris Agreement on Ending the War and Lasting Peace in Viet Nam shall enter into force upon signature of this document by the Minister for Foreign Affairs of the Government of the Democratic Republic of Viet Nam and by the Secretary of State of the Government of the United States and upon the signature of a document in the office of the Minister for Foreign Affairs of the Government of the Democratic Republic of Viet Nam, the Minister for Foreign Affairs of the Provisional Revolutionary Government of the Republic of South Viet Nam, the Secretary of State of the Government of the United States and the Minister for Foreign Affairs of the Government of the Republic of Viet Nam. The Agreement and the Protocols to it shall be strictly implemented by all the parties concerned.

Done in Paris on January 27, 1973, in Vietnamese and in English. Both the Vietnamese and the English texts are official and equally authentic.

FOR THE GOVERNMENT	FOR THE GOVERNMENT
OF THE DEMOCRATIC	OF THE UNITED STATES
REPUBLIC OF VIET NAM	OF AMERICA
MINISTER FOR FOREIGN	SECRETARY
AFFAIRS	OF STATE

(Text of the Agreement signed by the parties participating
In the Paris Conference on Viet Nam)

Chapter IX

OTHER PROVISIONS

Article 23.-- This Agreement shall enter into force upon signature by plenipotentiaries of the parties participating in the Paris Conference on Viet Nam. All the parties concerned shall strictly implement this Agreement and its Protocols.

Done in Paris on January 27, 1973, in Vietnamese and in English. The Vietnamese and the English texts are official and equally authentic.

FOR THE GOVERNMENT OF THE DEMOCRATIC REPUBLIC OF VIET NAM	FOR THE GOVERNMENT OF THE UNITED STATES OF AMERICA
MINISTER FOR FOREIGN AFFAIRS	SECRETARY OF STATE
FOR THE PROVISIONAL REVOLUTIONARY GOVERN-MENT OF THE REPUBLIC OF SOUTH VIET NAM	FOR THE GOVERNMENT OF THE REPUBLIC OF VIET NAM
MINISTER FOR FOREIGN AFFAIRS	MINISTER FOR FOREIGN AFFAIRS

58
Montgomery AFB—Debriefing

The scene now shifts to Maxwell AFB in Montgomery, Alabama, where I have been sent to debrief from my 7½ years in prison in Hanoi. My wife—I should say my Ex—had arranged for me to be stationed away from the West coast where she and our three sons lived quite comfortably in a nice home purchased with all of my Air Force pay, of which she received 100% of it tax free, plus what she put into it herself.

I had no input into this arrangement for me to be assigned to bases in the eastern U.S. But by this time, after all the haggling over our marriage and my release from prison, I was defeated in my efforts. I had given up hope of ever saving our marriage and relationship. So being able to visit with my three sons became increasingly important to me.

Maxwell AFB was a place where I had been stationed many times before. I liked it and also Montgomery. This gave me some comfort, plus the fact that Mom and Sis lived in Atlanta, had met me at the airport at Maxwell when I first arrived, and would be at my home after I completed my debriefing. Dad had died while I was in prison, but at least he was alive when the USAF announced that my status had changed from Missing in Action (MIA) to Prisoner of War (POW). So this was the scene as I was adjusting to being free again.

The Department of Defense was very interested in collecting all the prisoner names we had memorized. In what time frame did we know that name? Where were we? How did we learn of the name? Etc. We gave them every piece of information we could recall about everything. It was gut-wrenching to go back and pull all that up again, but we knew we had to help compile this information. Also information about diet, medical, torture, everything!

The nicest thing we had to do was to plot out our futures. As a full Colonel with a position in the top 2% of my peers, I had an opportunity to get into a Star-producing assignment. We were told that USAF personnel would be arriving in a day or two to discuss our individual futures, so I was excited about having that time with people who could be factual about my potential in the USAF. That night, over drinks at the Officer's Club Bar, all of us criminals discussed the futures we would like. We all got a bit fuzzy at the end, but what the hell? We were free to do that now.

My appointment with my personnel specialist was at 10:00 the next morning. This was like meeting a gal you might want to date or take on a trip—only it would probably be a guy since the fighter pilot business was my line of work. At any rate, my heart was pounding as I entered the office to arrange my next assignment. I took a seat with several of my friends who were also waiting for their names to be called.

"Colonel Quincy Collins," the airman called.

I thought, *Damn, that sounds good!* When I was shot down in 1965 I was a Captain. So yes, Colonel Collins did sound great to me. I walked through the door and there facing me was a big man who stopped me right in my tracks.

It was Major Rex Merritt, with one of the biggest s...-eating grins I had ever seen! He ran over to me, hugged me and asked how I was doing.

I grabbed him by the shoulders, and looking him square in the eyes said, "Merritt, this is no time to be trying to get even with me for your dumb ass mistake at the Academy Chapel!"

He laughed, put his arm around me and said, "Colonel, that was a long time ago and I'm a lot smarter now—thanks to you." He then got down to business and asked, "What do you want to do?"

I told him that was a mighty big question and I didn't know what kinds of options I had.

Major Merritt again laughed, and then added, "Quincy, you are the 800 pound gorilla. What do you want?"

After a lot of discussion we both agreed that the National War College was the assignment that would best prepare me to make Brigadier General. Rex said he would arrange it. We shook hands, hugged again, and went our separate ways.

I had that assignment within a week. Good things can happen in a Chapel. God will see to that!

(58.1) Lt. Col. Collins arrives at Maxwell AFB to debrief from his 7 ½ years in prison in North Vietnam

(58.2) Quincy meeting an old Air Force friend upon deplaning at Maxwell AFB

(58.3) Quincy deep in thought over what lies ahead!

59
A Decision To Make

What does a person think when he looks at the program for that event and sees the names of Jesse Owens, Senator Herman Talmadge and a guy named Colonel Quincy Collins? Is this for real or is he in the wrong place? As a former POW from Vietnam, recently released, I had often found myself in the midst of important people and prestigious groups and organizations. I certainly did not consider myself in the same league with a man who physically trained daily to become one of the fastest men alive nor was I on the same level as a politician who had been elected governor and then senator from the state of Georgia, but good Lord, there I was on the same program with these notables to address the prestigious Textile Manufactures Association of Georgia. Man, I am in high cotton, to say the least, and it may well portend another important phase of my life.

I told those hundreds of listeners that day about being shot down and captured in North Vietnam, and then spending 7½ years surviving some pretty tough times. I know enough about audience behavior to realize that my story and how I was telling it had captivated this audience because their eyes were glued to mine. I had them in the palm of my hand.

Earlier, I had heard Jesse Owens tell of his Olympic training, his races, and his run-in with Hitler at the Olympics in Germany in 1936. When he finished, the audience gave him a standing ovation. Then, Senator Talmadge told some interesting and funny stories, many of them about well-known people in the audience. But Talmadge was, in effect, the association's chief lobbyist in Washington who saw to it that legislation, beneficial to these manufacturers, was passed into law. They were motivated to contribute heavily to the senator's re-election campaign and he also got a standing ovation. But how was Quincy Collins going to be received?

This event was at The Breakers Hotel in Palm Beach, Florida, in late 1973, and I was still adjusting to re-entering civilization. My wife had dumped me upon my repatriation, and I was looking for a future while getting used to people not wanting to punish me, beat me and deprive me of life itself. But I kept those considerations close to my heart, as God and I wrestled with Quincy Collins. Without a doubt, my steadfast faith in and dependence on God carried the day for me and will until my last breath on this earth. I knew the audience heard that in every sentence I uttered that day. I guess that made me a preacher by definition. So be it.

I tried to be factual and accurate in my descriptions of how we were treated, how we fought back against our captors, how our senior officers lead us through years of suffering and how our loyalty to America and to each other never faltered. We were American fighting men and damn proud of it and we would never give up. And finally, I spoke about how wonderful it was to be home again in this country established by God for all mankind. God Bless America!

I thought the building was going to collapse. The Dean Dome in Chapel Hill or Cameron Indoor Stadium at Duke could not have matched the crowd response. I could never have predicted the reaction. Wow! I was looking at men in coats and ties crying and applauding. They were looking directly at me as if I had some secret answer they were looking for. It was contagious and I openly wept in happiness and sublime appreciation. I thought, "This is as good as it gets."

Jesse Owens put his arms around me and hugged me and said,

"Thank *you*." The senator shook my hand with a powerful grip and said, "See you back in Georgia." I stood there taking this all in, and eventually I sat down and bowed my head in grateful thanks. This event was the first step in that future I was seeking because I had begun to realize the power of persuasion that was becoming a part of me and the gift of leadership that was a big piece of that package.

My confidence was soaring as I headed back to Atlanta to discover my future.

60
The Second Time Around

I spent a lot of time in Atlanta speaking to civic clubs, professional organizations, churches and schools, and frankly, this was great therapy for me. Not only was I returning to earth from nearly eight years in space, but I was also still in shock over my wife's "welcome home" announcement that we were finished as a couple. The reality that my three sons didn't know me also clawed at my heartstrings. Being rejected and alone was not in my plans. I needed to be active—speaking and traveling and meeting new people to take the wire edge off my new life style.

One day I returned home from an event to find that my old Concord buddy, Joe Propst, had left a message for me to call him. Joe had married a beautiful gal, Mary Ruth Klutz, who was a sister to one of my high school classmates. Joe and Mary Ruth were in the class behind me. He had done very well through the years managing his father's business, an ESSO petroleum distribution operation. He also owned motels, a trucking company, and lots of real estate along with a company airplane. Joe's father and my Dad were good friends, so our relationship was deep and true.

The number that Joe had left for me to call was his car phone. Very few people had car phones at that time, so this was a different kind of call for me. He was out on the highway. We picked up from the last time we were together, which was my homecoming day in Concord. He finally got to the meat of his call.

Bruton Smith, who owned the Charlotte Motor Speedway, and Humpy Wheeler, his right-hand man, wanted me to be the Grand Marshal for the 1973 World 400 at the speedway. Joe explained the overall program to me, which involved the "Gentlemen, start your engines" announcement, driving the pace car around the track to lead off the race, and visiting various VIP suites to welcome the spectators. Of course, there would also be a lot of press coverage and interviews.

Joe gave me the timeline, I accepted, and we made plans to make this a great reunion time too. I was getting excited about this event, and began making reservations to fly into Charlotte.

Joe and Mary Ruth picked me up at the Charlotte Douglas Airport, and we went straight to the speedway. Joe led me through all the places I was scheduled to go, and finally to the stage in front of something like 150,000 people. Humpy was there waiting for me. I met all the drivers, and then gave the command, "Gentlemen, start your engines!"

I literally had to run in order to get into the pace car and take my place at the head of the line of cars. We gunned the engine and started moving around the track—I mean FAST was the operative word. The percentage of incline in the turns was unbelievable. It was like looking out the window on the third floor of a building. By then, we were scalding-ass-fast and looking for the exit arrow so that the cars behind us could begin the race. We exited, and the noise of wide-open high-powered engines vibrated through our bodies as the cars sped by, gaining more and more speed with each fleeting second. Man! This was exciting!

Joe was waiting for me. We had lunch and visited a lot of VIP suites. But frankly, I don't remember a soul I met. This event was like being in the middle of a landslide—except, rather than rocks, it was people and cars. Finally I told Joe that we had better start back to the airport so I could make my connection to Atlanta. Joe and I laughed about old times as we drove along. Then he asked about my family situation. We had discussed this at my homecoming in Concord earlier, and I told him nothing had changed.

He turned to me and asked, "Are you ready to meet someone, someone very pretty—a blonde someone?"

I replied, "Tell me more, Maestro!"

You might imagine my good friend's description was somewhere between Marilyn Monroe and Jane Mansfield, only bigger! Joe saw that I was intrigued and told me that her name was Elizabeth (not her real name), and that I knew something of her family—especially her father, as he had some association with my Dad.

By this time I was fidgeting and visualizing fair-haired blonde types and was somewhat breathless over the prospect of meeting someone who was obviously attractive. Joe appreciated good-looking women, so I trusted my friend's judgment.

Joe asked, "Do you want to talk to her?"

"Heck yes!" I eagerly replied. "Dial her up."

Joe did as I instructed, and the phone began to ring. He handed me the phone and it rang another time or two.

Then a soft, lovely, very feminine voice said, "Hello."

All the visualizations I had began to take shape as I nervously started to respond. "Elizabeth, this is Quincy Collins. Joe and I are on the way to the airport. Is it convenient for you to talk right now?"

It was, so we had about a 30-minute conversation that ended with a plan to meet the following Friday at the "old coliseum" where I was to be the commencement speaker for a joint Charlotte Mecklenburg High School graduation service to be held there.

Overflowing with anticipation, I thanked Joe for introducing Elizabeth and me. I informed him that I would take it from here and let him know how it all turned out. Joe dropped me at the airport. I checked in, got on board, and flew back to Atlanta, full of emotion and possibilities and looking forward to next Friday. This Grand Marshal was truly leading the parade—maybe my luck was about to change!

Next Friday I arrived at the coliseum as nervous as a widow on her first blind date. The kids really responded to my motivational approach for them, so I was very pleased with the first part of this visit. Now for the good part! I looked around to try to identify this blonde queen that I was supposed to be meeting. I mean I cased the joint like you wouldn't believe, but nothing appeared.

Suddenly a voice said, "Quincy. Over here!"

There she was. I was more than pleased. We hugged as we said hello, held hands, and started walking to her car. This was like a dream come true, and so a new relationship began. I wanted desperately for my last love episode to fade into history as quickly as possible.

Looking back, I can see that I wanted Elizabeth to be perfect in every way—the way she looked, the way she walked, the way she talked, and the way she dressed. I saw no flaws and no weaknesses. I desired to spend as much time with her as I could, but I had a job back at Dobbins Air Force Base in Marietta, Georgia, and Elizabeth and her daughter lived in Charlotte. These were the facts of life, and we had to deal with them.

We saw each other as much as possible. She would come stay with us in Marietta. I had purchased a home by this time, and Mom and Sis lived with me. I visited my girlfriend in Charlotte and met her mother and father and got to know her daughter. I will have to truthfully say that I felt her parents and daughter did not like me—especially when thinking of their moving to Georgia if things really got serious.

On the other hand, my Mom and Sis did not think Elizabeth was the right one for me. Moms never do! This dichotomy drove me nuts, and certainly rained on my parade in trying to make future plans for us.

Finally, in 1975, we married in Elizabeth's home in Charlotte, moved to Marietta with her daughter, and then I announced that I was making another run for the U.S. House of Representatives. Elizabeth did not like my house, so she shopped around until she found a townhouse she did like. Money became a big issue since I was retired and couldn't afford two houses. So we leased out my first house and each of us paid on the second house.

My wife was fairly well off, so we made it OK until I lost the election. Jimmy Carter's run for President had sunk every Republican candidate's ship in Georgia, so I was immediately in the job market as a two-time political loser with no shingle to hang up as a lawyer or doctor.

Often times during the campaign, Elizabeth would take the side of my opponent, and this really pissed me off. We began to have a lot of quarrels about insignificant things as well as some big issues. Our lives were not pleasant during these trying times, and we never seemed to be able to get on stable ground.

When I finally sat down with Elizabeth to discuss our dilemma and try to come up with a plan, she announced, "This is your problem, not mine."

I wondered—*What happened to for better or worse?* A huge gap had opened between us, and there was nothing available to me to fill that hole. So I told her that I thought it best that we separate, at least temporarily, and we did. I went back to live with Mom and Sis, and she stayed in the townhouse.

The only job offer I received that really gave me some future opportunity was in Charlotte in a risk management company. After interviewing with them, I decided it best to "get out of Dallas," so I moved to Charlotte to begin a new career and a new life.

I divorced Elizabeth, and she accepted that with no financial demands on me. I have not seen her since 1980.

This period of time is one of the Dark Ages of my life. I hope that I am now much wiser and have better judgment so that my future will be in line with God's will for my life. Beauty is definitely not the most important quality to look for in a marriage or in a relationship. Some of us are slow learners.

(60.1) My dear friend, Joe Propst, at my retirement ceremony-Dobbins AFB, outside of Atlanta.

(60.2) Joe, with dark glasses, to Quincy's right.

(60.3) Nelson Rockefeller, VP under President Ford, meets Quincy and Elizabeth at a campaign fund-raiser in Georgia.

(60.4) Former Texas governor John Connolly speaking on behalf of Quincy (far left in photo) as Elizabeth, far right, applauds.

61
Like Father—Like Son

You may recall that back in Chapter Thirteen I wrote about my Dad driving me to a secret location in the Jeep he had bought me in Concord. You also may recall that the destination turned out to be the future site of what is now The Concord Regional Airport. Dad had served on the board of the Airport Authority and was very interested in that issue. Little did we know that years later his dream would come true and his tow-headed son would be the dedication speaker. That one day also led to other events that would play a significant role in the future of Quincy Collins' life after my return home from the prisons of North Vietnam. Allow me to explain.

Politics had reared it's ugly head initially in my old hometown through a friend who saw a connection between all the publicity coming my way (as a returned POW) and the fact that a locally elected official might not run again at that point in time. At any rate I met with a bunch of folks to discuss the potential for me to run for public office in my old home area. This certainly gained my attention, but other green pastures also began coming to my attention. So the excitement of hearing prison guard keys rattling as a guard walked past my prison cell was being replaced with other interesting paths I might take.

I believe Mayor George Lyles of Concord was responsible for inviting me to be the speaker at the upcoming Airport dedication event. I was really excited over this development, and spent a lot of time preparing my remarks. I was living in Charlotte at that time so the trip to Concord was quick and easy. I also had accepted an invitation from the Charlotte Veterans organization to be the Grand Marshall for their annual Charlotte Veterans Day Parade that was to be held the same day at or about 11:00 AM. The Airport dedication was a bit earlier that morning, so time wise I felt comfortable regarding both events.

Upon arriving at Concord's new airport I began meeting a lot of people from my Dad's era so it was like another "Homecoming" for me. There were a lot of people that I had known when the Civil Air Patrol was popular during WWII. I used to fly missions with my Father, and landing at Douglas Municipal Airport in Charlotte was a big thrill for me.

Most of the time Dad's task was to deliver training films to military units based close to airports. As a kid, this was a big deal for me and, I am certain, was responsible not only for my going down the military path at college, but also for my career after graduation from The Citadel.

My message at the dedication was well received, especially when I told the audience about my Jeep and the part that it had played in Dad's search for the best future airport site. I kept looking at my watch so I would not be late for the Veterans' Day Parade in Charlotte, so after saying my goodbyes to my old friends and the newspaper and TV people, off I drove to the next event in Charlotte.

Charlotte was still a bit confusing to me, but I eventually found the "Reviewing Stand" location where I was to meet my hosts. Just as I had climbed up on the decorated flat bed the parade started, and various Veterans' organizations began to pass by and render their salutes to me, as the Grand Marshall.

I asked the gentleman sitting next to me how long they had been having this parade. "About seventeen years to the best of my recollection," replied the elderly Veteran. I then asked if the City of Charlotte was involved in any way with "honoring the troops". He then said that about all they did was allow the Veterans to parade uptown for about 30 minutes and that was it. There was no community involvement!

I just about fell out of my chair with amazement. That was it?

My head was spinning at the utter lack of appreciation for what our Veterans had done in their efforts to preserve our freedom and defend this nation! Something had to change. I began to wonder what I, as a new citizen of Charlotte, could do to make this recognition of Veterans really worthwhile.

I talked to a lot of people and accumulated a lot of ideas, but the main problem—as I saw it—was that there was no one driving this boat! There appeared to be little enthusiasm for Veterans and their programs and projects. So I decided to write a letter not only to Mayor Vinroot but also to the head of the County Commissioners, Ann Shrader. In my letter I tried to expose the lack of interest from a community standpoint in recognizing, much less honoring, the service our Veterans had rendered on behalf of the Charlotte Community—and I felt it was time to remedy this situation and honor them instead of their having to honor themselves on Veterans day.

I received a quick response from both of them acknowledging that this situation should be changed immediately. They appointed me to head a group to make recommendations for correcting the problem. They also selected some fairly high-powered citizens to assist me in this effort.

After several meetings, we decided to form a citizen's committee to be in charge of this effort. The group has evolved into what is now known as The Carolinas Freedom Foundation. It is now 25 years old and I am fortunate to have been the Founder. Obie Oakley was selected by me to be our Executive Director and he has done a magnificent job in that position. In 2019 we became an "organization driven" group instead of a "founder driven" one. This will ensure that The Carolinas Freedom Foundation will not die when I am gone.

Our events to recognize and honor our Veterans now include a FREEDOM BREAKFAST, a Parade for Veterans, a Freedom Award (presented to a person or organization who goes above and beyond what is normally expected of a PATRIOT), an event at Bojangles Coliseum recognizing and honoring the JROTC cadets in the Charlotte School System (who, by the way, have the highest graduation rate of any group at CMS). We also have a presentation to winners of our annual Patriotic Art Contest in the CMS system and adjoining counties, and to persons keeping American Flags in all of our classrooms and at every school. Additionally, we also provide around 30 scholarships for selected students to attend a one week leadership training class at the General Hugh Shelton Leadership Challenge held at the UNCC campus in Charlotte.

Finally, one of our board members has really stepped out by establishing an annual high school football classic called the Patriotic Bowl. Mark Brodowicz and his committee provide customized uniforms to each team and donate $10,000 to each school program participating. In addition to fly-bys, other military activities—like parachute jumps—are also arranged for the spectators to enjoy. These are some of the activities that our organization provides the youth of this area. We recently were listed in the "Guiness Book Of World Records" for arranging seven Flyby events at seven high school games within minutes of each other, on the same day!

I cannot be prouder of the men and women of our Board for their personal efforts on behalf of the citizens of this community, especially our young people! This is what "getting involved" is all about!

If you are interested, our web site is "CarolinasFreedomFoundation. org." Come take a look!

—— CAROLINAS ——
FREEDOM FOUNDATION

The Carolinas Freedom Foundation was founded in 1995 in response to former prisoner of war and retired Air Force Col. Quincy Collins' concerns about the lack of an organization in the area to promote patriotism and honor veterans. Working with then Mayor Richard Vinroot and former Mayor John Belk, a blue ribbon committee recommended that an organization be established for these specific purposes.

Our mission is to inspire patriotism and leadership in our community, especially in our youth. Our Values: Honoring our veterans and men and women in uniform. Character development. Patriotism. Selfless Service. Teach love of country and our freedoms.

Over the years, the Foundation has grown to become recognized as the "go to" organization in the community where promoting patriotism and honoring those who serve are concerned. The Foundation also now has an active part in working with the schools in the area sponsoring character development programs.

The foundation was chartered in 1995 as a 501 (c) (3) corporation, originally as the Charlotte Veterans Association. As the scope of the programs grew, the name was changed to the Carolinas Freedom Foundation to better reflect the initiatives in which the Foundation is involved. These range from Honoring our Veterans to Character Development programs within the schools.

HONORING OUR VETERANS

SUPPORTING OUR SOLDIERS

INSPIRING OUR YOUTH

62
Special Christmas Call to Bob Hope

25 December 1973 – San Francisco, CA

"Hello Bob—Hello Delores. I'm Quincy Collins. You may remember bumping into me at one of the many POW and Veterans Appreciation Celebrations in the past months. If you don't recall, maybe this little song will refresh your memory."

POW Hymn
By Col. Quincy Collins

Oh God, to Thee we raise this prayer and sing from within these
foreign prison walls.
We're men who wear the gold and silver wings and proudly
heed our nation's calls.
Give us strength to withstand all the harm that the hand of our
enemy captors can do to inflict pain and strife,
And deprive every life of the rights they know well we are due.
We pledge unswerving faith and loyalty to our cause, America,
and Thee. Amen.

"I don't know if you got a chance to hear our POW Hymn in May at the White House, but some of us sang it that night. Bob, that was the first time I had ever seen you in hip boots and tux—Man! Didn't it rain?

"I'm in San Francisco to spend a part of this Christmas season with my three sons—Chip, Chuck, and Corky. We're going to get together later today and whoop it up down at the Holiday Inn at Fisherman's Wharf.

"You know Bob, for many of us, this is our first Christmas at home— in the good old USA—in a long, long time. And I happen to know that your last Christmas at home with Delores was in 1941—just about the time I was born—or was that when I started losing my hair?

"At an rate, this Christmas should prove something to you all over again—it's easier to get laughs from a bunch of GIs than it is from your own family.

"Well, since this is sort of a first for you—being home this season—I appreciate very much being able, in my own small way, to share a few moments of this very sacred Christmas with you and your family—a kind of a "Turn About Is Fair Play" routine, if you will.

"The Serviceman, particularly overseas, always believed in Santa Claus—because he knew his real name was Bob Hope.

"Bob, for you, since you couldn't make it to Hanoi—you may recall that you were upstaged by some B-52's—here is a holiday song written by me in Hanoi in 1969. It's just corny enough to be kind of special. Hope you enjoy it. It's called 'It's Christmas Again In Your Hometown.'"

It's Christmas Again In Your Hometown
By Col. Quincy Collins

(1) The winter winds are blowing and in some states it's snowing.
It's Christmas again in your hometown.
Tom Turkey is acookin' and your good folks are lookin'
To gather the family all around.
The men are mixing eggnog while the girls prepare the food,
And at the festive table all heads bow in thankful mood.

So vanquish care and sorrow and plan a bright tomorrow.
It's Christmas again in your hometown.

(2)Bright carols fill the breeze, it's time to trim the trees.
It's Christmas again in your hometown.
The doors are bowed with holly, and everyone is jolly,
Yes, peace and goodwill on earth abound.
The gifts are wrapped and hidden, and the cards have all been sent.
Soon Santa will be coming, what a wonderful event.
So vanquish care and sorrow and plan a bright tomorrow.
It's Christmas again in your hometown!
It's Christmas again in your hometown!

"Thank you for still listening! Hey Bob, I must tell you something I heard on the way over here. Two guys were talking about the big energy crisis, and one of them said, 'You know, America should never have an energy crisis—never! When we run out of fuel all we have to do is pipe in Bob Hope!' I hope that doesn't break you up too much.

Bob, you've made a lot of 'Road' pictures in your time, but the most successful road you ever took was the road into the hearts of your countrymen—and how fortunate I feel to live in a country where I can tell it like it is.

"I graduated from the Citadel in Charleston, SC, and have been in the United States Air Force for 20 years. The military has been my life, and nothing have I heard about Bob Hope but applause, applause, applause!

"I am now stationed at Dobbins AFB, Georgia, and just the other day, while talking with a friend from Atlanta—before this little extravaganza even came about—he made a very interesting comment. It went like this: 'I am so happy that there is a sufficient level of peace in the world that Bob Hope can be home for Christmas this year!'

"Bob, there are literally millions of Americans who have received a unique 'Blessing' at Christmas due to your efforts—and, I might add—Delores' loss was our gain! For although I can only speak officially for myself, I know I really express the sentiments of those Americans who sat in the hot sands of North Africa during WWII, or on Guam or Okinawa, and on into Korea at Osan and Seoul, just to have a little "home away from home" at Christmastime.

"You played 'em all, Pardner"—Keflavik, Reflavic, Sharjah, Torrejon, and that great Berlin airlift show, and I guess every carrier in the fleet. And then there was Southeast Asia. You infiltrated that area about as much as the North Vietnamese—Saigon, Danang, Vietien, Phonom Penn, Bangkok, Korat. As the saying went, 'Wherever there were Americans, there was Hope!'

"Bob, I know you realize, more than most, that the true spirit of Christmas is much more than something material. It's an attitude—an attitude of the love, understanding, and compassion that one human being has for another as taught and practiced by the King of Peace, whose birthday we celebrate this day.

"My wish for you is that all your future Christmases will be at home. That's another way of wishing our country will always be at peace."

"So, I say from Quincy Collins and my family, and I know also from all those Americans who will never get the chance personally—thank you Bob and Delores for some fantastically memorable times. We will never forget!

"And what Bob Hope show would be complete without the old theme. Now, I'm not Perry Como, or Bing—but on the other hand they're not me either! So I guess we're even.

"Mr. Hope—your song!"

THANKS FOR THE MEMORY
Special Lyrics by Col. Quincy Collins
Thanks for the memory—of Christmases you shared,
Showing someone cared,
For flying to those trouble spots

Where no one else had dared,
We thank you, so much!

Thanks for the memory—I think was '41,
March Field in the sun,
You gave a show for G.I. Joe,
A legend had begun,
We thank you, so much!

Many's the time that we waited,
In rain, sleet, or snow just to smile
The jokes that you told were X-rated,
We did have fun and no harm done,

So thanks for the memory!
The rain at Camrahn Bay,
On Algier's "Cellar" day,
The "Big Red One," Danang was fun,
The world, you had to play,
So thank you, so much!

"Bob, my family and I wish you and Delores a very Merry Christmas, each day and forever!"

AND SINCE BOB AND Delores are no longer with us, it is very appropriate to say, "Thanks for the Memory!"

God Bless you both!

Hope Listens After 23 Years

For the first Christmas in 23 years, **Bob Hope** didn't sing "Thanks for the Memories" to the troops. They sang for him instead.

Hope s p e n t Christmas at home with his wife Delores, his children and four of his grandchildren.

The highlights of the day: Col. **J. Quincy Collins** of San Francisco, f o r m e r prisoner of the North Vietnamese, telephoned and played for Hope a recording of a POW choir singing a parody of "Thanks for the Memories," Hope's theme song and traditional s h o w closer.

"It's a great feeling to know that you don't have to go to the hospitals and see some of those kids who were wounded in combat," Hope said. "It's nice to know we don't have to go and there are no guys fighting . . . I bet there are an awful lot of people who are happy this Christmas because that's all over."

HOPE

(62.1) News article from December 1973— "Hope Listens After 23 Years."

(62.2) Getting Delores and Bob "On The Line."

(62.3) Quincy sings to Bob & Delores accompanied by the hotel pianist.

(62.4) Bob's cue card man helps Quincy with the script.

63
Ego—the Backbone of a Fighting Man

Here is a truth: "All human beings are the product of their personal egos." It drives us and causes us to react to life's circumstances. It can be like a bulldozer, moving under its own power, in its own direction, displacing anything in its path. Strong egos equate to people who are hard to handle because they feel that their conclusions on any issue are right and correct and that they have the answer to any given problem. They want to make their mark regarding life in general, and are motivated and committed to attaining a specific goal.

On the other hand, a weak ego (or none at all) causes that person to be a dandelion in the wind of life—a follower, one ruled by the currents of life. It tends to make one indecisive and unnoticeable. This type person will make few, if any, personal marks in life—unless an overriding need thrusts them into a leadership role. Otherwise he will just occupy space and go through the motions of living, but without making much of an impact.

My guess is that a majority of people probably fit into this category. My personal opinion is that one must make a conscious decision to be in this group, which also indicates a certain lack of motivation and drive. My conclusion is that ego is the sum of all of our life's experiences. It is the guiding influence of how we view ourselves, and everything that is around us.

Egos appear to be more noticeable when they are tied to politicians than to everyday citizens. Why is this? From the very beginning of America, representatives of the people were known as public servants. Religious freedom was the primary motivation among the peoples of this new democracy. The prevailing guide was, "Do unto others as you would have them do unto you." What a great ethical comparison for elected officials to pose to themselves each and every day on every issue facing them.

Can you imagine what the results would be if today our politicians had their decision-making apparatus tied to the correct guidelines? What has occurred in the past 242 years to cause our political system and government to be in the mess it is in today? The answer is *PEOPLE!* Find the causes of selfish behavior and lack of love, compassion and ignorance, and you will have the answer!

One other discovery I have made is this: It appears that we all have to be someone other than who we really are in order to be truly loved and respected. Our ordinary efforts in life are evidently not enough. We need to do more to be recognized and stand out in the crowd. Our parents and loved ones have hammered away at this since we were kids, and it never seems to end. So now I will try to measure all this against my own life's experiences to see if I can discover the real *ME!* What kind of guy is Quincy Collins? What makes me work?

My earliest years were spent in the presence of loving and caring parents and family. Life was good and I lacked for nothing. I received plenty of attention, was required to perform prescribed tasks, and on occasion was made to feel the pain of not doing my various assigned jobs. My one regret during my beginning years is that my parents did not read to me or require me to get into books! What a huge loss that was to me and to my development. In this day and time, it should not be condoned for a child not to be able to read as he reaches three to five years old.

I jokingly remember saying in high school that academics was interfering with my extracurricular activities. Band, sports, running the student store, and being in the Dramatics Club consumed most of my time. Fortunately, I was smart enough to pay attention in class and do enough homework to handle my school requirements. The same was true in college.

Then my military career began, and I became totally immersed in making the most of that opportunity. I was passionate about flying and the entire military system, and I performed my duties well. My Officer Efficiency Reports (OER) always reflected that I was in the top echelon of my peer group.

Then, one day I was in the wrong piece of sky at the wrong time. I was shot down, captured, and incarcerated for seven and a half years in North Vietnam. I look upon this as being my PHD learning experience, and indeed it was a growing time for me personally. And I was graded and evaluated on my performance during those trying years. Yes, I was given an OER by my superior officers after we were released. That is an official part of my records to this day!

On February 12, 1973, I graduated (was released), and reentered civilization as a hero. At least that is what the news media and hometown folks called us. We certainly did not look at ourselves in this light because we were merely doing our duty. Unfortunately, most Americans looked at us as having done something that they could never do. Living in a small cell with no ventilation, no utilities, and being exposed to torture and deprivation automatically elevated us to that exalted title of hero.

We heard it and read it every day, and what's more, we had a bunch of military medals hanging on our chests to prove it! Adulation is not a strong enough word to reflect what the American people felt about our service, but that is how we were painted. Even today that has stuck, forty years after the fact.

Picture yourselves in our shoes. Flying was our life, and impeding and destroying the North Vietnamese Communist forces was our mission— our reason for being! After being shot down and imprisoned, our mission changed somewhat. Survival became our number one task along with helping our prison mates do the same. We adopted the goal of "Returning

Home With Honor." The honor part put a completely different light on the issue of survival.

It is one thing to physically make it through years of imprisonment and finally be released. It is another to do this—and at the same time be able to look every American in the eye and proclaim, *"I have done my very best to uphold the American military fighting man's Code of Conduct, and to defend the Constitution of The United States of America . . . so help me God!"* This, my friends, separates the men from the boys!

Every year the enemy selected three POWs to be released. None of these men, save Seaman Doug Hedgal, were given permission by the Senior American officers to accept early release. In fact, all the guys who came home early violated the orders of our Senior Officers, and should have been court-martialed for their actions. They were not!

To this day, these misguided people have had to live without any contact with the rest of us and with no way of becoming a member of the official Vietnam POW Organization.

Special homecoming celebrations, parades, honors, radio and TV appearances and interviews, and tons on newspaper stories became a way of life. This gave each of us an opportunity to tell our story in a personalized and pertinent way. As might be expected, some of our group just wanted to fit in and get back to normal, and this was their right to do that. Many, like me, enjoyed the attention and the opportunity it provided to tell it like it was!

I remember an interview I had with a TV station and a newspaper reporter simultaneously. The question posed to me was, "You must really hate those North Vietnamese guards for punishing you and torturing you in prison."

I smiled and looked them right in the eye and replied, "Frankly, I expected some of that from my captors, but let me tell you what my wife did to me upon my release!"

She had sent a "Dear John" letter explaining that we were not going to be living together any more. Also, I was soon told that my wife had been given my entire pay for nearly eight years, tax free, and she had not saved or put aside one penny for my return. Here I was returned from prison, and I was, in essence, bankrupt!

The best part of the story was that I got to see my three sons again—Chip. Chuck and Corky—even though their Mother had told them that I would not be coming home. I was listed as MIA (Missing In Action) for a period of about two and a half years. Surprise! Surprise!

I felt more valued by ordinary citizens than I did by my wife and kids. Did that have an impact on me? Damn right it did! As a father and husband I felt lost—and a complete stranger!

What gave me the greatest satisfaction was standing in front of a group of interested listeners telling them of what had happened to me over seven and a half years, and then answering their questions. I particularly enjoyed speaking to young people. They hung on every word and asked the most interesting and entertaining questions. I think this turned out to be my Balm In Gilead, and I liked it.

Being on the same platform with Senator Herman Talmadge and Jesse Owens really convinced me that I had a message to give. I had the talent to speak to any audience, and I spoke with great confidence and conviction. I realized I was good at this and could get into the minds and hearts of my listeners. But for what purpose? Was I going to retire from the USAF and become a professional speaker?

The answer to this question would be forthcoming at a speech I made in Rome, Georgia, at the invitation of my new friend, Herman Talmadge, a born-again Democrat.

It was Flag Day, June 14, 1973, and the Senator's organization was in charge of my visit. It was a hot day. I spoke to several different groups before and after their big parade down Main Street. Our red, white and blue turns me on normally, but that day I was really with it. I could feel it, and the words came with all the emotion I could muster. At times I felt like General George Washington—at others like I felt in prison. My connection to our flag was solid, and my birthday of July 4th really topped it off! I had hit a home run in an unfamiliar ballpark, and I was as ecstatic and patriotic as I would ever be. This really felt good and natural and could easily become my personal *Song of the Siren*. (Homer couldn't do it any better!)

When I returned to my home in Marietta, the phone was ringing off the hook. Many voice messages awaited me. It seems that a group of Republicans had come to Rome to hear my message, liked my delivery, and had a plan in mind for me to run for the U.S. House of Representatives from that Congressional District. I decided it was time for me to stop talking and listen! We met the very next day!

I was told that the present Congressman, a Democrat, was not going to run again because of poor health. Politically that was welcomed news, though in over a hundred years no Republican had ever been elected to this office in this district. Of some concern was the fact that a Urologist and Davidson College graduate had run a decent campaign against the incumbent two years before, and would most likely run again this time too.

Well, what the hell! I had to start somewhere, and maybe this was it. After many political meetings and discussions I had all the information I needed to make an informed decision. On May 14, 1974, I announced my Retirement from the USAF and my Candidacy for the House of Representatives from the 7th District of Georgia.

The race had begun!

POW BRACELET — Sen. Sam Nunn, D-Ga., right, Saturday presented the POW bracelet he has worn for several months to Lt. Col. James Quincy Collins, Jr., of Atlanta, formerly of Concord, N. C., at the Atlanta airport after Collins arrived Saturday to spend leave with his mother, center, and sister. The bracelet bears Collins' name. The officer was recently released by the North Vietnamese.

(63.1) Senator Sam Nunn, Quincy and Mom.

(63.2) Quincy campaigning in a Jeep.

(63.3) "Please vote for me," when you get older.

(63.4) Quincy getting the message out.

(63.5) With Senator Barry Goldwater (far left) and others at Marietta, GA fundraiser.

64
The Candidate

Since I was leaping out into a political jungle that was filled with strange animals and unfamiliar paths, I needed some guides to assist me in my quest for a Congressional seat. The very first person that I called just prior to announcing was Sen. Sam Nunn, a well-known Democrat from Georgia. Sam had worn my POW bracelet while I was in prison, and had met me in Atlanta when I returned home.

Home was now with my Mom and Sis who lived together in an apartment off Piedmont Road. My Dad had died in Atlanta in 1968 after he and Mom moved there from Cedartown, Georgia. My sister, Carolyn, joined them soon after their move.

What I didn't know at the time was that my wife had already decided, shortly after my shoot-down, that she was going to divorce me, so I had nowhere else to go. My Mother knew of this but the USAF did not, as they probably would have stopped allowing her to receive my total Air Force pay tax-free.

At any rate, Sam suggested that I fly up to Washington and spend some time with him in the political arena that I would be doing battle in if I were elected. I agreed, and arrived at his senate office on the day he had suggested.

His staff was wonderful to me, and had arranged a number of meetings with other elected officials to give me a taste of what might lie ahead. Jesse Helms, Strom Thurmond, Bill Brach, Herman Talmedge, and several other well-known senators of that day and time greeted me with great interest and enthusiasm. This was 1974 and I, as a former POW, was still heralded as a hero—especially in the halls of Congress!

Sam and I had lunch in the senate cafeteria and got down to the bottom line on what was to be required of me in such a campaign. Money came up often along with political contacts. Sam knew that I was a Republican, but gave me advice that was well taken whether I was a Democrat or Republican.

At the end of lunch, Sam seemed to really get serious. His face tightened up as he leaned in towards me and said some words that have been a guide for me over my entire life in freedom. He said, "Quincy, no matter what you do the rest of your life you will be known as that former POW in Vietnam. Now what are you going to do with it?"

Wow! Sam really laid it on me, not just for that short time period, but forever! These words still guide me and challenge me as I forge my way through the latter years of my life. I can think of no better measuring stick to have than that penetrating question: *What are you going to do with it?*

The "IT" is my entire experience as a POW in Vietnam. "IT" is the torture and deprivation imposed upon us in our quest to serve America. "IT" is surviving, when giving in and succumbing to the pressures against living might have been easier. "IT" was the unknown of the next hour, the next day, the next year. "IT" was a future veiled in pain and sacrifice and the destruction of your own will to live.

I can imagine that Christ experienced some of the same considerations as he suffered on the cross for the sins of all mankind—then and now! "IT" was a heavy burden, and He asked God to relieve Him of "IT." But this was not God's plan nor His will for either Jesus' future or ours. God's Will Be Done!

Every day since then I have prayed, "God, what is Your will for my life?" No, I wasn't elected in 1974, nor was I elected two years later. Jimmy

Carter, Governor of Georgia at that time, ran for President, so all Republican candidates running for Federal office in Georgia—including my new friend, Newt Gingrich—were defeated. Newt went back to being a professor, but I had no shingle to hang out. So I found a position in the Risk Management business in Charlotte, North Carolina. But why did I put myself through the rigors of two political campaigns? What was my reason for running for Congress? This will require some analysis and reflection.

I was certainly influenced while in prison by the great American traitor—Jane Fonda. The messages that she recorded for our captors to play for us to hear were degrading to us as American fighting men, and demoralizing to us as citizens of the USA. How could my country allow her to remain a citizen?

Then there was the great presidential candidate, George McGovern. In late 1972 my prison guard opened my peephole in the cell door and tossed in a paper with Mr. McGovern's campaign platform typed on it. Of course we read it because of nothing else to do.

My reaction was, "Damn! If this ass is elected, I may not want to go home!"

I saw nothing that referred to the freedoms our founding fathers fought for, or how liberty and the free-enterprise system was an integral part of our culture and the foundation for our future. Also missing was God and the Christian principles that America had always embraced.

And then there were the traitors who were in prison with the rest of us, and who, against the orders of our senior officers and the content and meaning of our official US Fighting Man's "Code of Conduct" arranged and accepted early release.

What the Hell is going on here? Is there no loyalty or allegiance to the United States of America? I didn't expect everything at home to remain completely unchanged, but my patriotic nature did not allow me to accept a different set of standards from my government and the citizens it served. Little did I realize the extent of the changes that had swept through

America and that would be confronting me upon my arrival home in this new world.

It wasn't the seven and a half years I had been away. It was more like fifty years, and I had just been dug up in the Arctic after having been frozen all those years! Yes, my country had changed, and it wasn't over yet. The people were changing and the "work hard to get ahead" system was being replaced by "let government take care of all of us." That was to be achieved by electing these "give away" socialists who cared nothing about our Constitution.

Further, the labor unions of America were becoming all-powerful and influencing more and more of government and the officials running it. Finally, the American electorate appeared to care less about knowing what the political parties really stood for, especially about the candidates themselves. And the national news media had more to do with who got elected than the candidates and their party. I was one frustrated guy. It was all I could do to keep from yelling "Wake Up America," as I spoke to audiences about my POW experiences.

The day that I spoke in Rome, Georgia, about our flag, I really let go and said, "To Hell with being politically correct. Here is I what I really want to say." The crowds responded with standing ovations and really wanted more.

When the Republicans contacted me to offer help in a Congressional race, I almost fainted. "Me? Run for Congress?"

My first response was that this was the opportunity I was seeking to "right" some of the "wrongs" I had seen in my country. What better way to become part of the solution for a nation headed the wrong way. I had not given a thought to this path and it really took me by surprise. But from what I understood from those advising me, being elected as a Representative in the U.S. House was quite possible.

Not having to run against an incumbent was a great advantage. The fact that I would be, by far, the most recognized Republican primary candidate was also a plus in my considerations. All the TV interviews and radio broadcasts I had been a part of certainly gave me a name recognition advantage, and I soon learned that name recognition was one of the most sought after situations as a political candidate.

All of these certainly gave me confidence that the stars were lining up in my favor. My Mother, bless her heart, gave me the best advice I could have asked for. She reminded me, "Son, it won't be unanimous in your favor!" Time to get my feet back on the ground after floating around on the "could be" clouds of life. I had this opportunity—now what was I going to do with it?

The ego in me began to squeeze its way to the surface, and I began to picture myself as a Congressman in various scenes. The one I liked best was me addressing the full House on an issue where my POW experiences were pertinent to the issue under discussion. At other times, I was speaking to my constituents at home about an issue of concern to all citizens, and I was gratified with their support of my position.

These contrived situations were, of course, self-serving, as I began my research into the main issues facing our country at that time. Not all of the potential solutions were easy to come by or ones that the majority of citizens would support. On many issues, just as it is at any given time, there may not be an answer/solution that is obviously "right."

The Republican line of thought might be so and so, but that was not the answer I was seeking. I wanted to be right, and do what was best for my country and the citizens I represented. I had to determine, in my own mind, if I had the guts to stand up for my beliefs and take the heat when I opposed my party or my constituents. As hard as it was to measure this, I felt well prepared to represent the citizens of the 7th Congressional District of Georgia.

Here is an example of what I, as a candidate, had to face in the heat of an election. Big George Bush was the Chairman of the Republican Party nationally, and had authorized a poll to be taken to see what my chances were for winning. My opponent in the general election was a urologist who was a national council member in the John Birch society. He was, indeed, to the right of Genghis Khan and, at times, tried to make me look like a flaming liberal.

The poll indicated that only several points separated us. So the decision was made to invite Mr. Republican, Governor Ronald Reagan, to visit me in Marietta, get all the media coverage that was available, and give me a boost to take over the lead. I might add that my name recognition in the Atlanta area was already 82%, so the plan seemed feasible.

Many Democrats did not like my opponent because of his radical John Birch Right Wing philosophy, so my organization was able to arrange many events that might not have been ordinarily possible. At my invitation, Gov. Reagan flew into the city airport in Marietta, which was closed down because of the huge rally we were having there. He took his place by my side on the speaker's platform. Just as he began his remarks, a lone plane flew by carrying a sign that read, "Vote Larry McDonald." The crowd snickered. Reagan mentioned it comically, and the event went on.

After the rally we had a press conference in a local hotel and invited all the media in the Atlanta area. I introduced Reagan. He made a few opening remarks and then the media began. I was not aware of Reagan's full background, but I quickly became familiar with it.

Larry McDonald was not your regular liberal Democrat. In fact, it would be impossible to differentiate many of his positions from those of Republicans—including me! So the media had a great time shooting at me, the candidate—and comparing Reagan's views on issues with those of my opponent. This little visit changed my manner of campaigning and my positioning to defeat my very conservative opponent. We concluded our campaign with one of the closest Congressional races in many years. I lost by about 200 votes.

I may have lost the opportunity to sit in the halls of Congress and represent the citizens of the 7th District, but I was able to do something equally as important. I awakened thousands of people who had never voted before, and got a lot of them involved in my political campaign. I came to realize the strengths I had as a person, a citizen, a veteran and most important of all, a Christian.

Senator Sam Nunn's challenge to me rang true. I may always be known as that POW in Vietnam, but I had made a great decision as to "what to do with it." I was proud to be Quincy Collins, and to have the opportunity to serve my country in yet another way. I conclude most of my speeches with this quote: "To be born in Freedom is an accident; to live in Freedom, a struggle; but to die in Freedom is an obligation!"

Until I die I will always be looking for another way to serve my country.

(64.1) Quincy on the campaign trail, (1974).

(64.2) On the main drag of Calhoun, GA.

(64.3) Meeting my potential constituents in every city.

(64.4) My biggest supporter in 1974—Gov. Ronald Reagan.

(64.5) Enjoying a "Happy Moment" while campaigning.

(64.6) Catherine & Quincy working for his POW friend John McCain, and his wife Cindy, in John's race for the Presidency.

65
Governor John C. West

This 1942 graduate of The Citadel was born in Camden, South Carolina and went on to become one of the most popular elected officials
in South Carolina history. After a four-year stint in the Army, he got his
LL.B degree from the University of South Carolina and opened a law
office in Camden. In 1948 he was elected to the South Carolina Highway
Commission. From there he served on most of the important State Senate
Committees until he was elected to the office of Lieutenant Governor of
South Carolina in 1967. He actively supported many Democrat candidates through the years, and received tremendous support from within
the party when he announced for governor and was elected with 53% of
the vote.

I was living with my sister and mother in Atlanta when I received a
letter from Governor West asking me to serve on a special Board he was
establishing to advise him on veterans' matters. The timing was after my
trip to The Citadel and my visit with General Mark Clark. I assumed that
my visit there had prompted the Governor to track me down, as the South
Carolina news media had made me out to be a South Carolina native
since I was also born in Winnsboro, S.C. on the Fourth of July, 1931.

At any rate, I accepted the invitation and drove to Columbia in the

new car that Ford Motor Company had given me to drive for the first
year of my return. Each POW had received this offer and was given a list
of models to choose from. Of course this forced me to take a driver's test
and get a driver's license. I felt like a kid in high school getting my first car.
This was really exciting!

I finally arrived at the state capitol and found my way to the governor's office. As I walked in, there sat a gentleman I had known when I was
Aide to General Everest and accompanied him on trips to the Pentagon.

Colonel Jim Whitmire was a tall and distinguished gentleman who
had been Executive Assistant to the USAF Chief of Staff. I remembered
him well as we had discussed The Citadel, South Carolina and the great
beaches along the coast. He was now holding down the same type job for
the Governor as he had done when he was in the US Air Force. The fact
that he flashed his 1938 Citadel ring made me feel very comfortable and
I felt that I had a friend in, perhaps, unfriendly territory.

I was escorted into the governor's office and up jumped the man who
was sitting behind the big desk. His hand reached for mine, and he had a
jovial smile on his face.

"John West," he announced.

I countered with, "Quincy Collins."

I liked him immediately and got the impression that the feeling was
mutual. After some small talk about The Citadel he asked a few questions
about my experience in prison and what plans I had for the future. At that
time I had visions of flying again and working for my first star and I told
him that.

Finally, the governor said that he had a press conference to announce
this initiative about veterans and their returning home status, and asked
if I would like to attend. I accepted, and we walked down a corridor to a
small room already filled with media folk with recorders, pens and paper.
The Governor walked to his chair and indicated that I was to sit by him.
He seemed to know most of the reporters and called them by name as he
began to set the scene for the press conference.

In looking at the totality of the event, most of the time was spent in introducing me as a native South Carolinian who was fresh out of the prisons of North Vietnam. My Citadel affiliation was also a big point of interest. I got the feeling that this press crowd had never met or talked to a POW before, and that I was about to be bombarded for information on a happening they knew very little about. And I was floored as to how much the Governor knew about me personally and professionally. Some one had done his homework on me! Governor West finally started talking about some issues in the state, especially lack of jobs, unemployment and unions.

I was well aware that Democrats got much of their support from the unions and that putting citizens on the hand-out rolls was a big part of their election strategy. Right in the middle of an explanation the governor was giving, one of the media reporters yelled, "Colonel, you have been away for quite a time. As you return and begin to take your place in American society, what do you see that has changed—and is it for the better or worse?"

My God! What an opening for a Conservative to talk about the downfall of the American work ethic and the continuing promises of more jobs and more pay for the black population. Every statement I made had a follow-up question. I was really getting into the swing of things when Governor West realized that this was launching into a political discussion that he did not want to follow. He tried to bring back the issue of veterans, but my remarks were supporting the men and women who had put their lives on the line for freedom and the future of this nation.

From the back of the room came a question, "Governor, what do you think about the Colonel's conclusions on what has happened here in America since he was shot down?"

Damn! We might as well have pulled out our sabers and started whacking each other right there!

The consummate politician began to downplay my remarks, but he made one statement that every press person took as a backhand to me personally. "You've got to remember that Quincy has been out of touch with what is happening in this country."

I couldn't have asked for a better response. Damned right I have been isolated from the bad things happening to my country and its citizens! But now I saw it clearly from the patriotic eyes of someone who really cared. His answer made me mad, but it opened opportunities I never thought possible. All South Carolina newspapers carried the story the next morning and another political block took its place in the building process. Name recognition, name recognition, name recognition! Within three weeks a Republican poll indicated that I had a 28% name recognition in the state of South Carolina.

What next? I really liked John West, and understood why he was so successful in his political life. Can I do the same?

John C. West Bio
(from Wikipedia.org)

John Carl West, Sr. (August 27, 1922 – March 21, 2004),[1] was an American Democratic Party politician who served as the 109th Governor of South Carolina from 1971 to 1975. From 1977 to 1981, he was the U.S. Ambassador to Saudi Arabia.

Background

West was born in Camden, South Carolina. He was reared in the Kershaw County farming community of Charlotte Thompson. In May 1923, his father, along with seventy-six other persons, was killed in a fire at the nearby Cleveland School. His mother and maternal grandmother escaped unharmed from the fire. West was hence reared by his determined single mother. In 1942, he married his childhood sweetheart, Lois Rhame. The couple had three children, a daughter and two sons, Shelton, Douglas, and John, Jr. That same year, he graduated from The Citadel in Charleston, South Carolina, and enlisted in the United States Army as a major, an intelligence officer, during World War II, assigned to stateside service.

Political career

Following the war, West earned a law degree in 1948 from the University of South Carolina in the capital city of Columbia. From 1948 to 1952, he served on the South Carolina Highway

(65.1) John C. West.

Commission. In 1954, he coordinated the unsuccessful U.S. Senate candidacy of Edgar A. Brown, who lost in a write-in campaign waged by former Governor Strom Thurmond, then a Democrat but in 1964 a defector to the Republican Party.

From 1955 to 1967, West served in the state senate from Kershaw County. At the time he was a segregationist but felt uncomfortable denying basic rights to African Americans and by the time he was lieutenant governor was a "southern moderate" on racial issues. He was assigned to several committees which studied public school curriculum, investigated the activities of the Communist Party of the United States of America, monitored the state Development Board, examined state support for the nursing profession and junior colleges, and recommended revisions to the state constitution.

West was the 80th Lieutenant Governor of South Carolina, having served from 1967 to 1971. Elected lieutenant governor in November 1966, he and Robert Evander McNair, the governor, and Ernest Hollings, a former governor elected to a long-term stint in the U.S. Senate, succeeded in thwarting Strom Thurmond's daring attempt to stampede the white electorate of their native state from a century of Democratic hegemony into the Republican Party, which had prevailed in South Carolina in 1964 at the presidential level for the first time since the disputed election of 1876. Thurmond nevertheless won his first term as a Republican in that same general election. The GOP had also made a strong presidential bid in the state in 1960, but John F. Kennedy defeated Richard M. Nixon for the state's electoral votes that year.

In the 1970 gubernatorial election, in which McNair was constitutionally barred from seeking a second full term, West with 53.2 percent of the vote defeated U.S. Representative Albert W. Watson, a Democrat-turned-Republican who carried Thurmond's backing. Watson finished with 45.9 percent of the ballots cast. A former state legislator, Alfred W. Bethea of Dillon, polled 2 percent of the vote as the nominee of George Wallace's former American Independent Party. West's running-mate for lieutenant governor, Earle Morris, Jr., of Pickens defeated Watson's running mate, advertising executive James M. Henderson of Greenville, by about the same percent of the vote as West had prevailed over Watson.

As governor, West was known for his accessibility with the media and his openness with legislators. In carrying out his duties, he kept a recurring eye on history and left much archival material for future researchers. He worked to increase employment opportunities in the state. The Orangeburg Times and Democrat wrote that West's "greatest single success was in the field of economic growth. ... With the state's growing income and new jobs, the historic trend of out-migration ... was halted. Under West, South Carolina in October 1971 held its first ever integrated state fair in Columbia. On March 28, 1973, the South Carolina Legislature ratified an amendment to the state constitution that allowed restaurants to serve mixed drinks.

After his tenure as governor, West returned for two years to private law practice until he was appointed the ambassador to Saudi Arabia, a position that he held during the Jimmy Carter administration. Newly appointed as ambassador to Saudi Arabia, West outlined his plan to Dee Workman, high-ranking Mobil Oil executive, who reported directly to William Tavoulareas, to encourage communication between the public and private sectors of both the

U.S. and Saudi Arabia. He began by setting up visits by members of Congress, including Senator Jacob Javits, to allow them to see firsthand the "problems and opportunities" of the Saudi economy. In his 1997 oral history, West commented on his strategy of helping the Saudis with their image: "It didn't take a rocket scientist or a smart fellow to realize the public relations of the Arab world was just nonexistent." In a five-point formula for potential peace in the region, Carter endorsed the creation of a Palestinian state, an issue still opposed by conservatives. A leading Jewish Democratic Party contributor said that West was more "the Saudis' ambassador to the United States", rather than the U.S. ambassador to Saudi Arabia, as he had been appointed.

Death and legacy

After returning to the United States, he became a Professor of Middle Eastern Studies at the University of South Carolina.[1] He endowed a professorship at The Citadel, which currently resides in The Citadel School of Humanities and Social Sciences. From 1993 until his death from cancer in 2004 at Hilton Head Island, he had been a partner in the law firm of Bethea, Jordan, and Griffin. He was Presbyterian.

Philip G. Grose, a former staff member for both Governors McNair and West and later a research associate at the University of South Carolina's Institute for Southern Studies, wrote a 2011 biography of West entitled, Looking for Utopia: The Life and Times of John C. West. Grose took the "looking for Utopia" line from McNair, who once described his friend and colleague West as "an idealist ...always looking for Utopia".Grose depicts West as a determined statesman who shaped his career by championing causes of the underprivileged in a state with more than its share of poverty and denied opportunities to many of its citizens. Grose concludes that West "was right about a lot of things, as it turned out, and his Utopian quest left a permanent, undeniable, and irreversible impact on a state whose residents ordinarily did not like the idea of change."]

John "Jack" West, III, called his father "a combination of John C. Calhoun and Atticus Finch."

66
General Westmoreland—
His Nightmare Revisited!

No recollection of Vietnam would be complete without some mention of General William Childs Westmoreland, Commander of US Forces in Vietnam.

Born and raised near Spartanburg, South Carolina, he and his family seemed to come in contact with my family from time to time. His father, James Ripley Westmoreland, was in the textile business with my grandfather Doggett who lived in Cowpens, South Carolina. My mother remembered him as "Rip." But I was never in a position to call him that. My senior year at the Citadel, he was Chairman of The Citadel Board of Visitors and placed my diploma in my hand as I graduated in May of 1953.

His son, William Childs Westmoreland, also attended The Citadel for one year before being appointed to attend the United States Military Academy at West Point. He graduated from there in 1936 and was the ranking cadet as First Captain. He became one of the Army's fair-haired boys, and hit the promotion cycles in quick succession. His reputation was one of caring for the troops, and that reputation followed him until he made general and was in charge of the Vietnam Operation.

My next brush with a Westmoreland occurred in 1965, when I flew our Air division Commander from Yokota Air Base, Japan, to Saigon for a briefing. I knew that one of the officers stationed with me while at the new Air Force Academy was General Westmoreland's Chief of Staff, Colonel Kenny Talbert, so I called to make an appointment to see him. As a result, Kenny invited us to spend the night in General Westmoreland's complex on base, where we actually met the general and had an informal chat with him. Within 10 days I was shot down, captured, and held in Hanoi for 7 ½ years as a POW. Time waits for no man!

After my release from prison in February of 1973, I lived with my mother and sister in Atlanta and began to become active in the social, civic and political activities in the area.

Rankin Smith, who owned the professional Falcon football operation, and I became friends. One Sunday I was invited to sing the National Anthem and to join him in his VIP suite. Upon arriving, to my surprise, there sat General Westmoreland and his wife, Kitsy. We renewed acquaintances, and I answered his questions about my POW experiences.

I had a beautiful lady as a date that day, so I was anxious to cultivate her interest in me. My wife dropping me at my release was still a huge downer for me, and I was looking for some relief. This might well be the one! I quickly joined her by the front sliding glass window as the party in the suite was really cranking up. The food was great, the drinks were intoxicating, and the game was going the Falcons' way.

All of a sudden, out of nowhere, Kitsy plopped down beside me and said, "Quincy, the general would like for you to join him for a drink and a short conversation."

He was sitting high in the back of the suite, so this Colonel leaped to his feet and bounded up the steps. The general rose and invited me to sit by him as Kitsy slipped into the seat near the wall. After ordering refreshments, the General looked at me and said, "I understand that you are going to retire and run for Congress. Is this correct?"

"Yes, Sir," I responded.

Then he asked, "What political party are you going to associate with?"

I quickly replied, "General, after all we have been through in Vietnam, and all the dealings you personally have had with L.B. Johnson, I wouldn't think that you would have to ask."

I explained to him how the North Vietnamese had thrown a copy of George McGovern's campaign platform into every POW cell and how totally pissed off we were at the issues he was running on.

I think the General saw that he had ignited my fuse, so he coughed, lowered his voice and said, "Well, I am thinking seriously of running for Governor of South Carolina, but I don't know what party I should be in!"

I couldn't believe my ears! A four-star general who doesn't know what party he is in? *Wow! I hope no one else hears this.*

Our conversation shifted to the game and Rankin Smith and the general's father and my mother's family, the Doggetts, and eventually I went back to join my date. I didn't want to tell her how disappointed I was at General Westmoreland and the ignorance he displayed about politics in general, and especially in South Carolina.

However, I was quite anxious to tell Jim Edwards what I had discovered in hopes that that knowledge would benefit Jim. It most definitely did. Governor Jim Edwards became one of the best Governors South Carolina ever had.

It amazes me how an average citizen can sometimes make a huge impact on a political outcome.

(66.1) Col. James Ripley Westmoreland, Chair of the Board of Trustees of the Citadel and father of Gen. William Westmoreland, shakes the hand of Quincy Collins as he graduates in 1953.

William Childs Westmoreland Bio

(From Wikipedia.org)

William Childs Westmoreland (March 26, 1914 – July 18, 2005) was a United States Army General, most notably commander of United States forces during the Vietnam War from 1964 to 1968. He served as Chief of Staff of the United States Army from 1968 to 1972.

(66.2) William Westmoreland

Westmoreland adopted a strategy of attrition against the Viet Cong and the North Vietnamese Army, attempting to drain them of manpower and supplies. He also made use of the United States' edge in artillery and air power, both in tactical confrontations and in relentless strategic bombing of North Vietnam. Many of the battles in Vietnam were technically United States victories, with the United States Army in control of the field afterward; holding territory gained this way proved difficult, however. Public support for the war eventually diminished, especially after the Battle of Khe Sanh and the Tet Offensive in 1968. By the time he was re-assigned as Army Chief of Staff, United States military forces in Vietnam had reached a peak of 535,000 personnel. Westmoreland's strategy was ultimately politically unsuccessful. Growing United States casualties and the draft undermined United States support for the war, while large-scale casualties among non-combatants weakened South Vietnamese support. This also failed to weaken North Vietnam's will to fight, and the Government of South Vietnam—a factor largely out of Westmoreland's control—never succeeded in establishing enough legitimacy to quell defections to the Viet Cong.

Early life

William Childs Westmoreland was born in Spartanburg County, South Carolina, on March 26, 1914 to Eugenia Talley Childs and James Ripley Westmoreland. His upper middle class family was involved in the local banking and textile industries. At the age of 15, William became an Eagle Scout at Troop 1 Boy Scouts, and was recipient of the Distinguished Eagle Scout Award and Silver Buffalo from the Boy Scouts of America as a young adult. After spending a year at The Citadel in 1932, he

was appointed to attend the United States Military Academy on the nomination of Senator James F. Byrnes, a family friend. His motive for entering West Point was "to see the world". He was a member of a distinguished West Point class that also included Creighton Abrams and Benjamin O. Davis Jr. Westmoreland graduated as first captain—the highest cadet rank—and received the Pershing Sword, which is "presented to cadet with highest level of military proficiency". Westmoreland also served as the superintendent of the Protestant Sunday School Teachers.

Military career

Following graduation from West Point in 1936, Westmoreland became an artillery officer and served in several assignments with the 18th Field Artillery at Fort Sill. In 1939, he was promoted to first lieutenant, after which he was a battery commander and battalion staff officer with the 8th Field Artillery at Schofield Barracks, Hawaii.

World War II

In World War II, Westmoreland saw combat with the 34th Field Artillery Battalion, 9th Infantry Division, in Tunisia, Sicily, France and Germany; he commanded the 34th Battalion in Tunisia and Sicily. He reached the temporary wartime rank of colonel, and on October 13, 1944, was appointed the chief of staff of the 9th Infantry Division.

After the war, Westmoreland completed Airborne training at the Infantry School in 1946. He then commanded the 504th Parachute Infantry Regiment, 82nd Airborne Division. From 1947 to 1950, he served as chief of staff for the 82nd Airborne Division. He was an instructor at the Army Command and General Staff College from 1950 to 1951. He then completed the Army War College as a student in 1951, and stayed as an instructor from 1951 to 1952.

Korean War

Westmoreland was promoted to Brigadier General in November 1952 at the age of 38, making him one of the youngest U.S. Army generals in the post-World War II era. He commanded the 187th Airborne

Regimental Combat Team in operations in Korea from 1952 to 1953. After returning to the United States, Westmoreland was deputy assistant chief of staff, G–1, for manpower control on the Army staff from 1953 to 1955. In 1954, he completed a three-month management program at Harvard Business School. As Stanley Karnow noted, "Westy was a corporation executive in uniform."

After the war, Westmoreland was the United States Army's Secretary of the General Staff from 1955 to 1958. He then commanded the 101st Airborne Division from 1958 to 1960. He was Superintendent of the United States Military Academy from 1960 to 1963. In 1962, Westmoreland was admitted as an honorary member of the Massachusetts Society of the Cincinnati. He was promoted to lieutenant general in July 1963 and was Commanding General of the XVIII Airborne Corps from 1963 to 1964.

Vietnam War

The attempted French re-colonization of Vietnam following World War II culminated in a decisive French defeat at the Battle of Dien Bien Phu. The Geneva Conference (April 26 – July 20, 1954) discussed the possibility of restoring peace in Indochina, and temporarily separated Vietnam into two zones, a northern zone to be governed by the Viet Minh, and a southern zone to be governed by the State of Vietnam, then headed by former emperor Bao Đai. A Conference Final Declaration, issued by the British chairman of the conference, provided that a general election be held by July 1956 to create a unified Vietnamese state. Although presented as a consensus view, this document was not accepted by the delegates of either the State of Vietnam or the United States. In addition, China, the Soviet Union and other communist nations recognized the North while the United States and other non-communist states recognized the South as the legitimate government. By the time Westmoreland became army commander in South Vietnam, the option of a Korea-type settlement with a large demilitarised zone separating north and south, favored by military and diplomatic figures, had been rejected by the US government, whose objectives were to achieve a decisive victory, and not to use vastly greater resources. The infiltration by regular North Vietnam forces into the South could not be dealt with by aggressive action against the northern state because intervention by China was something the US government was concerned to avoid, but President Lyndon B. Johnson had given commitments to uphold South Vietnam against communist North Vietnam.

Chief of Staff of the United States Army, General Harold Keith Johnson, and subsequently historians such as Harry G. Summers, Jr. came to see US goals as having become mutually inconsistent, because defeating the Communists would require declaring a national emergency and fully mobilising the resources of the US. President Johnson was critical of Westmoreland's defused corporate style, considering him overattentive to what government officials wanted to hear. Nonetheless, Westmoreland was operating within longstanding army protocols of subordinating the military to civilian policymakers. The most important constraint was staying on the strategic defensive out of fear of Chinese intervention, but at the same time President Lyndon B. Johnson had made it clear that there was a higher commitment to defending Vietnam. Much of the thinking about defense was by academics turned government advisors who concentrated on nuclear weapons, seen as making conventional war obsolete. The fashion for counter-insurgency thinking also denigrated the role of conventional warfare. Despite the inconclusive outcome of the Korean War, Americans expected their wars to end with the unconditional surrender of the enemy.

The Gulf of Tonkin incident of 2 August 1964 led to a dramatic increase in direct American participation in the war, with nearly 200,000 troops deployed by the end of the year. Viet Cong and PAVN strategy, organization and structure meant Westmoreland faced a dual threat. Regular North Vietnamese army units infiltrating across the remote border were apparently concentrating to mount an offensive and Westmoreland considered this the danger that had to be tackled immediately. There was also entrenched guerrilla subversion throughout the heavily populated coastal regions by the Viet Cong. Consistent with the enthusiasm of Robert McNamara for statistics, Westmoreland placed emphasis on body count and cited the Battle of Ia Drang as evidence the communists were losing. However, the government wished to win at low cost, and policymakers received McNamara's interpretation indicating huge American casualties in prospect, prompting a reassessment of what could be achieved. Moreover, the Battle of la Drang was unusual in that US troops brought a large enemy formation to battle. After talking to junior officers General Westmoreland became skeptical about localised concentrated search and destroy sweeps of short duration, because the Communist forces controlled whether there were military engagements, giving an option to simply avoid battle with US forces if the situation warranted it. The alternative of sustained countrywide pacification operations, which would require massive use of US manpower, was never available to Westmoreland, because it was considered politically unacceptable.

In public at least, he continued to be sanguine about the progress being made throughout his time in Vietnam, though supportive journalist James Reston thought Westmoreland's characterizing of the conflict as attrition warfare presented his generalship in a misleading light. Westmoreland's critics say his successor, General Creighton Abrams, deliberately switched emphasis away from what Westmoreland dubbed attrition. Revisionists point to Abrams's first big operation being a tactical success that disrupted North Vietnamese build up, but resulted in the Battle of Hamburger Hill, a political disaster that effectively curtailed Abrams's freedom to continue with such operations.

Commander in South Vietnam

Westmoreland was sent to Vietnam in 1963. In January 1964, he became deputy commander of Military Assistance Command, Vietnam (MACV), eventually succeeding Paul D. Harkins as commander, in June. Secretary of Defense Robert McNamara told President Lyndon B. Johnson in April that Westmoreland was "the best we have, without question". As the head of the MACV, he was known for highly publicized, positive assessments of U.S. military prospects in Vietnam. However, as time went on, the strengthening of communist combat forces in the South led to regular requests for increases in U.S. troop strength, from 16,000 when he arrived to its peak of 535,000 in 1968 when he was promoted to Army chief of staff.

On April 28, 1967, Westmoreland addressed a joint session of Congress. "In evaluating the enemy strategy", he said, "it is evident to me that he believes our Achilles heel is our resolve. ... Your continued strong support is vital to the success of our mission. ... Backed at home by resolve, confidence, patience, determination, and continued support, we will prevail in Vietnam over the communist aggressor!" Westmoreland claimed that under his leadership, United States forces "won every battle". The turning point of the war was the 1968 Tet Offensive, in which communist forces attacked cities and towns throughout South Vietnam. At the time, Westmoreland was focused on the Battle of Khe Sanh and considered the Tet Offensive to be a diversionary attack. It is not clear if Khe Sanh was meant to be distraction for the Tet Offensive or vice versa; sometimes this is called the Riddle of Khe Sanh. Regardless, U.S. and South Vietnamese troops successfully fought off the attacks during the Tet Offensive, and the communist forces took heavy losses, but the ferocity of the assault shook public confidence in Westmoreland's previous assurances about the state of the war. Political debate and public opinion led the Johnson administration to limit further increases in U.S. troop numbers in Vietnam. Nine months afterward, when the My Lai Massacre reports started to break, Westmoreland resisted pressure from the incoming Nixon administration for a cover-up, and pressed for a full and impartial investigation by Lieutenant General William R. Peers. However, a few days after the tragedy, he had praised the same involved unit on the "outstanding job", for the "U.S. infantrymen had killed 128 Communists [sic] in a bloody day-long battle". Post 1969 Westmoreland also made efforts to investigate the Phong Nhi and Phong Nhat massacre a year after the event occurred.

Westmoreland was convinced that the Vietnamese communists could be destroyed by fighting a war of attrition that, theoretically, would render the Vietnam People's Army unable to fight. His war strategy was marked by heavy use of artillery and airpower and repeated attempts to engage the communists in large-unit battles, and thereby exploit the US's vastly superior firepower and technology. Westmoreland's response, to those Americans who criticized the high casualty rate of Vietnamese civilians, was: "It does deprive the enemy of the population, doesn't it?" However, the North Vietnamese Army (NVA) and the National Liberation Front of South Vietnam (NLF) were able to dictate the pace of attrition to fit their own goals: by continuing to fight a guerrilla war and avoiding large-unit battles, they denied the Americans the chance to fight the kind of war they were best at, and they ensured that attrition would wear down the American public's support for the war faster than they.

Westmoreland repeatedly rebuffed or suppressed attempts by John Paul Vann and Lew Walt to shift to a "pacification" strategy. Westmoreland had little appreciation of the patience of the American public for his time frame, and was struggling to persuade President Johnson to approve widening the war into Cambodia and Laos in order to interdict the Ho Chi Minh trail. He was unable to use the absolutist stance that "we can't win unless we expand the war". Instead, he focused on "positive indicators", which ultimately turned worthless when the Tet Offensive occurred, since all his pronouncements of "positive indicators" did not hint at the possibility of such a last-gasp dramatic event. Tet outmaneuvered all of Westmoreland's pronouncements on "positive indicators" in the minds of the American public. Although the communists were severely depleted by the heavy fighting at Khe Sanh when their conventional assaults were battered by American firepower, as well as tens of thousands of deaths in the Tet Offensive, American political opinion and the panic engendered by the communist surprise sapped U.S. support for the war, even though the events of early 1968 put the United States and South Vietnam into a much stronger military position.

At one point in 1968, Westmoreland considered the use of nuclear weapons in Vietnam in a contingency plan codenamed Fracture Jaw, which was abandoned when it became known to the White House.

Army Chief of Staff

In June 1968, Westmoreland was replaced by General Creighton Abrams, the decision being announced shortly after the Tet Offensive. Although the decision had been made in late 1967, it was widely seen in the media as a punishment for being caught off guard by the communist assault. He was mentioned in a Time magazine article as a potential candidate for the 1968 Republican presidential nomination.

Westmoreland served as Chief of Staff of the United States Army from 1968 to 1972. In 1970, as Chief of Staff, in response to the My Lai Massacre by United States Army forces (and subsequent cover up by the Army chain of command), he commissioned an army investigation that compiled a comprehensive and seminal study of leadership within the army during the Vietnam War demonstrating a severe erosion of adherence to the army's officer code of "Duty, Honor, Country". The report, entitled Study on Military Professionalism, had a profound influence on Army policies, beginning with Westmoreland's decision to end the policy that officers serving in Vietnam would be rotated into a different post after only six months. However, to lessen the impact of this damaging report, Westmoreland ordered that the document be kept on "close hold" across the entire Army for a period of two years and not disseminated to War College attendees. The report only became known to the public after Westmoreland retired in 1972.

Many military historians have pointed out that Westmoreland became Chief of Staff at the worst time in history with regard to the army. Guiding the army as it transitioned to an all-volunteer force, he issued many directives to try to make Army life better and more palatable for United States youth—e.g., allowing soldiers to wear sideburns and to drink beer in the mess hall. However, many hard-liners scorned these as too liberal.

Later years

Westmoreland ran unsuccessfully for governor of South Carolina in the 1974 election. He published his autobiography the following year. Westmoreland later served on a task force to improve educational standards in the state of South Carolina.

In 1986, Westmoreland served as grand marshal of the Chicago Vietnam Veterans parade. The parade, attended by 200,000 Vietnam veterans and more than half a million spectators, did much to repair the rift between Vietnam veterans and the American public.

You can visit wikipedia.org/wiki/William_ Westmoreland to read further.

67
Charleston—Where Good Things Happen!

Charleston, South Carolina, is the jewel of the South. It is a tourist Mecca, especially in the spring and early summer, and has an appeal that is universal. Besides that, The Citadel is located there. The city and its surrounding areas contain an endless supply of history, intrigue and Southern beauty. Through activities like Spoleto Charleston has started a new culture in music and literary enlightenment.

Did I mention that the food is out of this world? Well, it is, and every dish seems to taste better because it is in Charleston. Perhaps the moss hanging from the trees brings all this about, but believe me, Charleston is special!

After spending nearly eight years in the dungeons of the infamous Hanoi Hilton, I looked forward to my first trip to the "Holy City" and to returning to the incubator of my life, The Citadel. Fortunately General Mark Clark, President of The Citadel, invited me down for a visit and a little CID PR event. I had already been assigned to Dobbins Air Force Base in Marietta, Georgia as assistant to the commanding general of the Air Force Reserve in that sector, and was in my new Air Force uniform and gaining weight. Mom was taking care of that. Life was good, except for the occasional times I had to deal with the mother of our children out in California. *Miserable* is the best word I can use to describe that scenario. Going to Charleston would be like visiting heaven. I could hardly wait!

From the time I entered General Clark's office I became the center of attention. He was a great listener as I waded through my experiences in Vietnam. His questions were piercing and to the point, and I felt as though I had a new friend. Next, we were standing out on the parade ground, where the Corps of Cadets honored me by marching in review. I kept looking at the band drum major and comparing his movements and stature to what I recall I used to have. *Not bad*, I thought, and indeed the entire Corps looked magnificent. I was one proud guy!

The general's car pulled up after the parade, and we headed downtown to some event on Broad Street. I was to make a few remarks after being introduced by General Clark. That was an honor in itself, and I hoped that I would not disappoint him or the crowd. I spoke for a few moments and don't remember a word I uttered, but I received a huge round of applause. When this event was over, everyone mingled, shook hands and introduced himself or herself. I don't recall a single one—except Dr. Jim Edwards.

Jim shook my hand firmly as he looked me square in the eyes and made me feel like an old friend. I had a feeling that I would be seeing him again, at another place and for a different reason and purpose. This turned out to be true.

On the way back to the campus, General Clark commented favorably on my remarks and said, "You sounded like you were running for public office as a candidate!"

I laughed and then secretly filed it away to revisit at a later time. To return to The Citadel was like getting a new and invigorating outlook on life, and I loved it. My drive back to Marietta was filled with joy, suspense over the future and a huge question—*What was God lining up for me to accomplish?*

Within a week or so, Dr. Edwards called to invite me to speak to his civic club there in Charleston. He wanted to provide me a platform from which to *tell it like it was*. I agreed, and the date and time were set. The good Lord was already at work!

Ann Edwards was the ultimate Southern lady, with all the charm and manners you would expect from a person of Charleston lineage. I told Jim that he had married well above his status and that he should hang on to this one! Our first evening together was fantastic, and I learned a lot about my new friend. Jim was born in Hawthorne, Florida. He was a long- time Republican, an officer in the U.S. Maritime Service during WW II and was currently a member of the U.S. Naval Reserve. He graduated from the College of Charleston in 1950, received a D.M.D. in 1955 from the University of Louisville, and did some post graduate work at the University of Pennsylvania. Now he was a dentist in Charleston specializing in oral surgery.

Jim told me of his first Republican job, which was chairman of the party for the First Congressional District of South Carolina. Dr. Edwards became a candidate to replace Mendel Rivers when he died, but did not make it—although he gained a lot of name recognition in the process. Soon afterwards, he was elected to the South Carolina Senate and was presently serving in that capacity. Now the other shoe was about to hit the floor. Jim wanted me to run against Senator Fritz Hollings, a Citadel grad and an acquaintance of mine.

I just about fainted. Fritz was a well-established and long-term senator who had served many terms in Washington. Jim explained that I had a 28% name recognition in South Carolina by recent polls, which was a huge advantage, but that I probably would not win. Yet, like he had done, I would be running to establish credibility and even more name recognition for something down the road. I was flattered and somewhat frustrated, as I was seriously considering announcing for Congress in Georgia. We talked long and hard about the merits of each opportunity and what the realistic expectations would be. After my speech, I left Charleston with a lot of concerns. But I knew I really had a new friend who cared about me.

The very next week Jim called and wanted to talk about General Westmoreland. He was aware that we knew each other. Jim asked if I could shed any light on the general considering a run for Governor of South Carolina.

"What!" I exclaimed. "This guy doesn't even know what party he should be in." I told Jim of my experience in Rankin Smith's VIP suite.

Jim said that he was almost certain that General Westmoreland was going to throw his hat in the ring for the Republican Primary.

I encouraged Jim to throw his own hat there and go after him.

He said he was seriously considering such a move.

I again encouraged him mightily to run against the general because he was out of step with South Carolina and its citizens' needs.

I added a few more choice words to try to seal the deal, and we signed off.

A few days later, I read in the Atlanta Journal that both the General and Dr. Jim Edwards, state senator, had announced for governor. I was elated and called Jim to tell him of my joy at reading this. Then all hell tore loose!

The primary battle was between a warrior who wore four stars on his watchband, and a knowledgeable political candidate who knew his way around the political battlefield. Jim won in 1974 by 15% of the vote.

Now he would face Pug Ravenel, who had beaten Bryan Dorn by over 32,000 votes. But the South Carolina Supreme Court ruled that Ravenel did not meet the state's residency requirements, so the Democrats were forced to run Bryan Dorn against Jim. On November 5, 1974, Jim received 266,109 votes to 248,938 for Dorn.

During the Watergate scandal, Jim became the first Republican governor of South Carolina since Reconstruction. I received an invitation from the governor's office and attended the inauguration in Columbia, South Carolina. I, on the other hand, had just lost the closest congressional race in the country. Only 200 votes separated me from my opponent. My friend was to be a governor. What was I to become?

General Mark W. Clark Bio
(from www.citadel.edu)

Mark Clark was born in Madison Barrack, New York in 1896. He graduated from the United States Military Academy at West Point in 1917 and served in France during World War I.

In World War II, before the Allied invasion of North Africa, General Clark, as Deputy Commander in Chief of the Allied Forces in the North African Theater, made a secret and hazardous trip to Algeria on the submarine SERAPH to gather intelligence for the landing.

(67.1) Portrait of Gen. Mark Clark, President of The Citadel from 1954-1965.

In 1943, General Mark Clark became Commanding General of the 5th Army in Italy, and in 1944, he assumed command of the 15th Army Group, consisting of all the Allied Forces in Italy.

In 1945, General Clark was chief of U.S. Occupation Forces in Austria and U.S. High Commissioner for Austria. As Deputy to the U.S. Secretary of State, he negotiated a treaty for Austria with the Council of Foreign Ministers.

As commander in chief of the United Nations Command in 1953, he signed a military armistice between the United Nations Command, and the North Korean Army and the Chinese People's Volunteers in Korea.

In 1953, General Clark accepted the Presidency of The Citadel, where he served for twelve years. After retirement, he was named President Emeritus of the college. General Clark died in 1984 and is buried on The Citadel campus next to Mark Clark Hall.

James B. Edwards Bio
(excerpted from wikipedia.org)

James Burrows Edwards (June 24, 1927 – December 26, 2014) was an American politician and administrator from South Carolina. He was the first Republican to be elected the Governor of South Carolina since the post-Civil War Reconstruction Era in the 1800s. He later served as the U.S. Secretary of Energy under Ronald Reagan.

(67.2) Governor James B. Edwards of SC

Early life and career

Edwards was born in Hawthorne, Florida, and was an officer in the U.S. Maritime Service during World War II. He continued his service in the U.S. Naval Reserve after the war. Edwards received a bachelor's degree in 1950 at the College of Charleston where he was a brother of Pi Kappa Phi fraternity. He received a D.M.D. in 1955 from the University of Louisville, and did his dental internship at the University of Pennsylvania. Returning to Charleston, Edwards established a dentistry practice in 1960 that specialized in oral surgery. He subsequently held a variety of positions associated with dentistry in the community.

Political career

In 1970, Edwards became chairman of the Republican Party of South Carolina's 1st congressional district. In that capacity as a supporter of the Republican gubernatorial nominee, U.S. Representative Albert Watson of South Carolina's 2nd congressional district, Edwards claimed that Watson's Democratic opponent, John C. West, worked covertly in 1969 against the nomination of South Carolina's Clement Haynsworth to the United States Supreme Court. The Nixon nominee failed in the U.S. Senate, 55 to 45, on grounds of alleged bias against organized labor and a lack of supports for civil rights. Edwards predicted that West as governor would install "an ultra-liberal, minority-dominated state government," citing West's political ties to Hubert H. Humphrey and Roy Wilkins, longtime executive director of the NAACP.

Edwards first ran as a candidate in 1971, when he entered a special election to fill the vacancy in the Charleston-centered 1st congressional district caused by the death of longtime Democrat L. Mendel Rivers. Edwards narrowly lost to one of Rivers' staffers, Mendel Jackson Davis.

Edwards gained enough name recognition from his strong showing in the special election that he was elected to the South Carolina Senate as a Republican from white-majority Charleston County. Two years later, he entered the governor's race as a long-shot candidate. Edwards upset General William Westmoreland in the Republican primary, and he defeated Democratic Congressman William Jennings Bryan Dorn of South Carolina's 3rd congressional district in the general election. Dorn had become the Democratic nominee after the winner of the runoff election, Pug Ravenel, was disqualified on residency grounds.

Edwards was elected as the first Republican governor of the state since Daniel Henry Chamberlain in 1876. 1974 was otherwise a dismal year for Republicans nationally because of the Watergate scandal and lingering opposition to the Vietnam War, both of which may have contributed to the primary defeat of Westmoreland, commander of U.S. forces during the late 1960s.

Later career and death

At that time South Carolina Governors were not allowed to serve two terms in succession, so Edwards was unable to seek re-election in 1978. In 1981, U.S. President Ronald W. Reagan appointed Edwards to be the Secretary of Energy. He resigned two years later to serve as the President of the Medical University of South Carolina, a post that he held for seventeen years. In 1997, Edwards was inducted into the South Carolina Hall of Fame. In 2008, Edwards endorsed former Governor Mitt Romney of Massachusetts for his party's presidential nomination.

As governor and thereafter, Edwards developed a close friendship with his Democratic predecessor, John C. West, whom he had earlier accused of undermining the Haynsworth nomination.

In 1994, the state legislature renamed a portion of the Mark Clark Expressway that crosses the Wando River the James B. Edwards Bridge. In 2010, the new MUSC dental building and the dental school was renamed in his honor as the James B. Edwards College of Dental Medicine. Edwards died at his home in Mount Pleasant on December 26, 2014 at the age of 87 from complications from a stroke.

68
The One Who Really Counts!

As a man, I have often wondered what really goes on in the minds of two people who are about to be introduced to each other through a mutual friend. Does the friend truly believe that a "match" is about to take place that will be the most important event in their lives to this point? Have the descriptions passed along from the matchmaker to the two recipients adequately expressed the real essence of their being? Should the opinion of the matchmaker be the most important element in this event?

In my case, the matchmaker was a very attractive member of my new Sunday School Class in Charlotte. She had caught my eye from the very first time I attended the class. Shortly, I discovered she was married with children. After our initial introduction was completed and I had the marital status squared away, she seemed to want to continue talking with me. But now it was about someone else, a good friend of hers who was also a member of our Church—Myers Park Presbyterian Church—and was about to be single as the result of a pending divorce. The description she gave me was enticing and certainly sparked my attention, so I told her that I was indeed interested.

Virginia was the Matchmaker, and she and her friend worked in a dress shop in the exclusive Myers Park area of Charlotte. The Christmas of 1979 was just around the corner, and I planned to drive to Atlanta to visit with my mother and sister who lived together in Marietta, Georgia, right outside Atlanta.

I had already concluded that no man should visit two ladies at this time of year without bringing good tidings of great joy, so I began thinking about presents for my two favorite people. Both of them loved clothes and all the associated intricacies like scarves, belts, and the like. I concluded that Virginia and her friend might provide a possible solution to my Christmas dilemma, plus I would be able to meet her friend in more of a business atmosphere rather than a staged romantic selection process. So off I went to accomplish the two objectives.

December 20, 1979, was a beautiful day, and the Christmas lights added to the delight of shopping for my two ladies. Also, little did I know how important this day would be in my life!

The area around the Ladies Shop was filled with all kinds of stores from shoes to foods, and I enjoyed browsing amongst them. All of a sudden I heard my name being called by a voice I recognized—Virginia! She was standing right outside the shop in which she worked, and by chance had seen me as she came out for a breath of fresh air.

We embraced and exchanged holiday greetings, and then she went straight to the point—her friend was in the shop with a customer. Nothing would satisfy Virginia but for me to follow her back into that store to meet Catherine, her friend. I had no alternative but to do exactly like she wanted, so "follow me" became my order for the day!

Christmas music was flowing from the shop's speakers and a spirit of joy seemed to pervade the entire area. My escort took me to a balcony overlooking a downstairs area that was stuffed with possible gifts for the store's customers at this time of year. My gift was walking around on two gorgeous legs with high heels that accentuated every curve this woman dared to show.

Catherine has commented many times since then that the brown suit she was wearing was the worst outfit that she owned and she felt somewhat bedraggled as a result. I didn't see things in that same light, however! She was my kind of woman and I wanted to meet her *RIGHT NOW!*

LET'S BACK UP A minute to see what had transpired between Virginia and Catherine, since my name had come into the equation. In explaining me to Catherine, she pointed out that I had been a POW in North Vietnam for over seven years, was balding, but had two piercing blue eyes that held everything together!

I know that Catherine must have thought that any man held captive that long must be a raving sex maniac by now. That just wasn't true. I had already been one of them for years before being shot down! She didn't like the balding part either, as her present husband had the same malady.

My eyes were my only saving grace, and she reluctantly agreed to at least meet me before writing me off completely. That was the situation as I said hello and began the Herculean task of trying to satisfy any expectations she may have had relating to having a new guy in her life.

She was impressed that a bachelor would be shopping for presents for his mother and sister at Christmas. Her concrete shell was beginning to crack and I sensed opportunity lay ahead. Our conversation flowed very smoothly, and an aura of acceptance surrounded us. I had no idea what to say or ask, so I blurted out, "Are you busy this evening?"

She seemed to stumble for an instant before saying she was going to a neighborhood Christmas cocktail party.

I decided to pursue this further by asking, "May I escort you to the party?" A shy glance with a smile and an interested look prompted her to reply, "Yes, of course!"

We chatted briefly about the party, who was coming, where it was, what time, and where she lived? But the most important item just flipped in my mind. I asked if she would join me for a cocktail after work that very day?

Catherine accepted!

As it was already closing time, I found something else to do until she was ready to leave. She had led me to purchase two gifts for my ladies so I was set for Christmas. It was now time for me to relax and explore a relationship with a very attractive woman that—until twenty minutes ago—I had never seen and knew little to nothing about.

As I've said before—Fighter Pilots live the best lives!

Jenkos was the cellar bar that was in that area, so we went down the stairs into a more darkened environment with romantic music floating about. The waiter seated us at a nice comfortable table, and we began to pick up on the conversation we had started earlier in Catherine's dress shop.

I told her about the condo I had initially rented on Queens Road across the street from Myers Park United Methodist Church.

She immediately perked up and said her parents' home was right next door to the church, and it had been the old Joe Cannon home years before.

I quickly added that I had seen several political signs in that yard advertising for Democrats.

She acknowledged that her cousin was married to John Ingram, the current Insurance Commissioner for North Carolina. One thing led to another and eventually Albemarle became the center of our conversation.

When I was in high school in Concord, my Dad had opened furniture stores in Albemarle and Kannapolis, and I had worked in those stores in addition to the Concord store (Maxwell Brothers & Collins). My uncle, Ralph Setzler, had moved to Albemarle to run that store for Dad, and of course his family and all my cousins ended up in Albemarle.

Wouldn't you know it? Catherine knew all of them because she had spent a lot of time at her Grandmother's home in Albemarle and walked past Uncle Ralph's house every day. Small world, isn't it?

I had dated several girls in Albemarle during my high school days and Catherine knew all of them, although I was eight years older than she. I had met many of the Albemarle High athletes because Concord played them in football and basketball. I also had some marching band contacts, but most of my dates had come through my first cousins—the Setzlers—and their friends.

Wow! We had better get out of there because the party I had invited myself to was coming up fast. I got all the information on where she lived and when to pick her up, and we went our separate ways. Life was beginning to get interesting. My attention now centered on a new lady in my life named Catherine.

As I drove back to my new place on Thermal Road, my mind was spinning faster than I could keep up with. So many new twists and turns in the last two hours. Where was all this leading me? To put things in their proper prospective, I was forty-eight years old, drove a Ford Thunderbird provided by the company for whom I worked—Pat Ryan & Associates out of Chicago—and I had just purchased a new townhouse in east Charlotte.

Man, I struggled to pick out the best outfit I could assemble and I was throwing clothes around like I was shopping at a bargain basement sale. Finally, I picked the right trousers along with a jacket as colorful as Jacob's jacket in the Biblical story. To bring all these colors and patterns together, I slipped into a red turtleneck sweater that fit me like a glove. *Smashing!* I thought.

I had never looked in the mirror so much. What was so different about this date? I just wanted everything to be perfect! I kept looking at my watch to be certain I was on time tonight of all nights. One more look in the mirror, a final comb-through of hair that simply would not lie down, and I was out the door. I was truly as excited as if this were my "Coming Out" party. But I should be calm, Fighter Pilot laid-back, and as sharp as I could be.

I was ready as I pulled into Catherine's driveway on Colville Road in Eastover—one of Charlotte's finest residential areas. My Charlotte debut was about to begin.

Catherine had told me about her three daughters, but the one whose name really stuck with me was her youngest, Adelaide Quincy Scott, an eight-year-old wiser than her years might indicate, and very close to her mother. I walked up to the front door and was about to ring the doorbell when the door opened and there stood this cute little girl wearing glasses and blonde curls and looking me over like I was a new bicycle.

I introduced myself, and she blurted out that she was Quincy too. Did this portend a battle for future position or status? Only time would tell. Addle informed me that her mother was still upstairs dressing and would be down very shortly.

In the meantime, Addle introduced me to her piano in their living room. It looked like a Baby Grand version, but was also a player-roll piano. Because I played by ear, this was of interest to me. I anticipated sitting down and knocking out a tune or two, but my little hostess beat me to the punch. She slipped into the piano seat and started playing the Spinning Song at breakneck speed. I knew the song and tried to slow her down a bit, but she thought faster was better and, I guess, more irritating. She quickly finished the song and disappeared up the stairs. (Now it was *my* time.)

The tone of the instrument was excellent and it was in tune, so I chose *Tenderly* as my first selection for the evening. I will have to say that this rendition was probably the best that I had ever played, and I was hoping that Catherine was getting an earful of the nice chords and melody I was producing.

Suddenly, she rounded the corner with praise and admiration for the song that I was playing. It certainly was a change of pace from the Spinning Song, which sounded like a musical truck with no brakes heading straight down a mountainside at breakneck speed. But as a new student, Addle was doing her best, and I, as a stranger, should not be judgmental of her performance. I was here to make the best possible impression on Catherine and her daughters—although I had only met Sally very briefly and Caroline not at all.

Catherine informed me that we had better depart for the party, so we gathered our wraps, got into my car, and drove the short distance to the scene of the festivities. My Charlotte introduction to the local social scene was about to begin.

I parked the car, and we walked to the front door of this beautiful brick home. Party noise was escaping from the inside and beckoning us to enter and participate. The host and hostess welcomed us both. And then it happened! For the first time, I could see Catherine as if she were under a spotlight. Beautiful blonde hair down to her shoulders and her dress was a wonderful light tan wrap that showed her magnificent figure perfectly. *Poised* was not the word to describe her movements around that home. Everyone wanted to hug her and say hello.

I felt as if I had escorted the Queen to this Christmas party. Without a doubt, Catherine was the prettiest woman I had ever been with, and I was to find that her beauty was deep and challenging. My personal Fighter Pilot Angel must have been working overtime for me that night and I loved it!

The drinks were great, the food was fantastic, and everyone was nice and friendly. I met many new friends that evening. They would become lifelong acquaintances. My date was unbelievable, and she looked at me from time-to-time with a penetrating depth that excited me and stirred my passion to want her company as much as she would allow. Somehow, I had to test what progress I was making with this lovely damsel. So I held her hand and led her about halfway up the stairs to the second floor. I stopped, put my arm around her, and put my face nose to nose with hers. I was thinking that the kiss I wanted to give her should be the softest and most provocative that I could muster. I pulled her closer until our lips met and I could get no closer to her.

Wow! This was it! I wanted this woman long term, but I didn't want to scare her. I loosened my grip on her, but she didn't move away. In fact, her lips began a shy search for mine and we met again. I could feel the sparks flying, so I just held on like my boat was sinking and she was my life jacket. What a great feeling!

We looked at each other with a stunned look of amazement, and moved down the stairs. People were beginning to leave, so we said our good-byes to our host and hostess and some of Catherine's close friends, cranked up my chariot and drove away.

The evening was too early to end, so I asked if I might show her my place—you know, *etchings* and the like?

Without hesitation, she said, "Fine."

Man! I was shaking and stuttering a bit as I searched for the words to describe my place. A few minutes later we arrived and I escorted her into my abode. As I closed the front door I pulled her over into an embrace and kissed her like this was for real and I wanted a lot more of this.

She physically surrendered to my actions, and Catherine and Quincy were to be close from that minute on. The passion was there, the desire was there—this night was right for us!

JUST AS MY "WIFE to be"—Catherine—was divorcing her husband of twenty years, and shortly before Sir Lancelot—that would be me—appeared on the scene, she and her three daughters had purchased a Pekingese-Poodle puppy named Pooh while at Pawley's Island, SC. This was during the summer of 1979.

I was introduced to this lovely lady December 20, 1979, and we were married December 20, 1980, in Charlotte. Of course "Poohsie" was part of the deal, and we became closer with each passing day. I even referred to him as my son. Poohsie Woosie became a big part of the love of my life. Catherine and I developed our own dog language so that we could talk directly to Pooh. Life was not just good—it was terrific!

Sometime in mid-1987, Pooh started becoming irritable at night, and would bark and raise hell until one of us would tend to him. I, too, became irritated, and decided it was time to close him in the laundry room at night. This seemed to work until I came down one morning and he wasn't in the laundry room. Actually, he was in the room, but he had climbed over behind the washer-dryer and had broken his neck trying to reverse course to get out. This was like one of our kids passing. The entire family was in mourning.

To this day, Catherine and I lapse into Pooh language when we express caring for each other or love for one another. Pooh would have given me many happy hours while I was in prison, but now he enhances my life and enforces my love for Catherine and our family.

God Bless You My Little Friend!

(68.1) *Quincy & Catherine take their marriage vows, Dec. 20, 1980, Myers Park Presbyterian Chapel. Officiating is Rev. Randy Taylor.*

(68.2) *Quincy & Catherine enjoying their beautiful backyard & pool in Charlotte, NC.*

(68.3) *Here they are "playing the role" of the U.S. President & First Lady at a fundraiser at the Charlotte Museum of History (Quincy was Board Chair).*

(68.4) Quincy's final jet flight at Randolph AFB, Texas, on April 3, 2003.

(68.5) Quincy & Catherine dressed as characters from "Grease" at the Cypress Club's Halloween party

69
Letter To Santa—December 1993

D_{ear Santa,}

I'm a little old to be doing this, and I'm a little embarrassed for anyone else to know I'm writing to you, so please treat this with great confi-
dentiality. My reputation, you know!

My name must be in your archives because it's been nearly 80 years
since I first corresponded with you. If you remember, I am the kid who
wanted a Flexi-Flyer on wheels. Now I didn't mean for just one Christmas—I meant for *every* Christmas!

As you can see, I just flat liked Flexi-Flyers. My best buddy was Lee
Kinard, and he ended up being a big TV celebrity in the Greensboro-High
Point area. We both loved our Flexis, and spent hours and hours down in
the red hills behind our homes making Flexi trails. Boy! That was really
living! Frankly, I haven't felt as good about life until a few years ago when I
lost my freedom while serving my country, and became a Prisoner of War
in North Vietnam. Please let me explain.

I was a Fighter Pilot flying a great airplane—the Republic F-105
Thunder Chief. My flying career came to an abrupt halt as my plane and
I were shot out of the sky over North Vietnam on September 2, 1965.

Quick as you can flick your finger, I lost my freedom and began a 7 1/2 year tour as a POW in a Hanoi prison cell. It was really tough Santa, but I started to appreciate the wonderful things that America and freedom have to offer.

Now that I have been released and am back home and free again, I will never forget the lessons I learned there. Enjoying the love and true meaning of Christmas and the spirit surrounding it makes me feel like a kid again. What a refreshing feeling!

Well Santa—I am going to be with a lot of friends during the Holiday season who are in their own personal prisons. I didn't realize that there were so many people in this hostile condition, but radio, TV, and the newspaper tell about them all the time. And you know what? I know a lot of them personally. I see and talk to them every day. They seem to be chained to something that keeps them distracted, disinterested, and divided from paying attention to the things in life which really matter.

My personal Christmas experiences have taught me that it is not the gift that is important—it is the *giver!* It is not the price of the gift, but rather the sentiment that is attached to the gift—the love and true meaning that flows from the giver to the receiver and back again. These are the most important items. Not only at Christmas, but also at any time one's true feelings are being expressed to another.

The spirit of Christmas is a sacred and observable joy that only God administers to us humans. Like the smile on a small child's face when the secret gift is—or becomes—known for all to see and enjoy. Gift giving is always a pleasure and a privilege for young and old.

Santa—you and God must be first cousins!

Merry Christmas!

(69.1) Santa (Quincy), Mom, and Carolyn's dog Sugar at Quincy's Marietta, GA home, Dec. 1974

(69.2) The east side of Quincy's home in Marietta, GA.

(69.3) The north side of Quincy's home.

70
The Real Estate Business

I had never sold a home since I had been in the USAF, so I decided it was time for me to at least learn something about the business end of that endeavor. My present job was in Public Relations, and I had just completed a joint venture with Coach Jim Valvano of NC State University. We had contracted to do a life-sized statue of the first Kentucky Derby winner, Aristides, who had won in 1875. We were fortunate to have great connections through the Churchill Downs organization and had landed Cornelius Vanderbilt Whitney to dedicate the statue prior to the next Derby.

Everything came off without a hitch until I discovered a big error in Jim's staff's sales and commission payments to me on the project. I wrote a letter to Jim informing him of my finding and suggested he should buy me out or I should buy him out in order to settle the issue. He bought me out and we closed on friendly terms.

Shortly thereafter, I met a sculptor from Texas who was also a big-game hunter and was interested in a project I had dreamed up. A good friend of mine had a Jaguar dealership in South Carolina and also had a list of all Jag dealers in the US and Canada and South America. My idea was to market a medium sized and numbered statue of a Jaguar to all dealers in North and South America as gifts to their customers. I composed the letter. My sculptor had already completed the Limited Edition Jaguar, so I mailed the letters and the responses started arriving. It was better than I thought it would be!

Now I had to be thinking of my next move and my inclination seemed to be leading me into the real estate business.

In North Carolina at that time, the first step to getting a state license to sell a residence was to attend a real estate school and take an exam. Then if you passed the exam, you would receive a real estate license and become registered. About half the students failed the test on their first attempt and would have to take the course again and pass the exam in order to become a real estate agent. I found the course to be interesting and challenging and I passed the Mingle Real Estate course the first time. I made fast friends with a lot of strangers during my attendance at the school.

Most of my new friends had already decided to go into commercial real estate. That required additional schooling and examinations so I just followed them and signed up too. Some wanted to be the Broker In Charge of their firm. Others, like me, were only interested in selling and leasing commercial properties like office buildings or warehouses and shopping centers. Several of my closest friends were sent to the school to gain the knowledge needed to return to their firms to perform specific tasks, but I was not one of them. I had no idea where I was going to be working or what I might be doing so I started making a list of firms with which I might interview.

One of the oldest and most reputable firms I came across was Southern Real Estate, begun in 1899 and owned by the Rose family. At the time I interviewed with them, they occupied an entire floor in the big savings and loan building near the square in uptown Charlotte. On my first visit I was introduced to Louis Rose, Jr. whose family owned the business. He looked familiar and I later determined that I had seen him and his wife at Myers Park Presbyterian Church when I was first church-hunting back in 1979. All of the brokers and their staffs seemed to be "top notch" and Louis and I became fast friends. He had two sons, Louis III and Caldwell, who both worked there. I concluded that this would be a great place to hang my hat so I accepted their offer to join them.

About that same time, the *Charlotte Observer* came out with a story about a new uptown Convention Center. It outlined several sites that might be of interest. One was the Young Ford site located by the big Merchandise Mart. I had been the General Sales Manager at Arnold Palmer Cadillac across the street from Charlie Young's Ford dealership. These items had stuck in my mind and when I quickly discovered that one of SRE's big clients controlled the Merchandise Mart, my mind started twirling and I began to envision my first big deal at Southern!

I made an appointment with Louis, Jr. and told him of my thoughts and what we might do to make this happen. He listened very carefully and suggested we make an appointment with Charles Young to feel him out on this issue. I agreed to be the contact person since I already knew him from being at the Cadillac dealership. I really felt good about Louis allowing a new guy to take the lead on this size project. I quickly realized that I could learn a lot by listening and observing Louis doing what he did best—working with land assemblage for project development. It took us three years to complete this deal, but it was worth it, both financially and in helping develop the uptown area into a thriving business district.

In my 23 years at Southern Real Estate, many interesting projects came my way. One of the most challenging was a project involving Duke Energy and a huge lake project in the Gaffney, SC area near the Broad River. The project was connected to the Atomic Energy plants that were to be constructed in that area, and the resulting lake we were working on was to act as a coolant if ever any plant got overheated. This involved many acres and many families who would have to relocate. If the terms *atomic plant* or *water to cool down an overheated facility* ever reached the ears of the public, we would be dead in the water, so to speak. We had to have a plan!

A fairly new broker named Vince Sumner was assigned as my assistant. We spent hours together working on this project. Most of the time we had to drive to the Gaffney area to locate the exact address and names of the owners of the parcel we were interested in purchasing for our client. Before we could even do that we would have to spend hours going over county maps to keep as references for owners of interest, and try to develop a plan for assembling the most land in the most efficient manner.

We could never reveal whom we represented. This complicated our task tremendously and made it more difficult for the owners to accept dealing with us. If you can imagine—your doorbell rings. There stand two city slickers trying to purchase property that has been in your family for over 100 years, and they won't tell you what they want the land for. Man, this was a huge obstacle to overcome. We realized that this was going to take a lot of time and effort on our part to pull this off. It was a sensitive process and we had to handle it just right.

One of our best selling points was that people who are neighbors like to talk to each other. If we could convince them that we were good human beings and were decent and honest people, then the word would spread, making our task a little easier. After all, we were offering top dollar for their property—and money does speak with a loud voice! We made a lot of new friends during the year or so that we worked on this project, and we both learned a lot about people and ourselves. I enjoyed this one a lot.

Another large project was one near Clinton, NC. I had already done a lot of work for BFI, a landfill, trash and garbage disposal operation. They wanted me to assemble land near Clinton for a large garbage dump in that area. The name BFI could never be mentioned because people did not like garbage dumps near them, and BFI had a reputation for paying high prices for property. The area I was assigned to cover was in a fairly poor section of Sampson County. I spent a lot of time at the Registry Of Deeds looking up ownerships and putting together maps. I could see this was not going to be easy as one large parcel had 17 different owners and one of them lived in Paris. This became an 18-month project, but finally closed successfully for both Southern Real Estate and me.

The worst experience I ever had at SRE was the day I received a phone call from someone I used to know in Concord, my old hometown. I will call him Stratton. One of his relatives was a High School classmate of my Sister, Carolyn. Les Stratton wanted to meet with me to discuss his bringing a huge company from Chicago to Charlotte to establish Charlotte as the new headquarters for the operation. I recognized the name of the company, and of course I was really enthused over this opportunity. I thought it best to include my boss, Louis, since some contacts might be required that I didn't have. Mr. Stratton arrived at our office as arranged and I introduced him to Louis as we sat down at our conference table to learn of Stratton's plans.

Les had prepared a folder to include some of his investors from both the US and England. This seemed reasonable since a lot of their business was in Europe. He went into a long narrative of how he became involved in the project and then began telling us of his plans and his new firm's needs.

A Headquarters-type office was high on his list along with several large warehouse requirements. Also, a part of his total real estate requirement was a home, which had to be in Concord in an up-scale section of town. He had not lived in Concord since high school days so he wasn't familiar with the current status of availability, prices, etc. So this was to be a total move-in for the business and his personal home.

Finally, he wanted to bring select executives to the area and it was his desire to provide them company cars. I certainly had those contacts from my days at Arnold Palmer Cadillac so that would not be difficult to solve.

Of course Louis had me check out his references and credit, which I did quickly and my initial inquiries gave positive results. Now came the task of locating an office and warehouses. It took about 2 months to accomplish this and for Les to sign the leases and decide on upfitting the property to accommodate his requirements. I also found time to actually lease 6 cars, one Cadillac and 5 Buicks to satisfy the Executive car requirement.

Then I was tasked with finding a home that suited Les and his wife. I did not want to be officially involved in the residential part of the project, but I was aware of an historic home on Concord's main drag that was on the market, so I made that contact for the Strattons. Then came the pitch from left field!

My wife, Catherine, and I invited the Stratton family to dinner one night. That morning Les had called me asking if it might be possible for me to join his firm as a vice-president with a very good salary, and also the Cadillac would be mine to drive. I just about fell off my chair! I felt like a traitor to Louis for just considering the offer, but after heavy discussion, Catherine and I decided that this might be the break I needed.

I composed a letter of resignation, reviewed it thoroughly with Catherine, then presented it to Louis the next day. Man, that was hard! I couldn't keep the tears from running down my cheeks. Louis didn't say much other than we had a job to complete, so I excused myself and got back to work. Little did I know that this entire project was about to fall apart right in front of me and there was nothing I could do to stop it.

Les had told me that he and his wife were going to have to fly to Chicago to complete all the administrative matters involved in the closing. Around noon he called in a twit—saying that the airline's schedule would not accommodate his schedule and did I have any contacts that would fly them there and back on such short notice. I told him I did, and that I would get busy right away to line this up—and I did!

The timing was closing in on me as I called him to tell him to get moving this way and I would meet him at the private terminal at Douglas Airport in Charlotte to see them off. He said he wouldn't have time to go cash a check and could I have about $800 available for him to take to Chicago and he would pay me back after they arrived back in Charlotte the next day.

My head was spinning as I got the cash and headed out to the airport. "What the hell is happening?" Nothing made sense to me and I began to feel like a lamb being led to slaughter. Shortly after I arrived, my friend was there with his jet aircraft, and very soon Les and his wife arrived. They were very calm, but enthused over going to the closing, so I calmed down a bit and sent them off with a smile and a prayer that all would be well!

That evening I got a call from my friend who flew them to Chicago. He said Les was not prepared to pay them anything for flying them up, and he wanted me to know that this whole exercise was not on the up and up. I started trying to call Les, but with no success. I had been had!!

Finally the next day, Les called me to say that the closing did not happen and the deal had fallen apart. Wow! Here I am having sent Louis my letter of resignation, had Les sign six big car leases and two huge rental agreements for warehouse and office space, and he had also signed a sales agreement for a wonderful house in Concord, courtesy of me! This wonderful real estate "deal" has just melted in front of me and now I have to try to undo everything I have done! Can I do it? My answer was YES!

So I got the cars involved in this horrible tale back to the dealers, managed to negate all the property leases and the home sale, and worked up the nerve to sit down with Louis and tell him the truth. I wanted my job back! He opened his top drawer to his desk, pulled out my letter and had me read it to him. Embarrassed, humbled, humiliated—these words describe me fully at that time. What I didn't know was that every year after that, on this important date, Louis would invite me into his office, pull out this letter, and have me read it to him! How fortunate I was to have a boss who loved me and wanted me to be successful! Thank you Lord!

By the way, I think Les ended up in prison.

Turn about is fair play! Glad I'm out and he is in!

(70.1) First Kentucky Derby winner, Aristides.

(70.2) The Jaguar.

71
Support Staff Angels

"*Hello, Southern Real Estate. Julia Speaking!*"
This telephone message was delivered to every human being who called our business phone for years and years. It was the "voice" of our firm and set the scene for whatever transpired afterwards. Julia Livengood was that voice and her ethereal demeanor charmed all callers, and enticed them to want to talk more to her.

Whether it was to check on a specific property or to follow up on a sales call by one of our brokers, this lady made you feel comfortable and at home discussing your needs, and how Southern Real Estate might assist you.

Many of our customers commented on the effect Julia had on them, and the mood that she fostered just by answering the phone. She was great and much appreciated by all of us sales people at SRE. She made each of us feel as though we were special people to her, and that she was a part of each broker's team. Almost everyday I would select a song to sing to her. It might be a famous love song, or an old WWII USO song. I tried to make her laugh as much as possible and just enjoy the time we would spend together.

Her husband was a Veteran and suffered from some injuries he had received. He sported a Purple Heart License plate and displayed it with great pride and satisfaction. He died while she was an employee and we all tried to ease her pain as much as possible. When Julia finally retired, we suffered a great loss! She will be remembered as long as Southern Real Estate exists because she was a part of us! God bless you, Julia, wherever you are!

IT WOULD HAVE BEEN impossible for me to work at Southern Real Estate for the past 20 years without administrative assistance to help me accomplish the career achievements I have made. For every deal I have closed, and every project I have been a part of, there are hundreds of pages of data, contracts and summaries that have to be completed in order to verify the results. Through the years I have had several associates who have performed these tasks quite well. However, there is one who has been superior in every way one might evaluate performance—she is Olivia McDaniel!

Olivia and her husband, Gary, have become an important part of my life, and have taken roles in many endeavors to which I have committed. Southern Real Estate has been very gracious in allowing Olivia to continue to be a part of my public life—by typing my speeches and keeping up with my busy personal schedule in addition to my work as a very active broker there at SRE.

They (SRE) also participate in my annual Carolinas Freedom Foundation breakfast that is one of the largest patriotic events in Charlotte. Most of the time our Governor, the Charlotte Mayor, and key Mecklenburg County Commissioners, along with Board of Education members and elected Federal Officials attend these events. Over the years we have come to expect around 700 attendees at these breakfasts.

Olivia has had a big role in seating arrangements and crowd control. To say that she has been my right arm during these times is a gross understatement. She is my friend, my fellow co-worker and a fine Christian woman. I use her as my life's mentor and guide. Man, do we need more Olivias in this world!

Thank you Lord for this one!

(71.1) Julia Livengood, a voice to remember.

(71.2) Olivia and Gary Mc Daniel—"
The Best of The Best."

72
Fun at Work!

Working at Southern Real Estate really was fun. Louis Rose, Jr., our boss, was a hoot and loved to provide the occasion to have a good time. Golf was one of his favorite pastimes, and he enjoyed being with brokers who also were golfers. Unfortunately, I was not one of those people. Although I had a set of clubs and shot in the low 70's—that was just on the first three holes! I never had a chance for a hole in one because I rarely could get to the green—but I kept trying and everyone gave me high grades for the effort.

One weekend we hung up our real estate badges early and headed to Charleston for a round. I thought this was to be a drinking trip—and it was to a certain extent—but all the people brought their clubs. After checking into the hotel we headed up towards North Charleston where the alligators ran free and our golf balls seemed to disappear in a single gulp! This was a little too much of nature for me, and not enough of Charleston's famous cuisine. Every evening, however, our dining experiences brought us the best food and drink known to man. It was tremendous, and well enjoyed by all of the SRE golf club buddies.

This was just one of the trips Louis took us on. The most impressive trip, however, was SRE's 100th Anniversary soiree to California. That trip included our ladies, and golf clubs were not allowed. We all boarded an American Airlines aircraft and flew to San Diego, California. Louis really wanted to celebrate this one and had arranged a bus to take us to George's Cove at La Jolla for a wonderful dinner with exquisite wine. The place was beautiful! Catherine and I now claim La Jolla as our favorite vacation spot in the US. The sunsets are glorious!

Another trip arranged by Louis was our outing to the golf capital of the world—Sawgrass Golf Club in Florida. You may recall seeing its most famous hole on TV. There is a small lake with an island green rising out of the water. I sank 13 golf balls in that lake and finally had to get close enough to throw my ball onto the green. This one hole will test a golfer's patience and tenacity more than any I have ever encountered. Just seeing all that water and a postage-stamp-size-green is enough to cause one's knees to start shaking. This hole will wrap what confidence you have around your neck and turn you into a mere mortal! Maybe one of these days I will be able to hit my ball onto that miniscule green island and become a golf legend—at least in my own mind!

One other event stands out in my mind—the SRE Christmas Party. Louis invited everyone at SRE and our sister company, DMI, to be his guests at Quail Hollow Country Club for cocktails and dinner and some special entertainment. It might be a terrific magician or sleight-of-hand expert. It was always fascinating and interesting to watch.

In addition to that, I was always called upon to write a piece that (1) used "The Night Before Christmas" as its basic format; (2) everything had to rhyme; (3) I had to mention every member of the SRE/DMI staff; (4) it had to be funny or at least embarrassing to the person being talked about.

It would take me weeks to write this epistle, and at least 30-40 minutes to read it. Everyone would quiz me as to what I might be going to say about him or her that evening. It became a very popular part of the program, and I spent hours trying to dig up interesting tidbits on everyone.

Closing the evening with "Hummers" was another "must do" for this Christmas Special. *And Special it was!* For Louis Rose, Jr. was Santa in every way, and he will hold a place of honor in my memory for as long as I live on this earth!

Happy Heaven, Louis!

(72.1) Yeaman's Hall Club—Charleston, SC, where alligators will eat your golf balls like frogs eat bugs

(72.2) SRE's 100th Anniversary at La Jolla, CA's best restaurant, "George's At The Cove"

(72.3) The Players' 17th hole, Sawgrass, FL

(72.4)The Hummer, Official drink at SRE parties

73
September 11, 2001

This is the day that was! It is an historic day—December 7, 1942. Or was it 41? Or did it even happen at all? President Franklin Roosevelt declared that it was a day that would live in infamy!

As we humans try to place events of long ago in present recall, time has a corrosive element that wipes out the certainty that you know is real and has actually already happened. Pearl Harbor will never be forgotten. But why is it more in our recall and memory than the first actual attack by a foreign people on these United States of America? How long will it take for us to forget the details of this catastrophic event?

Where were you and what were you doing that morning when United Airlines Flight #11, at exactly 8:46 AM, crashed into the North Tower of the World Trade Center, immediately killing all 92 people on board? Did you actually see this happening on TV?

At 9:03 AM local time, United Airlines Flight #175 slammed into the southern façade of the South Tower at an air speed of 590 mph. It is estimated that 637 people were killed instantly at that moment.

American Airlines Flight #77 crashed into the western side of the Pentagon at 09:37 local time killing 184 people. These victims are memorialized in the Pentagon Memorial adjacent to the crash site.

United Airlines Flight #93 crashed into a field near the Diamond T Mine in Stonycreek Township, Pennsylvania. It is believed that the ultimate target for this aircraft was either the White House or the Capitol Building. Some of the passengers on this flight decided to "revolt" and this recorded message went around the world.

"Are you guys ready? OK! Let's roll!"

At 10:03 local time the plane went into the ground, killing all 40 passengers on board and the 4 hijackers. The aircraft went in inverted at a 40-degree nose-down attitude and made a crater that was 10 feet deep and 50 feet wide. Today, there is a memorial on site.

Remember the *unity* that gripped America during this time? It didn't take too long for it to diminish to a whisper, did it? A Dallas Morning News reporter found that a national poll taken in 2003 showed that our American pride level was at 70% then, but by June of 2016 that number was down to 52%.

My conclusion is that if the USA wants to be united and our people getting together to accomplish some goal—like winning a war or beating ISIS—then we are going to have to have one hell of an explosion—maybe nuclear—in this country to even get our attention!

This makes me want to throw up and run the other way!

That is why we need to *PRAY! PRAY! PRAY!* And ask God to forgive us for our arrogance and our propensity to forget when America has so much to remember. Please think about this and then do something about it.

God Bless America and God Bless Us!

(73.1) United Flight #175 crashed into South Tower at 9:03 am

74
Pensacola and the Bad News

Pensacola, Florida, is a beautiful place right off the Gulf of Mexico and a short distance from Destin. It is an historic area and the home of the famous U.S. Navy Aerial Demonstration Team, *"The Blue Angels."* Pensacola Naval Air Station is one of the Navy's finest training centers, and since the end of the Vietnam War, has become the home of the Robert E. Mitchell Center For Prisoner Of War Studies.

The Department of Defense established the center as a clinic to examine the POWs held in North Vietnam so that medical and psychological data could be collected and used to analyze the results. No other American fighting men had been incarcerated for the durations of these men, and the information about the effects of diet, torture and general deprivation would be of great benefit to future generations of the military.

In order to get the very best comparative data, the center selected an equal number of men of the same general ages as the POWs and scheduled them for annual visits to Pensacola Naval Air Station. These were people who were not in combat, were not captured, but who agreed to receive a free physical every year to be a part of this important program. It was a thorough examination, and—as my Dad used to say—"covered everything from Asshole to Appetite." It was during one of these sessions that my bad news surfaced.

Each of us POWs had a medical summary folder that was filled with charts, graphs, reports and all the information pertinent to our individual health and welfare. In essence, this folder contained the cumulative results of every physical we had received there at the clinic.

In early May of 2010, I arrived in Pensacola for my annual check-up. In the course of my examinations several blood samples were taken to be analyzed. This was standard procedure and served as a comparison—last year's results against the current year's results. One of the most important items to be compared was PSA (prostate-specific antigen). Researchers had searched for years for a male version of the Pap smear, and the PSA blood test appeared to be the best answer to providing information on the presence of cancer in the male genital area. The prostate is a gland composed of muscular and glandular tissue that surrounds the urethra at a male's bladder.

I knew little to nothing about an organ I had that was called the prostate, but this mysterious little organ was responsible for the deaths of thousands of men when cancer attached itself to the prostate. The real problem is that prostate cancer is fairly easy to cure and control if discovered early on. Unfortunately prostate cancer rarely produces observable symptoms until it spreads outside the prostate—then it may be too late! Men are, by nature, very vain about anything having to do with their "manhood." Couple that with a huge case of ignorance and you have a crisis about to happen.

Well, in my case, the current blood test for PSA was a lot higher than last year's reading. A huge red flag was unfurled and the military doctors advised me to get with my family physician as soon as possible to follow up on this finding.

When I returned to Charlotte I did just that, but my doctor saw no reason to be concerned even though I insisted we do further tests. I decided to fire him because I saw no reason for me to have to fight *him* to preserve *my* own health. When I started asking other men friends about a Urologist they might recommend, I was amazed at how many of them had experienced prostate problems.

Finally, I selected the doctor I thought would do me the best job and made an appointment with him. He had me come in for several tests with his associates prior to meeting with him. On the big day, I took Catherine with me because this ailment involved more than just me. Besides, she could remember medical terms and I wasn't too hot on that. In fact, I gave her the name of "Nurse Good Body," taken from the TV show *Hee Haw.*

When we walked into his office he was facing away from us while sitting at his computer. I thought it rude that he didn't greet us in a normal way—handshake and welcome—but he did ask us to be seated. He asked several questions to complete whatever he was working on then suddenly pushed back in his chair. Almost in a yell he announced, "I'm going to have to castrate you!"

The blood drained from my face and my knees got weak. But my vocal chords strongly blurted out, "The *HELL* you are!" With my own announcement, Catherine and I exited his office—never again to return!

Mind you, this doctor's office had already performed a biopsy and had implanted a medication in my left arm called *Vantas* that would take a year to completely disperse an element that would kill my testicle's ability to manufacture testosterone. I was actually on the road to castration and didn't realize it. This was the first part of my treatment, and radiation was to be the second part.

I had already selected a radiologist and was scheduled for 8 ½ weeks of treatment for 5 times per week. During this time of consternation and uncertainty, I found a program at Walter Reed Hospital in Bethesda, Maryland, that provided consultations to active duty military and to veterans who had prostate cancer. (The Vietnam Agent Orange project had caused a lot of prostate cancer among those connected with spraying the jungles so as to kill the jungle growth and expose the enemy.)

This was a special one-day program with the best specialists in the world. The hospital doctors accepted six military each day to examine, and then they made recommendations as to what treatment each man should receive. They acknowledged that what I was planning to do in Charlotte was very appropriate for my condition. Man, was I pleased with their findings! Catherine and I flew home enlightened and pleased that we now had a great second opinion. Bring on the treatment!

In order to offset the fatigue factor associated with this treatment, I decided to double my time spent exercising. This was one of the best decisions I have ever made! Not only was I not fatigued from all the medication and radiation I was taking, but the extra exercise also helped in my recovery. After nearly 7 years of treatment, I have been declared, "CURED!"

There is a saying: *God looks after old Fighter Pilots who drink Martinis!* I guess I qualify on both counts.

Amen!

Gentlemen: Have a PSA blood check today!

PROSTATE FACTS
AND CANCER SYMPTOMS
(from prostrcision.com/prostate-facts)

About the Prostate

The prostate is located behind the pubic bones in a man's pelvis and is sandwiched between the bladder on top and the rectum underneath. A normal-sized prostate is about the size of a walnut. Similar to a shell around an egg, a capsule covers and contains the prostate except at the apex (bottom). The urethra, a tube that runs through the middle of the prostate and out of the penis, empties urine out of the bladder. Very small tubes, called ejaculatory ducts, run from each testicle into the prostate and empty into the urethra in the middle of the gland.

About two-thirds of the prostate are normal prostate cells, and the remaining part is the urethra, muscles that act like valves to prevent leakage of urination, fibrous tissue that holds the prostate together, blood vessels and ejaculatory ducts. The purpose of normal prostate cells is to produce seminal fluid, which when mixed with sperm from the testicles is called semen – the white-colored fluid visible upon ejaculation. Prostate cells also secrete various proteins into the blood stream, one of which is called Prostate Specific Antigen (PSA).

Prostate Specific Antigen (PSA)

Your best defense against prostate cancer is the PSA test which can lead to early detection, a critical part of being successfully treated. Recommendations for initiating testing for elevations or changes in PSA vary based on age, history and ethnicity. Current recommendations to start PSA testing include:

- All Men over the age of 50
- African American men 45 years old, or older
- Men with a family history of prostate cancer at age 40

74.1-Questions & Answers about curing Prostate Cancer

A rising PSA may be a sign of prostate cancer; however, a rising PSA may also be caused by Benign Prostatic Hyperplasia (BPH), an enlarged prostate.

Prostate Cancer Symptoms

Prostate cancer rarely causes any urine symptoms, such as a weak, slow stream. The urinary symptoms are normally caused from compression (squeezing) of the urethra due to an enlarged prostate, called Benign Prostatic Hyperplasia (BPH). **The first sign or symptom of prostate cancer** (other than an elevated PSA or positive digital rectal exam) is usually bone pain from cancer cells that have spread to bone, and then you are not curable.

If you have been recently diagnosed with prostate cancer, it's critical to personally research prostate cancer treatment options to make an informed decision that is best for you and your family. And, with few exceptions, **your first treatment method gives you the best chance for success.**

75

Bone on Bone

Can you believe that fifty-two years after being shot down in North Vietnam and, upon ejection, breaking my left femur (sometimes called the thigh bone) that I have bones in my left knee that are rubbing together and making it very difficult for me to walk? The Vietnamese doctor who originally operated on me did a good job of resetting and repairing my knee, but now time and wear have put me in a different place with different circumstances, and I am hurting every day.

God, I hope I will not require a knee replacement! I have heard very bad reports from those who have had that operation.

Finally, I had to make an appointment with the best-known knee surgeon in Charlotte. He confirmed that I was a candidate for having my left knee replaced. This did not thrill me. I detest pain—especially when the pain is administered by an enemy who wants to force me to do something against my will. I had experienced this many times in prison. However, in this case, my doctor is a personal friend, and I hope he doesn't want to inflict pain on me.

I left the doctor's office with a lot of questions I needed answers for. I arrived home, went straight to my laptop computer, and typed in "partial knee replacement," which was what my friend had said I would need. It took only seconds for an image to appear on my laptop screen. The video had titles and a big arrow in the middle of the screen that, I assumed, would start the video showing the operation. I clicked the arrow and sat back to view the proceedings.

Damn! Here was a guy sitting there with a black line drawn down from above his left thigh to just below his knee. Some doctor was narrating the video like this was how you get a banana split at a soda shop.

The next thing I saw was a hand with a scalpel in it cutting down that black line and stopping about four inches below the knee. I was up and out of my seat and already hurting—even though the cutting was on someone else's knee. Then the most gross thing I had ever seen happened. The doctor pushed his hands into the cut and pulled it apart like he was opening a cantaloupe. And this is a "partial." Damn! I'm happy I'm not getting the full deal!

Then the final part of the operation came into view. The doctor grabbed a chisel that was about a foot long and started chipping away at bones near the knee. Then he banged on the chisel with a hammer—and I almost passed out. Do I get the Congressional Medal Of Honor for doing this? Wow! This is unreal. Is it too late to call this butchering off?

I called Catherine into my office to view this, but she would not stay. This may have been the worst part of my operation—having my wife be a witness to my treatment. My operation was on February 6, 2017, and I am almost completely healed now. Modern medicine is still just one step from being Medieval, and I still do not like pain!

76
What has God got to do with it?

Yes, I am a Christian! Yes, I believe in GOD!

Yes, I was "shot down" by an enemy. That didn't have to happen to me, did it? That is only one side of the issue.

Here is another. I don't remember getting out of my F-105 Fighter when I was shot down over North Vietnam in September of 1965. After I had been hit by anti-aircraft fire, my wingman saw I had been hit, closed in on me and was flying right next to me as we were into a steep and speedy descent. In fact, years later, my wingman told me that we were doing around 700 knots right before he had to pull off or go into the ground with me. That is how close it was.

Keep in mind that 700 knots at sea level is approaching the speed of sound. As he pulled off, he noted that I was bent over my stick and not responding to his radio transmissions to *EJECT!* He also said he had almost waited too long to pull up, and there was no doubt in his mind I had gone in with the airplane. The point is this—there was little "wiggle room" for me to use in escaping the fate that goes with "going in with the airplane!"

Looking back, this raises some issues that I would like to understand.

(1.) Did my aircraft explode before it hit the ground and blow me out as if I had used the ejection seat?

(2.) Did I regain consciousness and have enough control over myself to go through my normal ejection procedures?

I concluded one indisputable fact…. God wanted James Quincy Collins, Jr. to survive certain death at that moment in time. *He* made it happen! If all the above is true, and I feel that it is, then I must ask, *Why?* What does/did God want me to do? Why did he save me from death?"

As a Christian, I know there are reasons for all things that happen under God's watch. He knows the present and the future and the part that each of us is to play in this drama of life.

In another part of this book, I tell of my relationship with a great American, Sen. Sam Nunn of Georgia. I was visiting with him in Washington to get his advice on my retiring from the USAF and announcing for the US House Of Representatives from the 7th district of Georgia. Sam asked me a lot of personal questions then "eyed" me with the look of a serious father and uttered this statement, "Quincy, no matter what you do the rest of your life, you will *always* be known as that former POW from Vietnam."

And then he asked the question that has stopped me in my tracks every time I think of this occasion. "Now—what are you going to do about it"?

Sam was reminding me that God had already issued the challenge to me. He had already provided me the platform from which I was supposed to help others and carry out his will for my life! Were all of my POW mates receiving the same challenge? Not necessarily. We are all different, and we all have different talents to present to our Master. Our motivations are not the same.

Some of us can deliver speeches that can mesmerize an audience and cause them to want to be followers of what they are hearing. Others of us can cause that same audience to sleep soundly and not remember a word or idea we expressed. And others would not have the slightest inclination or desire to stand before a crowd of people to talk about anything.

It takes a brave person, indeed, to have the guts to talk to another human being about their afterlife and being "saved" and to answer the question of what God expects of all of us in our role as Christians. So you see, not everyone is prepared to do some of the tasks God would like for us to do, even though He tells us that if we make the commitment, He will give us what we need to do the job!

I do not know what my mission is here on earth, but I do know this: I either have now—or will have at some time in the future—whatever I need to accomplish any task God wants me to undertake. I am not afraid of the unknown future nor am I reticent to face whatever God wants me to do. I am convinced and believe religiously that He will give me what I need to be successful in His will for my life!

Here I am at this very moment writing my memoirs—and for what purpose? I don't have the answer to that question, yet! I do know that I am telling truths about what has happened in my life that may be of interest to my family and descendants of the Collins Clan. And, perhaps, of interest to other human beings who may feel unprepared for the real challenges of life and who may lack the motivation to put the extra effort into life to be successful. Whatever that word means to you who are reading this dissertation, I pray that my experiences will be of help to each of you as you face the challenges of your future. And now to answer the question this Chapter asks: "What has God got to do with it?"

Everything, my friends. *EVERYTHING!* GOD BLESS YOU!

77
Retirement—is it Time?

Catherine and I lived for something like 32 years at 4641 Mullens Ford Road in Charlotte, North Carolina. Looking back is a pain to do because time is a very fleeting thing and neither of us keeps accurate records. We think the year was around 1982 when we bought our house there. Over the years we made many changes to the backyard such as replacing the existing vinyl liner in the pool and replanting various plants and flowers.

All of this took a lot of work and effort on my part because each year brought a different outlook and plan for that particular year, and I had to work around a schedule that would produce a result I really wanted. Bottom line: I was working my fanny off just to keep up with Mother Nature's normal growth pattern.

We had met Don Dela Mea of Spain Construction in Charlotte. Don was the son-in-law of Jack Spain whom I had met while at The Citadel in Charleston. Don had done some work for us around the house and had proven himself to be not only very reliable but also quite good in whatever task he was assigned.

So when we eventually decided to put in a new pool, rehab the patio and replace the gazebo, we selected a pool company and put both it and

Spain Construction under contract to complete the renovations in our backyard.

This became a huge project as our backyard began to look like London during World War ll. I hope I will be able to find photos I took of all this construction as it amazed me to see how well it all turned out.

In addition to all the demolition and construction going on around the pool, our hero—me, the Master Gardener—was busy replanting most of the greenery and plants and flowers in the backyard. This job continued for months, even after the big reconstruction project had been completed. I normally was in the yard from around 8 in the morning until 8 at night. My face would be red as a beet and I would be breathing like I had just run a mile. I told Catherine that I needed to make some drastic changes in my work schedule or she might find me in the bushes having a stroke!

Our reward for all this hard work was that we were really enjoying our home, especially when grandkids began to come on the scene to enjoy the pool and backyard and add so much love and caring to our daily routine.

As time went by, we began to receive invitations to various retirement homes in the Charlotte area. Now, as a former USAF Fighter pilot, retirement was not a lifestyle I wanted to embrace. To my thinking it is like being put into a coffin and planted in the ground. This is neither very enticing nor desirable for a guy who is supposed to be full of piss and vinegar and ready to shoot down the next bogey that crosses his sight path. I do not want to be a Zombie who is led around the premises while in an old age coma. I think you get the idea! I ain't ready to go just yet!

Don't let me get ahead of myself because a lot of things had to happen before I started thinking about hanging up my spurs. But we did begin to seriously consider a move to another place where I would not be exposed to this type wear and tear on my body!

About that time came invitations from several retirement communities to come inspect their facilities for our use. The Cypress even invited us to lunch. We arranged to visit several places and were pleased to see a lot of people we knew from Myers Park Presbyterian Church, especially when we had lunch at The Cypress.

My point of view after seeing all these homes was that they all had a lot of older people there. Catherine commented that she was not yet old enough to become a member of any of the places we had visited. Since then we have both adjusted our thinking and have joined everyone else in being as old as we really are.

We decided that The Cypress offered us the best values so we lined up Spain Construction, signed a sales contract with The Cypress, and put our home on the market. After all the work we had completed there, I thought our place would sell the next day. Nine months later we got our first offer to purchase our home. This little glitch caused me to have to get a "Bridge Loan" in order to afford the unit we bought at The Cypress. We moved in there on October 2, 2014.

We are very happy in our new home, love all the new friends we have made and look forward to many happy years in the future. God will look after those who look after themselves. Amen!

78
Our Political Dilemma

The date was July 23, 2015, the day after Catherine's seventy-sixth birthday celebration, and we were almost back to "normal" again!

She and I had been lounging at a gorgeous resort area near Pawley's Island, South Carolina, for nearly three weeks. We embraced the motto, "Eat, Drink, And Be Merry" during the time we had been at our condo at "Litchfield By The Sea." The weather had been nearly perfect, except for a few boiling days when the temperature pushed or exceeded 100 degrees. An umbrella does nothing against a sun that is so hot you must wait until the sun sets and the night air cools to a respectable level before you can get out on the beach. Then it may be too dark to walk the beach safely.

We buy a Charlotte Observer each day at "Eggs Up" to keep track with Charlotte and the activities in both North and South Carolina. This was, and still is, the best place in the Carolinas to have breakfast, say "Good Morning" to a lot of folks, drink a ton of coffee, and just get the right direction for the day. It is truly a mood-changer kind of place.

I am told that there is a famous tropical plant that blooms at specified intervals and produces a smell so bad it will make you go blind and completely wipes out the functions of your taste buds. I also understand that it will straighten out curly and kinky hair. At any rate, you get the idea.

I compared this to the 2015-2016 election cycle for President. To put it into proper focus...it stunk!!

The Republican Party had some of the most qualified candidates to ever be on the scene, and I looked forward to the debates to witness the selection of the most talented and best prepared to be President. That finally appeared to be Donald Trump!

He, for some unknown reason, brought up Sen. John McCain and his campaign against Obama in 2008. Trump then made a public statement claiming that my old POW cellmate was not a hero, and that the military guys who were "not captured" were the ones he really liked. Well, La De Da!

I told Catherine it was a good thing that we weren't at home or our phone would be ringing off the hook trying to get radio and TV statements from me regarding my POW relationship with John McCain. Evidently only one media guy in Charlotte had my cell phone number. He was David Perlmutt of the *Charlotte Observer*. After he interviewed me here is part of what he wrote:

Quincy Collins of Charlotte wasn't sure he'd heard right last weekend when Republican presidential candidate Donald Trump questioned whether Sen. John McCain was a true war hero because he'd been captured during the Vietnam War.

But when he heard Trump say at a campaign event in Iowa: "I like people who weren't captured," Collins got angry. He was a fellow POW for more than seven years and in 1970 shared a cell with McCain and about 40 other prisoners at the infamous "Hanoi Hilton."

They were all tortured repeatedly for years, especially McCain after their captors discovered he was the son of a Navy admiral who commanded American forces in the Pacific, Collins said.

"Obviously this guy (Trump) didn't have much of a brain in his head when he arrived at that conclusion," said Collins, 84,

a retired Charlotte real estate executive. "John was shot down. He didn't ask to be there. None of us did. And they really tore into him because his daddy was an admiral and so was his granddaddy."

Collins, an Air Force fighter pilot who was captured in 1965 after his plane was shot down, knows what McCain endured during his five years as a POW.

"Being a POW isn't the easiest thing on Earth. I doubt our friend Trump or any of the other politicians on the scene at that time would have the will to endure it," Collins said.

By the time he met McCain in prison, Collins had been held for five years and McCain for three.

McCain, shot down in his Navy Skyhawk dive-bomber, was taken prisoner with fractures in both arms and his right leg. He was given minimal care. "He was in rough shape," Collins said. "But we all were. They knew almost right away who John was and made him a special case. They never allowed his arms to heal."

Yet their captors did offer McCain early release as a propaganda ploy to show American leaders the POWs were not being mistreated. McCain refused, saying he wouldn't go without his comrades. That brought more torture, every two to three hours over four days.

"He told them to 'stick it'," Collins said. "Our rules did not allow a release without the permission of the senior officers. They were being tortured too so this thing went on and on. John could have left, but he said no. In my mind, he was absolutely heroic."

AT THAT TIME, MOST people would have been pleased if I had been a little tougher on Trump for his remarks. Once you get covered with manure, stirring it up does not change the odor!

At any rate, at this specific time a few years later, Trump appears to be taking a reasonable position on the issues.

It does not take a rocket scientist to see very clearly that the thousands of immigrants headed to our southern border are not coming there to attend a party. They are there to disrupt our nation and cause the Trump administration to fail. Yes, there are those who want America to disappear from the face of the earth so that Socialism can replace Democracy and Capitalism. Wake up my friends—because it is already on top of us!

God help us!

Whether you like it or not, Donald Trump is President of the United States of America. The American people elected him, fair and square. I predict that he will again be elected because he makes good things happen to our people and to our nation. I also believe the Democrat leaders are setting their party up to fail in the coming election.

May God's will be done!

79
February 21, 2018—a Memory!

B illy Graham died this morning! I never met him personally, but I did see him in action in Atlanta in 1973 at a Crusade in Fulton County Stadium in Georgia. There had been a lot of protests from minorities, but Martin Luther King had led a prayer at one of the sessions, and the crowd's temperature cooled down quickly.

I went to the first session because of something that happened a week or so before Rev. Graham preached. Having just returned from my seven and a half years as a POW in North Vietnam, I had been in the news a lot with TV and newspaper interviews and speeches about my experiences.

One phone message I received was of great interest to me because it was from Cliff Barrows, Billy Graham's musical director. The fact that I had been the first Protestant Choir director at the new Air Force Academy when it opened in 1955, and that I had formed a POW choir in prison may have sparked his interest in calling me. Of course, I returned his call as soon as I got his message. Cliff wanted me to come to his hotel and meet with him. I agreed, and the time was set.

By now I had selected the car that Ford Motor Company had offered each POW when we returned home, had gotten my driver's license, and was ready to go. It took me a while to navigate to Cliff's hotel, as this was my first solo drive into the big city of Atlanta. My heart began to thump and bump as I pulled into the hotel parking lot. What did Cliff want of me? Did he want me to sing or lead the choir? Maybe he wanted me to be interviewed and answer questions—all in front of the entire world! Well, dumb cluck, why don't you go in and find out!

I went to the check-in desk and asked them to call and tell Cliff that I had arrived. He told them it was OK for me to come up, and so I did. I stood there pushing the doorbell, thinking of all sorts of possibilities. The door opened, and there was Cliff, talking on the phone while shaking my hand. He was a good-looking man with curly black hair and an *I'm in charge* type of personality.

Shortly, he hung up the phone, put his arms around me and said, "Quince, I have really been looking forward to meeting you. God bless you for coming." We sat down, had a soda, and he began asking me about my return.

He had heard about my musical endeavors while in prison, and spent a lot of time quizzing me on what part my personal faith in God had to do with my survival.

"Everything!" was my answer.

Then he asked about my treatment and how I felt about it.

I don't think Cliff was too pleased with my response. I told him that I expected some of what I received from my enemy, but none of what I received from my wife—a *Dear John* letter stating we would not be living together now that I was back home. I think his issue was to forgive and move on. We prayed together, had a firm Christian hug, and I left.

I could tell very quickly that Cliff was truly a man of God. What an opportunity I had been given to meet him and talk a short while! His association with Billy Graham certainly kept his religious motivation at a high peak. How wonderful it would be to have that opportunity on a daily basis!

To tell the truth, God is available to each of us at any time we want.

We just need to call on HIM! And I do just that, because I realize that I have constructed a huge obstacle in my path to doing God's Will in my life—forgiving my first wife for the way she treated me—and it must come down if I am ever to be released to do His Will!

God help me. Amen!

80
Time Waits For No One

My wonderful sister, Carolyn, was living in Marietta, Georgia, and had made an appointment to have Sunday lunch on August 19, 2018, with a friend who was to pick her up at her apartment. We now know that on the evening of Saturday, August 18, Carolyn passed out in her apartment and lay on the floor all night, unable to notify anyone of her condition, although I had purchased an emergency contact necklace for her to wear around her neck in the event she needed help. I discovered later that this emergency piece lay on her bedside table, out of reach and of no use to her.

Sis's Sunday luncheon date showed up at the appointed time, but could not get a response from Carolyn to open the door. The friend went to the apartment office and got someone to go over to open Carolyn's door. Finding her on the floor, they called an ambulance and sent her to a local hospital. That was on Sunday, August 19, 2018.

I received a call at my home in Charlotte from the hospital on the morning of Monday, August 20, explaining Carolyn's dehydration problem. This condition had occurred several times in the past so I wasn't overly concerned, although the nurse said Sis was having a little difficulty talking right now. I asked her to keep me apprised of Carolyn's condition and said I would call back in a day or two. I called Carolyn on her cell phone Thursday afternoon, August 23, and she was talking very well and showed no weakness in her voice.

Catherine and I had planned on traveling to Marietta that weekend as we had been looking at possible places for Carolyn to live in the Charlotte area. We wanted her to be closer to us because the drive to Marietta was getting tougher and tougher to handle for an 87 year old, namely me! I didn't mention that to her, but I did ask if she would like for us to come down. Without hesitation she replied. "Come now."

We made immediate plans to drive down Saturday morning, arriving at the hospital around 2 PM. She said that would be fine and she looked forward to seeing us. That would be my last voice contact with Carolyn!

When we arrived at the hospital and checked in at the admissions office, Sis had been moved to a different room than when I last talked with her. We went up to the room number provided us, and the door was partially opened. Catherine pushed the door for us to enter and someone was standing in our way. He asked who we were. When I told him I was the patient's brother, he pointed down the hall and asked us to go wait in the waiting room at the end of the hall. As we walked down the hall, I said to Catherine, "Something is wrong here!" She agreed as we sat down to await hearing from the medical staff. We really didn't know what to say to each other so we sat in utter silence.

Finally the man who had stood in our way in Carolyn's room and a black lady doctor entered the waiting room and came directly to me. The lady doctor said, "Colonel, we did all we could do, but your sister has passed!"

My jaw dropped, my eyes teared up, I gasped for a breath and I looked at Catherine. "What?"

Then I thought, *How can this be? Sis sounded strong the last phone conversation I had with her.*

The Doctor then explained that all Sis's vital signs had gone south very suddenly and the staff could not stop it. The Doctor escorted us to Carolyn's room, opened the door and there was my wonderful sister lying in bed as if she were asleep. I touched her forehead and her skin was still warm and pliable. She was so peaceful and still had an aura of holiness about her. She had truly been an angel to our Mother and Father and to me also. I said a prayer of thanks to God for allowing such a person to be in our midst. I kissed her face and walked away, but I shall never forget God's special Angel! I miss you my love!

(80.1) My wonderful sister, Carolyn

81
My Final Thoughts.

I hope that you have enjoyed being exposed to my life and the events that have christened me on my voyage around God's green earth. I can say with great certainty that my "tour guide" has made it interesting, challenging, and exciting in every way possible. I think that, as a human being, My Maker has thrown me into just about every pothole He has created in my road of life. For that I am so very thankful, because it has drawn me so much closer to knowing what His will is for my life.

I firmly believe that a smooth-sailing life does not make one a better Christian, nor does it prepare one for the big tests that life uses to evaluate one's personal performance on this planet. Even with all the stress and strain that has come my way, God has provided me the strength and the will to overcome all the adversity I have had to endure.

And how can I forget my many friends who have made my life worth living—my loving wife, Catherine, and her wonderful daughters, and all 12 of our Grandchildren; my sister, Carolyn, who had to endure the task of caring for our parents—not an enjoyable task to say the least; and my handsome sons who grew up in spite of my being absent during their formative years. Of all the places I have lived, Concord, North Carolina, has had the most positive impact on me. In my youth, the Baptist Church in Concord showed me the way. Then Ridgecrest, the Southern Baptist Training Center in the mountains of North Carolina, made life a lot clearer to me.

But the *one person* who has made me into what I am today is my beautiful wife Catherine. She is the essence of Love, and has taught me the true meaning of the word. I will love her forever and seek her counsel at every turn.

When you have lived for 88 years and begin to think about whom you want to mention in your "Book of Life," you discover there is not enough paper and printing ink to do that. Yes, there are many, many people who have loved me. I loved them and will never forget them. Events of my early youth, Citadel memories, USAF experiences, POW trials and tribulations, and adjusting to life after prison—these have all become a part of me and are, at this very moment, shaping the rest of my life. I can hardly wait to see what happens next. Perhaps there will be more…a lot more!

You can never tell what will come

Out of the Blue!

(81.1) Col. James Quincy Collins, Jr. USAF Ret.

Some of My Favorite Photographs

I have used many photos in showing various parts of my life. A visual is a lot more effective than just verbal descriptions. So where possible, rather than just descriptions, I have used visuals of events, people and places to make my life become more alive for my readers. This technique is most useful to my relatives, particularly to my descendants, in following my life and that of the people closest to me—the Doggetts and the Collins Clan.

This section of my book is really a "filler," so that there is a visual record of things that I may not have explained in detail in the main part of the book. I hope that you find this interesting too.

(Fav1.01) Quincy with Chip, Chuck and Corky, 1965.

(Fav1.02) Chip, Corky and Chuck, November 1965.

(Fav1.03) Chip, Corky and Chuck, Easter 1966.

(Fav1.04) Chip, Corky and Chuck, 1966.

(Fav1.05) My sister Carolyn with Chuck, Corky and Chip, 1967.

(Fav1.06) Corky, Chuck and Chip, 198?

(Fav1.07) Corky, Chuck and Chip, 1987.

(Fav1.08) Corky, Chuck and Chip, 198?

(Fav1.09) (Fav1.08) Corky, Chuck and Chip at Chuck's college graduation

(Fav1.10) Chuck, Chip, Quincy and Corky at Corky's graduation.

(Fav1.11) Chuck, Corky ,Quincy and Chip at Corky's wedding.

(Fav2.01) First step of freedom, February 1973.

(Fav2.02) First visit with my sons.

(Fav2.03) Chuck with his daughters.

(Fav2.04) The Collins clan, when Quincy was 75..

(Fav2.05) Our hero as a Citadel Junior — note the hair!

(Fav2.06) Photos of a skinny colonel, Feb 12, 1973

(Fav2.08) Quincy makes a new friend in uniform.

(Fav2.09) Quincy with his new 1957 Cadillac convertible.

(Fav2.10) Quincy's "co-pilot" in Spain.

(Fav2.11) Quincy in Concord, NC parade, in front of his old house.

(Fav2.12) Quincy had a young man, confined to a wheelchair and who had never visited an airport, as his special guest for his retirement ceremony at Dobbins AFB, GA on May 4, 1974.

(Fav3.01) Colonel Quincy Collins retires, May 4 1974.

(Fav3.02) Two ladies pet a dog — figure it out!

(Fav3.04) The Colonel telling Chip what to do.

(Fav3.04) President Ford telling the Colonel what to do!

(Fav3.04) The Colonel telling the crowd what to do!

(Fav3.09) Some Concord boys stepping out! (Quincy seated in front on right.)

(Fav3.10) The Colonel gets "A big head" at the Citadel, November 1999.

(Fav3.11) The Wing at the USAF Academy gets ready to pass in review.

(Fav3.12) The USAF Academy Chapel.

(Fav3.12) Quincy leading his POW Choir at the Nixon Presidential Library.

(Fav3.12) Quincy's wife Catherine.

(Fav3.12) Quincy reviewing the troops with General John S. Grinalds, President of The Citadel.

About the Author

Quincy Collins was a 4th of July baby back in 1931. Raised in Concord, NC, he graduated from Concord High School, attended The Citadel in Charleston, SC, and graduated with a Bachelor of Science Degree in Commerce in 1953. Quincy immediately entered the Air Force as a 2nd Lt. and began pilot training. Twenty-one years later he had accumulated over 3,000 hours of jet time with a Command Pilot rating, and had flown all the jet fighters of the day. He earned his Jump Wings at Ft. Benning, GA, while a Flight Commander in an F-104 unit at George Air Force Base, California.

He had an illustrious Air Force career, from opening the new Air Force Academy in 1955 as an Air Training Officer, to being the Aide to the Four Star Commander-in-Chief of U.S. Air Forces in Europe, to being shot down by the North Vietnamese Communists and spending 7 ½ years in prison cells in and around Hanoi.

Quincy retired as a full Colonel in 1974, ran for Congress in the 7th District of Georgia in 1974 and again in 1976. He has since been involved in insurance, was the General Sales Manager for 4 ½ years at Arnold Palmer Cadillac, and was President of his own marketing firm in Charlotte. For 22 years he was a commercial and industrial real estate broker, and a Senior Vice President of Southern Real Estate in Charlotte.

He is married to Catherine, his wife of 40 years. She has 3 daughters and Quincy has 3 sons. They have 12 grandchildren—triplet girls (26 years), boy/girl twins (25 years), and four grandsons and three granddaughters, ages 10 to 25.

Quincy is very involved in the Charlotte community through his civic and political activities. He is a Deacon and Stephen Minister at Myers Park Presbyterian Church, and has served on the Boards of the Carolinas Carrousel Parade, the Carolinas Concert Association, the Board of Charlotte's Friendship Trays, was President of "The Collector's Circle" of the Mint Museum, and former Chairman of the Board of Directors for the Charlotte Museum of History. He is the founder of the Carolinas Freedom Foundation and Chairman of the Charlotte-Mecklenburg World War II Memorial Foundation. He was a candidate for Charlotte City Council in 1995. In 1999, Quincy was President of the Citadel Alumni Association headquartered in Charleston, South Carolina. The Colonel was recently designated a "Distinguished Graduate" by his Alma Mater.

He was a 10-year member of the prestigious Multi-Million Dollar Club of the Charlotte Commercial Board of Realtors and became a member of the Ten Million Dollar Club for three years in a row. In 2003, the Board of Realtors, for only the second time in their history, awarded Quincy their coveted "Realtor Citizen of the Year Award" for his contributions to the betterment of the community and for outstanding public service in the Charlotte Region. He also was recognized as one of the top Commercial Real Estate Producers in the Charlotte Region, and achieved the SIOR designation awarded by the Society of Industrial and Office Realtors, an international association of professional commercial real estate brokers.

General Hugh Shelton, former Chairman of the Joint Chiefs of Staff, asked Quincy to serve on the Board of the "Shelton Leadership Initiative" at N.C. State University, and he was selected to join the South Carolina State Guard Foundation Board to advise the South Carolina Adjutant General on military matters. Quincy also serves on the Boards of the USO and Operation Homefront for the State of North Carolina.

The Carolinas Freedom Foundation and its founder, Col. Quincy Collins, have been awarded the 2009 World Citizen Award by the World Affairs Council of Charlotte. In addition, Pat McCrory, then Governor of North Carolina, awarded Quincy the Order of the Long Leaf Pine for his many contributions to his community and state. After he delivered the commencement address for the 2014 graduating class at the College of the Ozarks in Point Lookout, Missouri, Quincy was awarded an honorary Doctor of Laws degree. He is now retired and is in constant demand as an event speaker.

His military awards include:

2 Silver Stars

2 Purple Hearts

2 Air Medals

POW Medal

Air Force Commendation Medal

Air Force Longevity Service Award

Armed forces Expeditionary Medal

Republic of Vietnam Campaign Medal

Air Force Outstanding Unit Award

National Defense Service Medal

Vietnam Service Medal

Acknowledgments

It is one thing to decide to write a book, it is another to have the motivation and will to actually sit down and start typing! In my case, there are multiple reasons to want to put words on the pages of a book that tells the story of my life. No matter what the reason might be, it takes the support of others to make it actually happen.

This comes in the form of good friends who are inquisitive about what has happened in your life. Sometimes this happens over cocktails where one's mind is allowed to bounce around and bring up situations you wouldn't ordinarily mention. It is known to be a fact that Veterans do not relish talking about themselves so entire families often never hear the true military experiences of close relatives.

Hearing and listening are two different activities that anyone can participate in, but putting the stories on paper requires people with the proper training to type, format, punctuate and use correct grammar—a herculean task, to say the least! Then the piece must be proofread. This function requires a special talent and a lot of patience and is so important to the author, because agents and publishers often require strict adherence to their instructions for preparing manuscripts. Misspelled words, bad grammar, faulty punctuation, etc. can cause your book to end up in the trashcan of your agent or publisher.

This is why your friends or staff are so important in assisting an author in getting his/her book published. First, I want to thank all the people who have entered my life, either on purpose or by chance, and have made my existence richer as a result. All of my Concord buddies and playmates come to mind. High School classmates and my Citadel contacts—what an impact they have had on my life! Next are my USAF friends and my POW buddies—sometimes called prisoners!

Now to be specific: Sheila Evans (an author herself) and her good husband, Slick, are at The Cypress with me and have led me through all the twists and turns of authorship. Next is Margaret Bigger who invited me to attend her class on writing memoirs. I knew her from Myers Park Presbyterian Church and her encouragement got me going.

My good friend David Hays has also greatly impacted my life and has become one of my closest friends. He has lined me up for many speeches and appearances and brought me into Gen. Hugh Shelton's Advisory Board at the Leadership Center at N.C. State. He also serves on that Board. Col. Rick Kiernan, former PR Director for Gen. Norman Schwarzkopf, has been a stabilizing influence along with David Hays. Finally, Melissa Schropp has put this book together along with arranging all the photos and cover. She is one of the best!

I cannot ignore the part that Catherine, my wife, has played in this little scenario. She is the one who has taught me about love and my book is definitely about LOVE! Loving this nation, loving its people, loving our God and loving life. Catherine has been a great teacher to me, and someone against whom I will always be able to measure LOVE!

Thanks to you all!

9 780578 969312